CAMBRIDGE LIBRARY COLLECTION

Books of enduring scholarly value

Egyptology

The large-scale scientific investigation of Egyptian antiquities by Western scholars began as an unintended consequence of Napoleon's invasion of Egypt during which, in 1799, the Rosetta Stone was discovered. The military expedition was accompanied by French scholars, whose reports prompted a wave of enthusiasm that swept across Europe and North America resulting in the Egyptian Revival style in art and architecture. Increasing numbers of tourists visited Egypt, eager to see the marvels being revealed by archaeological excavation. Writers and booksellers responded to this growing interest with publications ranging from technical site reports to tourist guidebooks and from children's histories to theories identifying the pyramids as repositories of esoteric knowledge. This series reissues a wide selection of such books. They reveal the gradual change from the 'tomb-robbing' approach of early excavators to the highly organised and systematic approach of Flinders Petrie, the 'father of Egyptology', and include early accounts of the decipherment of the hieroglyphic script.

Tell el Hesy (Lachish) ~ Hyksos and Israelite Cities

A pioneering Egyptologist, Sir William Matthew Flinders Petrie (1853–1942) excavated over fifty sites and trained a generation of archaeologists. This reissue brings together two of his well-illustrated excavation reports. The first, originally published in 1891, covers his 1890 dig in Palestine at Tell el-Hesi. Although he identified it incorrectly as the biblical city of Lachish, his work here was significant in Near Eastern archaeology for the stratigraphic method of excavation and use of pottery to establish chronology. The second report, from 1906, records the work carried out at a number of Hyksos and Israelite sites in Egypt, such as Tell el-Yehudiyeh and Tell er-Retabeh. It also includes chapters by John Garrow Duncan (1872–1951) on the cemeteries of Suwa and Goshen. Each report contains a section of photographs and drawings of sites, artefacts and inscriptions. Petrie wrote prolifically throughout his long career, and a great many of his other publications are also reissued in this series.

Cambridge University Press has long been a pioneer in the reissuing of out-of-print titles from its own backlist, producing digital reprints of books that are still sought after by scholars and students but could not be reprinted economically using traditional technology. The Cambridge Library Collection extends this activity to a wider range of books which are still of importance to researchers and professionals, either for the source material they contain, or as landmarks in the history of their academic discipline.

Drawing from the world-renowned collections in the Cambridge University Library and other partner libraries, and guided by the advice of experts in each subject area, Cambridge University Press is using state-of-the-art scanning machines in its own Printing House to capture the content of each book selected for inclusion. The files are processed to give a consistently clear, crisp image, and the books finished to the high quality standard for which the Press is recognised around the world. The latest print-on-demand technology ensures that the books will remain available indefinitely, and that orders for single or multiple copies can quickly be supplied.

The Cambridge Library Collection brings back to life books of enduring scholarly value (including out-of-copyright works originally issued by other publishers) across a wide range of disciplines in the humanities and social sciences and in science and technology.

Tell el Hesy
(Lachish)

~

Hyksos and
Israelite Cities

W.M. FLINDERS PETRIE

CAMBRIDGE
UNIVERSITY PRESS

CAMBRIDGE
UNIVERSITY PRESS

University Printing House, Cambridge, CB2 8BS, United Kingdom

Published in the United States of America by Cambridge University Press, New York

Cambridge University Press is part of the University of Cambridge.
It furthers the University's mission by disseminating knowledge in the pursuit of
education, learning and research at the highest international levels of excellence.

www.cambridge.org
Information on this title: www.cambridge.org/9781108067263

© in this compilation Cambridge University Press 2013

This edition first published 1891 and 1906
This digitally printed version 2013

ISBN 978-1-108-06726-3 Paperback

This book reproduces the text of the original edition. The content and language reflect
the beliefs, practices and terminology of their time, and have not been updated.

Cambridge University Press wishes to make clear that the book, unless originally published
by Cambridge, is not being republished by, in association or collaboration with, or
with the endorsement or approval of, the original publisher or its successors in title.

The original edition of this book contains a number of colour plates,
which have been reproduced in black and white. Colour versions of these
images can be found online at www.cambridge.org/9781108067263

TELL EL HESY

(LACHISH)

From "The Illustrated London News,"]

VIEW ALONG EAST FACE OF TELL EL HESY.

[with kind permission of the Proprietors.

TELL EL HESY

(LACHISH)

BY

W. M. FLINDERS PETRIE

Author of " Pyramids and Temples of Gizeh," " Tanis," I and II, " Naukratis," I,
" A Season in Egypt," " Hawara, Biahmu, and Arsinoe," " Historical Scarabs,"
" Kahun, Gurob, and Hawara," &c.

LONDON :
PUBLISHED FOR THE
COMMITTEE OF THE PALESTINE EXPLORATION FUND
BY
ALEXANDER P. WATT, 2, PATERNOSTER SQUARE.

1891.

LONDON :
HARRISON AND SONS, PRINTERS IN ORDINARY TO HER MAJESTY
ST. MARTIN'S LANE, W.C.

CONTENTS.

CHAPTER I.

INTRODUCTORY.

CHAPTER II.

SITE OF TELL EL HESY.

CHAPTER III.

REMAINS AT TELL EL HESY.

CHAPTER IV.

IDENTIFICATION OF LACHISH.

CHAPTER V.

HISTORY OF LACHISH.

CHAPTER VI.

STRUCTURAL DETAILS.

CHAPTER VII.

THE POTTERY.

PLATES.

ILLUSTRATIONS.

CHAPTER I.

INTRODUCTORY.

1. The work of excavation at Tell el Hesy, the ancient city of Lachish, was the fruit of a permission which the Palestine Exploration Fund had long been endeavouring to obtain from the Turkish government. The first idea was to explore Umm Lakis and Khurbet Ajlan, two sites which were supposed to be Lachish and Eglon; but happily the area asked for included some other ancient sites, and among them Tell el Hesy. I left Egypt and arrived in Syria in March, 1890. On going to Jerusalem, I found that the permission granted by the government had been delayed owing to a verbal error. I was thus detained for three weeks, during which time I carefully examined the remains at Jerusalem with Prof. Hayter Lewis, Dr. Chaplin and Herr Schick, each of whom are authorities on their own subjects there. I also measured most of the rock tombs about Jerusalem; and made an apparently successful essay to recover the cubits of the excavators, by an examination of the measurements on the principles worked out in 1877 in my " Inductive Metrology." The results of this work will shortly appear.

2. Having at last obtained the permission, and seen His Excellency Reshid Pasha, I went down to the village of Bureir, the nearest inhabited place to my area of work. After waiting for ten days more, at last the needful Turkish official arrived to watch the excavations, and to take for the government all antiquities that might be found. I began work on Umm Lakis, about three miles from Bureir. But three days' work there were amply enough to prove its late date, as I had supposed at my first view of it. It is strewn with rough rounded stones, the remains of rude walls. The soil is from 4 to 8 feet deep; all organic mould and humus, without any ancient consolidated stuff. Roman pottery was found throughout it, and a coin of Maximian Hercules about 300 A.D., at only

B

2 feet above the native clay. At a little distance to the north, on a rise, we cleared part of a building of concrete and small stones; which, from the large bath in it, seemed to be a Roman villa. I therefore settled that no reasonable prospect of anything important could be seen here.

3. I had, while waiting at Bureir, gone over the district allotted to me, and seen each of the ancient sites. Khurbet Ajlan seemed far more unpromising than Umm Lakis; only a few stray scraps of late pottery lie strewn about, and there does not seem to be any depth of soil. But Tell el Hesy from its height, and the pre-Greek style of its pottery, seemed to me to be a very promising site; and I settled on attacking it, although it was in the midst of the Bedawin, and mostly cultivated. The Turkish official was here of use, in doing all the communications with the innumerable Bedawi Shekhs and visitors who came about, and so relieving me of much attention to them. I had six weeks of work there, including the whole of the month of Ramadan, when work is very difficult to the fasting and thirsty Muslims. But in that time, and without disturbing the crops, I succeeded in unravelling the history of the place, and obtaining a long series of pottery approximately dated. It was well that I had not reckoned on continuing my work longer, for at the last all my men deserted me to go to harvest, and I could not get one even to guard my tents.

4. I had usually about thirty men employed, each with a woman or girl to carry the basket. But only a small proportion of the natives there are fit for work; each group of men that I engaged rapidly dwindled down by weeding out the hopelessly lazy ones; so that in two or three weeks half of any lot would be dismissed, and in six weeks but an eighth of the original party remained, all the rest having come in later. At first it seemed as if watching them made no difference; if away one never saw them doing anything, and when there one always saw them doing nothing; that was the only variation. But gradually by steady weeding, and by regular work, the average quality improved; and at last there were some tolerably good workers among them. The Bedawin were troublesome, though not actually quarrelling. Some of the head shekhs appeared civil enough, and as far reasonable as such folks can be. But the common herd were always in mischief; lounging about the excava-

tions, carrying away things that were found, overthrowing any masonry, driving off the workmen's donkeys while out grazing, worrying about supposed injuries to crops, and generally being about as much in the way as they could. It would have been a treat to have made them do a hard honest day's work ; for nothing is more annoying than a pack of ne'er-do-weel, quarrelsome, loungers insisting on hanging about. No villager dare say a word to them, or object to anything they did, for fear of the ever-present sword and pistols, which they were only too ready to flourish about. What with needing to be always conciliatory to the Turkish official, and to the Bedawin shekhs, and yet never allowing anyone to obtain any authority over the men or the work, the course of an excavator is not of the easiest.

After closing the work, as I did not see a prospect of doing more without much greater expense and time, I then went to examine several important sites in Judaea. Ed Dhaheriyeh, Hebron, Beit Jibrin, and so to Jaffa, being my route. I thus found some very promising sites for work, where early towns lie exposed, as seen by the style of the pottery strewn about.

Various friends rendered much assistance to my arrangements in Palestine. Besides advice from Dr. Chaplin's intimate knowledge of the country, and from Herr Schick's long experience at Jerusalem, I also learned much from my old friend the Revd. J. Longley Hall, of Jaffa, whose constant visiting about Palestine renders his information very practical ; and Dr. Elliott, who has a large work in the medical mission at Gaza, also was most cordial. The principal difficulties of excavating in Syria arise from the insecurity of the country, and the tenacity of a weak government.

CHAPTER II.

SITE OF TELL EL HESY.

5. The mound of Tell el Hesy stands 16 miles east of Gaza, a little
to the north : that is rather more than half way from Gaza to Beit Jibrin,
and a third of the distance from Gaza to Jerusalem. Though in the
bottom of a valley, yet its height of over 100 feet makes it a conspicuous
mark, both from the hill country—when looking over the wide plain of
Philistia,—and also in the view up the broad Wady Hesy from the west.
This mound, for over 60 feet of its height, consists of successive ruins of
towns piled one on the other. The houses were built of sun-dried clay
bricks ; every storm washed down somewhat from the walls, and deposited
the mud around the houses ; every house that was ruined was partially
broken down and helped to fill up the surrounding space ; every gust of
wind left some dust in the streets ; and little by little the surface was thus
raised, about half an inch each year, until, instead of a low swelling
ground 50 or 60 feet above the stream at its foot, the mound when it was
last occupied rose over 120 feet from the water. This gradual piling up
of a mound of ruins is well known in Egypt, where sun-dried mud bricks
were also used ; the mound of ruins of Damanhur is over 40 feet high,
and the mound of Tanis is as much as 80 feet.

The stream of the Wady Hesy—or rather its branch the Wady
Muleihah, which joins it here—is a torrent during the winter rains,
though about dried up in summer ; it runs past the east side of the
mound, and since the time when the town was built it has eaten its way
further into the soil of its western bank, undermining the ruins, and thus
leaving a steep cliff, sloping down at about 45° in irregular ledges from
the top edge to the stream below. The other sides of the mound are
less steep ; the north and south are rather below the angle of rest, and
on the west the mound slopes gently down to the natural ridge on which
it stands. The surrounding soil and the top of the mound are now

cultivated by the Bedawin; and it is only on its steeper sides that excavations can be made without the need of buying out the crops, and of restoring the surface of the land for cultivation.

6. The hill of ruins is about 200 feet each way (Pl. I); it stands in the north-east corner of an enclosure nearly quarter of a mile across. The bank around this will be seen from the plan to skilfully occupy the natural crests of the ground, between the small drainage valleys; on the southern side the ridge is yet 7 feet high of artificial stuff, banked up on the highest edge of the ground; on the western side the space is marked partly by a ridge, partly by the steep edge of a plateau; and on the northern side there is a sharp edge to the plateau, with the foundations of a brick wall which originally defended it on this side. The nature of the soil greatly aggravates the scouring action of the rainfall, as it is a deep bed of sand with a cap of clay on the top of it; hence the rain cannot penetrate the ground gently, but is shed off to the watercourse which has already cut through into the soft sand, and it rapidly deepens and lengthens that channel. The small watercourses are, therefore, here about 10 feet below the surface of the soil around, between walls of soft sand; and this accounts for the strangely furrowed state of the ground, the steep slopes of the little valleys, and the marked importance of what would otherwise be insignificant drainage lines.

Within the area thus enclosed there is no great depth of remains, except on the mound; on an average only about 4 feet of humus and artificial soil overlie the native clay, in some parts only one foot, and nowhere more than 10 feet. The depth of soil is marked in feet on the plan wherever it was tested. In the northern parts some pottery is found, and it appears that the earliest town extended along the northern side; perhaps before the restriction of walls and fortifications built to defend the place, as the pottery is like that of the earliest part of the mound. No late pottery was found in this enclosure, and it only seems to have been used during the earlier history. Probably it was intended for a refuge for the country people and their herds, during the invasions of foreigners.

CHAPTER III.

REMAINS AT TELL EL HESY.

7. We will now turn to the remains of the town. First it must be said that there is not any inscription, nor have any accurately dateable objects been found, which would give a precise age for any of the lower levels of the mound: we must therefore proceed by less direct methods. Happily no Roman pottery or remains occur anywhere on the mound, and I only saw one chip of Roman pottery in the enclosure, accidentally dropped there; the same may be said of the Seleucidan and Ptolemaic ages which have not left any remains here. The latest objects found are pieces of regular black and red Greek pottery, which occur in the top foot or two of the mound, on the east side and north-west; the most dateable of these is a part of a small vase, made about 450 B.C., and none of the other fragments indicate a later age than this. The close of the history of this place is then in the fifth century B.C. And as only a few fragments of this age are found, and those confined to less than half of the town, it seems that this last occupation was but partial and not of much importance. If then the top of the mound is of 450 B.C., how far before that are we to date the bottom of the 60 feet of ruins beneath us? Unfortunately no Egyptian objects were found which would give us a fixed point; and the only help we can get in estimating what must have been a long period, is in the Phoenician pottery. Not much of this occurs in the mound; but as many vases were found associated together in burials outside of the town we know all the contemporary varieties, and can help our dating by each of them. The thin black vases with long necks (called *bilbils* by the Syrians) occur from about 305 feet level up to 325 feet on the east side, about the pilaster building; the black bowls, which we know to be contemporary with the *bilbils*, occur from 295 feet at the S.E. to 315 feet at the pilaster building; the white juglets and the ladder-pattern bowls, both of which are also contemporary with *bilbils*, have just the same

range. So we may assign the Phoenician pottery to from 295 to 320 feet, at the middle of the east side. Now this pottery is not yet dated in Phoenicia, but in the past two years I have found it in Egypt; the earliest examples being late in the XVIIIth dynasty, about 1400 B.C.; the greatest number about the close of the XIXth dynasty, or 1100 B.C.; and some as late as about the XXIIIrd dynasty, or say 800 B.C. So the date of this Phoenician pottery may be roughly said to range from about 800 to 1400 B.C.

8. The problem then reads thus. The top level is of 450 B.C., the middle period of the Phoenician is about 1100 B.C.; and the middle of the Phoenician levels is at 307½, or 32½ feet under the top. If 32½ feet corresponded then to 650 years, this gives just 5 feet per century as the rate of average accumulation. Applying this scale we find that about the region of the pilaster building the dates should be,—

Top of mound	...	...	...	340 feet = 450 B.C.
Latest Phoenician ...	...	...	320 ,, = 850 B.C.
Earliest ,,	...	...	...	295 ,, = 1350 B.C.
Earliest dwellings ...	...	...	278 ,, = 1670 B.C.*

We therefore see that not only is this scale fixed by the middle point of the Phoenician, but the extent of the range of the Phoenician period according to the mound is just in accord with the duration of it in Egyptian remains. No doubt there were irregularities in the rate of accumulation; the captivity of the Jews, the desolation of the Canaanite towns after the ravages of the nomadic Israelite invaders, and such causes, would make a much slower rate of accumulation in some centuries than in others; but yet the scale cannot be so far wrong as to land us in a wholly different period to the truth, as we have it fairly fixed by three points,—the Greek pottery, and the beginning and end of the Phoenician.

---

* This scale is concordant with the rate of accumulation of the Egyptian towns of the Delta which have risen about 3 to 4 feet per century; with the greater rainfall of Syria therefore 5 feet per century is a very probable rate of deposit, as the walls would be destroyed more quickly.

9. Can we then see any other historical clues in the remains? I think we fairly may. The most prominent stage in the history of the town is pointed out by the widespread beds of ashes (see section of east face, Pl. III) and the underlying stratum of stream-bed stones. These ashes were certainly spread by the wind. Alternate layers of black charcoal dust and white lime ash streak the face of the mound for a depth of about 5 feet; and the lines are always unbroken and continuous, often a streak not over half an inch thick being traceable for 10 or 20 feet, and gradually thinning out at the ends. No deposit by hands could effect this, the stuff must have been wind borne, and dropped by the breeze without interference. The source of these ashes was doubtless the burning of plants for alkali, as is now done by the Bedawin. This custom has led to the heaping up of large piles of the lime, and insoluble substances remaining after lixiviation, near the north side of Jerusalem. At Tell el Hesy the charcoal layers were the result of the sparks and dust of the burning, and the breaking up of the fires; while the white lime layers were the dust blown about after the lixiviation had washed away the alkali. The town must then have been deserted, or almost so, at the time when the alkali burners resorted here, and when their ashes blew about and settled undisturbed over a great part of the hill.

Beneath these ash layers there is a stratum of rounded stones from the stream; showing a time when no regular brickwork was used, but when huts were roughly piled up out of the nearest material; a barbaric period followed by a desolation. The level of this time is from about 298 to 308 feet; which would on our approximate scale correspond to 1300 to 1100 B.C. Of course we cannot say that these stones and ashes accumulated at the same rate as the town ruins did before and after them, though probably the rate would not be extremely different. Hence we cannot be certain of the duration of this barbarism, but only of its general period, about 1200 B.C.

10. Now this we see just corresponds to the great break in the history of Palestine, between the destruction of the Amorite civilization, and the establishment of Jewish civilization under the Kings. The period of the Judges was a terribly barbaric age; its fragmentary records speak of savage retaliations, and the fierce struggles of disorganized tribes.

Judge after judge rises out of a mist of warfare, only to disappear and leave a confusion as black as before. Ehud, Barak, Gideon, Gaal, Abimelech, Jephthah, Samson, with their bloody record, lead up to the hideous tragedy of the slaughter of Benjamin. Not a trace of peaceful arts do we find; not even the arts of civilized warfare, in the making of weapons. Deborah sings "Was there a shield or a spear seen among forty thousand in Israel?"; Ehud made his own dagger, not having one, nor apparently able to get one otherwise; Shamgar slew the Philistines with an ox-goad; "there was no smith found throughout all the land of Israel," so that "there was neither sword nor spear found in the hand of any of the people that were with Saul"; and even as late as David the Hebrew warfare was so rude that the rich booty of a thousand chariots was nearly all destroyed, as being useless, only reserving a hundred. The invasion of the nomad horde of Israelites on the high civilization of the Amorite kings—such as we see it shown on the Egyptian monuments —must have seemed a crushing blow to all culture and advance in the arts; it was much like the terrible breaking up of the Roman Empire by the northern races, it swept away nearly all the good along with the evil; centuries were needed to regain what was lost, along with the further gain of a better moral order than that which had been destroyed. That the Amorite cities were almost deserted, and that rude huts of the stones of the stream stood in the place of brick and stone work, is just in accord with the history; and the wind-swept desolation of the alkali burners' ground, shows when even the barbarous dwellers had left the place.

11. We can now gain a further standpoint in the history of Tell el Hesy, by looking at the series of town walls shown on the northern side in the section. We there see that the stratum of stones which we have just found to represent the age of the Judges, divides the series of successive walls, at the level of 286 to 291 feet. The massive walls which lie below this we must accordingly date to the Amorite times, while those which stand above it must belong to the age of the Jewish Kingdom. Having now shown on what grounds we can succeed in settling the chronology of this site, we will next consider its identification, and then the historical results to be drawn.

CHAPTER IV.

IDENTIFICATION OF LACHISH.

12. As no inscriptions have been found here we can only rely on literary remains for discovering the name of the site. This city was one of the most important places in the low country, or Shephelah. No settlement so large and so ancient is to be seen for a long distance around it; excepting Tell Nejileh, 3½ miles to the south, in the same valley. The reason for these places having been so early settled, and so strongly held, is evident in the nature of the country. Here alone are natural springs, no others existing in all the neighbourhood; nor, so far as I have seen, are there any nearer than the "upper and nether springs" of Caleb some 19 miles off in the Hebron mountains. In a country where deep wells, over a hundred feet in many cases, are the only constant source of water, the possession of springs is as much coveted as it was by the bride of Othniel. To hold the springs means life for the flocks and herds, and the interposing of a serious difficulty for any intruder who might try to occupy the thirsty land around. To the present time thousands of animals are watered here daily, and there are far more Bedawin camps within easy reach of this water than in any equal patch of country. Springs also rise at Tell Nejileh, and a massive dam of concrete has at one time retained their water as a lake at the foot of the tell. This must have been an early work, as that place does not appear to have been occupied since the invasion of Nebuchadrezzar, or perhaps that of Sennacherib. Another great concrete dam lies across the Wady Hesy close to the tell, to retain the rainfall coming down from the eastern branch, or Wady Jizair, showing that even more water than that of the springs was needed here.

13. We therefore see both from the natural features, and from the great Amorite fortification, that this site of Tell el Hesy was probably the most important in the whole district, and Tell Nejileh only second to it.

Turning now to the list of the principal Amorite towns, who united together in the league against the invasion, we find Jerusalem, Hebron, Jarmuth, Lachish, and Eglon, whose rulers Adonizedek, Hoham, Piram, Japhia, and Debir were called "the five kings of the Amorites." Of course Jerusalem, Hebron, and Jarmuth are out of the question; and we only have to consider the claims of Lachish and Eglon. As Eglon disappears from history much before Lachish, and as Tell Nejileh was evidently deserted centuries before Tell el Hesy, there is good presumption that Tell el Hesy should be Lachish, and Tell Nejileh the ancient Eglon. Turning to Jerome's assignment of the ancient sites we find this confirmed, as he states Lachish to have lain near the district of Daroma, which was the Shephelah or low country, and at 7 miles from Beit Jibrin, Tell el Hesy being rather more, or about 10 miles, which is not far out. Again in Joshua it is implied that Lachish and Eglon were close together, as they are described as being taken in one day; and this situation would well accord to the nearness of Hesy to Nejileh. The identity of Tell el Hesy with Lachish was proposed before by Major Conder, on the ground of its position; but now that we know for certain its importance as an Amorite fortress, we see far more reason for accepting this view.

14. There remains the question of the modern names to be considered. Near Tell el Hesy there are two sites of villages, called Umm Lakis and Khurbet Ajlan. These names seem to correspond with Lachish and Eglon, and for some time they have been supposed to be those ancient towns. But as I have mentioned, in the earlier chapter, neither of the sites can claim a history before the Greco-Roman period, and therefore neither can be Amorite cities. Yet so near are they to the sites which we have seen good reason to identify with Lachish and Eglon, that some connection would seem very probable. Now we know that the Jews returned to this district in but feeble force after the Captivity, as it was the southern limit of their occupation then; Eglon is not mentioned at all, and of Lachish we read that "the children of Judah dwelt . . . . at Lachish and the fields thereof," not as in most other towns "and the villages thereof"; this shows that the small sites of the neighbourhood were not occupied, and that the numbers who returned here were but scanty. Now after the removal of the fighting population, and the breaking down of all resistance in Judea by Nebuchadrezzar, we cannot

doubt but that the Bedawin would greedily seize on such valuable watering-places as the springs of the Wady Hesy, for their cattle. And when the feeble fringe of the returning Jews spread down here they would hardly be strong enough to regain their old possessions. Thus the families of Lachish and those of Eglon might very likely found new settlements, as near to the older ones as possible ; and Umm Lakis and Ajlan are just on the opposite bank of the Wady Hesy, within sight of the older settlements, Ajlan being 5 miles from the old Eglon, and Umm Lakis 3 miles from the old Lachish. The name Umm Lakis should also be noted ; the Arab usage of naming parentage is to say "his father (or mother) so-and-so," Suleiman abu David meaning Solomon his father (was) David ; so Ummu Lakis "her mother was Lachish" might readily be corrupted to simply Umm Lakis or "mother Lachish," especially as the Arabs invented a meaning for it, Umm Lakis being "mother of itch." The form of the name therefore suggests a derivation one way or the other, of Lachish and Lakis, and the remains in the ruins at once show which way the derivation ran. That the sites of towns are often known to have shifted a few miles is certain. We only need to remember Jericho, Bubastis, Cairo, Delhi, and even Old Sarum to see that there is nothing new in supposing the Lachish and Eglon of the Greek period to be a short way from the Lachish and Eglon of the Amorite and Jewish history.

CHAPTER V.

HISTORY OF LACHISH.

15. Having now settled the outline of the history of Tell el Hesy from its pottery and strata, and discussed the identification of the site, we will turn to the history of the place as filled in from other sources. From the depth of the accumulations we saw that the town was probably founded in the seventeenth century B.C. This corresponds to the beginning of the XVIIIth dynasty, the age when Egypt began its foreign conquests, and when the Syrians would find the need of massive walls to resist the invaders. The section of the east face (Pl. III) discloses at the lowest level a grand wall 28 ft. 8 ins. thick, of unburnt bricks, which are thin in proportion to their length, more like the Babylonian than the Egyptian form ; the sizes average $22 \cdot 8 \times 12 \cdot 6 \times 4 \cdot 2$ inches, and the bricks are laid in alternate courses of headers and stretchers. Such then were the great walls of the Amorite cities which discouraged the Israelites, "cities walled, and very great." After it had been partly ruined, down to 10 or 11 feet high, it was heightened again by a still thicker wall built on it ; when that was ruined another wall was founded on that, somewhat set back on the outer face ; and that in its turn supported another thick wall of which only two or three feet remain. On both the inner and outer sides of the lowest wall there is a great accumulation of ashes and rubbish, from among which we recovered a large amount of fragments of the earliest Amorite pottery. These Amorite walls were traced along for some 50 feet on the north side, and reached again by two cuttings made in the side of the mound, one cutting disclosing a gateway ; and then a cutting further west, and a tunnel which we cut 13 feet long into the hill, showed us again the same brick wall ; beyond that it was not found owing to the depth of earth over it. The extent of it actually traced will be seen on the plan (Pl. II) ; and the level of the base of it is without much varia-tion, only rising 5 feet in the whole length. I suspect that it did not go

much further westwards, under the N.W. corner, as there was no sign of it found on the west side; it may perhaps turn to the south, and so come in to the outline of the S.W. wall and corner.

16. Of the time of the Judges there is no building to be traced; the stream-worn stones picked up in the bed of the valley, and used for rough building of huts, are all that remain of that age. The evidence of the desertion of the site, and its being used by alkali burners, we have already noticed.

17. The first mention we have of a fortifying of Lachish is that by Rehoboam, in whose list of fenced cities it occurs; and we should, therefore, attribute to him the wall based at 291 feet level, which I have traced along the northern side. This level accordingly we must set to 970 B.C. It is not likely that David or Solomon would fortify places so near home; the Jewish kingdom had too much vitality in it then to need defences in its midst; and it was not till the weakened power of Rehoboam laid him open to foreign invasion, that strongholds were needed within the country. The site was very likely inhabited, however, so soon as the kingdom was well established; and therefore the 5 feet of accumulation under the pilaster building, above the great bed of ashes, may well represent the century from 1050 to 950 B.C. We may, therefore, reckon that building as being of the time of Rehoboam; and the stonework of it, which was reused from some earlier building, is probably of the age of Solomon.

18. The purpose of this structure is unknown; and I could not examine it completely, as it was buried under 30 feet of earth. The walls were all of mud brick, so unified by damp and pressure that they appeared like indistinguishable earth; thus the east side was almost all cut away in the excavations, while in search of more stonework, without any suspicion that it was brickwork. We continued clearing away the face of the mound for some thickness, to uncover the building; but the depth of earth, and the difficulty with the Bedawin about restoring the cropland on the top (which would have been impossible to do had we cut further in), prevented our slicing more away. We therefore worked the cliff face into bays, leaving buttresses to support the vertical section, and then ran tunnels inward to trace the walls. In this way we found the S.W. doorway, and the beginning of the western wall, proving this

building to have been square; but the remainder of the west wall, and the inner half of the north wall, were not traced. The limits of the wall certainly traced are shown in full line, and the parts drawn by analogy in dotted lines (*see* enlarged plan of pilaster building, Pl. II). Within the building is a bed of ashes and pieces of charcoal, evidently from the burning of its roof; but no small objects were found excepting four pottery vases placed in pairs one on the other (Pl. VIII, 128, 134). It is evident that this was not a private house by the number of doors, but rather some public building, probably connected with other structures more to the west. On the south side there were no other walls or constructions as we cleared and tunnelled considerably into it.

It is certain that much of the stonework here was reused from some older works; not only were the blocks in many cases fragmentary, and unsuitable to their positions, but they showed plain marks of adaptation, and the stone jamb of the S.S.E. door had a *graffito* of an animal scratched on it upside down, proving that it had been reversed since its first use. The stone facings seem to have been restricted to the doorways. Each doorway has a threshold and paving of stone; the four eastern doorways have jambs, and a lining on one side; and also the fragments of a deep and thin stone lintel, with a cavetto moulding, closely like that around the rock-hewn chapel or altar at Siloam, which has been reasonably attributed to the early Jewish kings.

19. The slabs bearing pilasters in low relief are the most important objects found at Lachish (Pl. IV). As we have seen, they probably date from the time of Solomon, and they show for the first time an example of early Jewish architecture. They were placed here, each lining the side of a doorway, next to the lock—the side which was exposed when the door stood open. And, moreover, they were upside down, according to our notions of which part is base and which is capital. But, as we have already noticed, there is plain evidence of the stonework being reused here and inverted, and these slabs themselves being only 4 feet high are far too short for the doorway; so we should not attach much importance to the positions in which

PILASTER CARVED
ABOUT 1,000 B.C.

they were found. Two were fallen over, face down, upon the ashes which lay on the thresholds, at the S.E. corner : and the two slabs at the N.E. doorways stood in place. There is no such slab at the S.S.W. doorway. The reason for inverting these slabs may be found in the wish to obtain the dovetailed recess to hold the metal fastening of the lock at the right level, when the stone rested on the ground.

The limestone is a fine white quality, rather soft. The dressing of the block has been first by rough flaking, probably with a stone pick or hammer, as is seen on the back of the slabs ; this is similar to the first dressing of the unfinished column by the Russian church at Jerusalem, which has been considered Solomonic. Most probably a narrow chisel-ended pick (or a chisel and mallet) was used, such as we see the marks of in the later cutting in the slab, about half-inch wide, and making strokes about an inch long, or else the face was pounded flat with a pointed pick-hammer. Lastly, the face of the slab is all smoothed by scraping down with flint scrapers, leaving long scores and scratches on the surface, corresponding to the notches and jags in the flint, a method of dressing which I have not seen elsewhere in Judaea. The surfaces and lines are somewhat wavy, the angles not sharply worked out, and the volute at the top is irregular, the bottom surface between the turns being quite rough. The design of it is stumpy and ungraceful ; but it is much what might have been expected of such a period.

20. The elements of the form are of great value to us in estimating what Jewish architecture—and particularly that of the temple—must have been. The absence of capital is remarkable ; only a volute at the side of the pillar marks the top of it, without any line or break across the pillar. The form of the volute, its thickening close to its attachment, and its position as fixed against the pillar, recall strongly a ram's horn nailed up against a wooden post. And we may well see in this the type of the horns of the altar, so often mentioned in describing the temple decoration. There is nothing in the text to imply whether these were bulls' horns standing upwards, or rams' horns curving downward ; and though the bull's horn has been more favoured by imaginative restorers, this evident ram's horn decoration seems rather to give us the correct idea. On comparing this with other architecture, the Ionic volute capital is known in Assyrian art ; on the sculptures of Sargon, columns with a

volute head are seen ; but as these are two or three centuries later than these pilasters, they do not so much affect the question of the origin of the ornament.

We see on this slab at Lachish the earliest type of the Asiatic volute, and glean from its simple and primitive outline whence the origin of the form arose. The use of rams' horns to decorate a pillar is much like the bulls' skulls affixed by the Greeks to the architraves of their buildings ; and the position of the horns of a sacrifice decorating the corners of the altar is evidently natural. The shaft of the pilaster is doubtless more sloping than would be the case in pillars, but it suggests that the pillars were greatly tapered in proportion to those of other architectures. There is on each slab a slight expansion of the shaft close to the base, apparently to accentuate the recess below it. The base itself is of a simple curve, but unlike the idea of Egyptian bases, which always were very wide, spreading far beyond the column, and rounded both to the upper and lower sides. What may have been the original purpose of these slabs is not certain. They are all left halves, and in two cases had a ridge of stone remaining projecting down the mid line, showing that they were never bilateral. Being only about 4 feet high, they are too short for a doorway by themselves. But varying somewhat in height (45 and 49½ inches), they cannot have been placed close together, as around a room, or casing a pedestal. Altogether there seems no more appropriate use for these unilateral decorations .than the side of a doorway (see Pl. IV) ; though in their first design they probably stood on a plain stone dado some 3 feet in height, and so reached high enough to appear suitably in support of the lintel.

The lintels that were found were all fallen over, and much broken up, that of the N.N.E. doorway was almost entire, lying on its .face inside the doorway just as it had been overthrown. The form seems evidently borrowed from Egypt ; but it is singularly bare and plain, for there is no trace of ornament on the large flat surface under the roll. The cavetto in each example is somewhat drooping at the front ; an excessive curvature reminding us of the exaggerated outlines of the style of Ramessu III, rather than the lighter style of previous Egyptian work. The slabs are about 2½ feet high (varying, 29·7 and 31·1 inches), and the thickness is but 7 or 8 inches at the bottom, and 2½ or 4 inches

D

behind the hollow.   So they were of little value for strength, and must
have been mainly intended as a decoration.   The successive sections of

PORTION OF CORNICE, XTH CENTURY, B.C.

the lintel, and outlines of the pilaster are copied from different examples
(Pl. IV) in order to show the extent of the variations.

21. The next step in the history of Lachish, after the Rehoboam
period, is seen probably in the building of the thin wall on the front edge
of Rehoboam's wall, to heighten and strengthen it.   The older wall
must have been decayed down to only 6 feet high, and this suggests that
some time had elapsed since it was built, about 974 B.C.   If it had been
destroyed by Shishak in his subsequent (2 Chr. xi, 9, xii, 2) invasion, it
would have been more overthrown ; probably decay, and the rise of
ground in the city, needed its renewal.   So far as we can judge, this
refortification is due to Jehoshaphat ; he had subdued the Philistines and
Arabians (2 Chr. xvii, 11), and so needed a fortress in this position ; and
he garrisoned all the fenced cities (ver. 2), and built fortresses and store
cities in Judah (ver. 12).   This wall therefore at 298 level, on the N.
face of Rehoboam's wall, may well be of about 910 B.C.

After that we do not read of any further fortifying for a century. Amaziah fled to Lachish in 810 B.C., and was there slain (2 K. xiv, 19). But the next fortifying seems to have been due to Uzziah. He specially attacked the Philistines (2 Chr. xxvi, 6), and therefore would need a fort at Lachish as a base of operations. Also he built much (ver. 10); and he raised much cattle in the Shephelah, for which the watering-place of Lachish would be very valuable (ver. 10). For all these reasons it is highly probable that one of the walls of Lachish would be his work; and perhaps the fragment left inside of the wall of Jehoshaphat (298 to 300 level) may be the base of Uzziah's wall, about 800 B.C.

22. After a short time that wall was intentionally destroyed; this we gather from the very low fragment left; for it would not be naturally decayed away so low, and if used for long it would be flanked with rubbish so much that a destroyer would not remove it so thoroughly. This razing of the wall is probably due then to the ravaging of the country by Rezin and Pekah in 735 B.C. during their fruitless beleaguering of Jerusalem. (2 K. xvi. 5). But immediately another wall rises on that (300–305 level), which is probably due to a renewal by Ahaz, whose architectural tastes are recorded. Apparently the stone steps at the south side of the city are also about this period. On the plan, at the S.E. edge of the fortification, will be seen a piece of wall with a doorway; and adjoining it on the west a flight of steps leading up into the city. (*See* lower part of Pl. IV.) This construction is rough; but of great interest as showing the masonry which is certainly of the time of the Jewish kings. The stones have drafted edges with a rough central boss; but there is no trace of the comb pick (or " claw-tool ") on the dressing. On the contrary, the only tool marks are the long stroke of a pointed pick, like the marks on the fort of Tell Safi (Gath) and on the first building of the Beit el Khulil near Hebron.

23. Behind the wall of Ahaz on the north side of the town is a foundation of a thicker wall (303 to 305 level), which has evidently been ruined very shortly after it was built. And on the south side of the town we find a long glacis slope, of some 30 feet breadth in all; formed of blocks of stone, bedded in the earth, and faced with white plaster (*see* enlarged section Pl. III). This belongs apparently to some hasty defence, as it bears but a very small wall on the top of it (333 to 335 level); and

this wall, like the thicker wall on the north, has evidently been razed to the ground soon after its erection.   These details correspond with what

DRAFTED MASONRY AND·STEPS, VIIITH CENTURY, B.C.

we should expect at the time of Sennacherib's invasion in 701 B.C.   The cities of this district had been put in repair, either by Hezekiah when subduing the Philistines (2 K. xviii, 8), or in view of the Assyrian invasion ; and very soon afterwards Sennacherib besieged and destroyed Lachish.   And we see above this level on the north side (305 to 310), that the town was greatly injured, and that the buildings after that were largely of rude stones, as in the old barbarism of the Judges.

24. At this point we will turn back for a moment to notice the chronology shown by the south side of the town, as we have hitherto been mainly dealing with the north walls.   The pilaster building was of about 950 B.C.   After that was ruined, filled up with its own rubbish, and entirely passed over out of sight (*see* enlarged section Pl. III), a long range of building was set up at 319 level ; this, by its position, would be of about 800 B.C.   This may well, therefore, be one of the establishments of Uzziah.   On the plan will be seen the long line of wall, 85 feet from N.

to S., with cross walls forming chambers. The section shows us how that this became buried in rubbish, which covered up as much as 13 feet high of the building, and which must have taken long to accumulate. This building was however completely covered before the making of the glacis and wall of Hezekiah about 701 B.C. We thus can trace a series of building on the south as well as on the north side of the city.

25. After the destruction of Lachish by Sennacherib, there does not seem to have been more than one refortifying of the site. This is the wall at 310 to 319 level on the north, which though thin at the east end, is much thicker in the middle of the side. This can be traced around the city (see the plan) to the thick wall built over the glacis on the south. This large work is most likely that of Manasseh ; as about 660 B.C. he fortified Jerusalem, and put commanders in all the fenced cities of Judah. This cannot have been done to resist Assyria, as he was a dependent of that power (2 Chr. xxxiii, 13) ; but just then Egypt was rising under Psamtek, and defence was needed at Lachish, as that city guarded the high road from Egypt to Jerusalem. These therefore are the walls which were besieged by Nebuchadrezzar (Jer. xxxiv, 7) in 590 B.C. After that destruction, the place was probably desolate and left to the Bedawin and their cattle. Even after the return of the Jews, about 445, Lachish appears to have been hardly reoccupied, as we have seen ; at least the surrounding villages were not restored, and before long the settlement was moved to the later site of Umm Lakis. On the top of the city mound is found at the N.W. part some amount of Greek pottery of the Vth cent. B.C. But after this was a desolation, and neither Greek nor Roman attempted to occupy the site.

We have now traced the history of the place, as seen in the remains, and in the Jewish records ; the correspondence is complete ; and though there may yet be some question as to the attribution of the successive city walls between that of Rehoboam, and the last one, that of Manasseh, yet in the historical relation of the other remains, we have reached a material form of what has hitherto been only literary history without a solid resting point.

CHAPTER VI.

STRUCTURAL DETAILS.

26. In this chapter we shall notice the plans and sections, and consider the details of the measurements and levels.

Pl. I. Tell el Hesy.—The Wady Jizair and Wady Muleihah join into one stream, which is named Wady el Hesy below the junction. Originally the Wady Jizair ran into the Wady el Hesy about quarter of a mile more to the north ; but it has brought down a bar of shingle which has gradually forced it further south, so as to form a detour around a wide shoal, which is a few feet above the water, and is cultivated with a scanty crop of barley. The small watercourses which run down at this point have a rapid fall, and only contain water during storms ; but the Wady Muleihah runs with water from springs above this point as late as June ; and a fine spring about a furlong north of the Tell in the Wady Hesy yields a constant supply of water. The watercourse on the west of the site runs down into the Wady Hesy, which turns along the north of the town.

The contours are marked for every 20 feet, with dotted lines ; and in two cases 10-foot contours are marked with broken lines to explain the form of the ground. The absolute level was taken from the Survey of the Fund, which fixed the top of Tell el Hesy as 340 feet above sea level. From the top I levelled up and down the site, using a suspended mirror leveller. This is rapid to use, and quite accurate enough for such work ; the discrepancy on going down one side of the hill, along the base, and up the other side was not a foot ; and on levelling all round the hill there was only 5 inches difference on 1,000 feet. This is as close as naked eye observations can be expected ; and is amply enough for chronological levels. The contours were drawn by eye, on a plan on which details were entered, by sighting around at each level with the mirror.

The most prominent object is of course the great mound of the city,

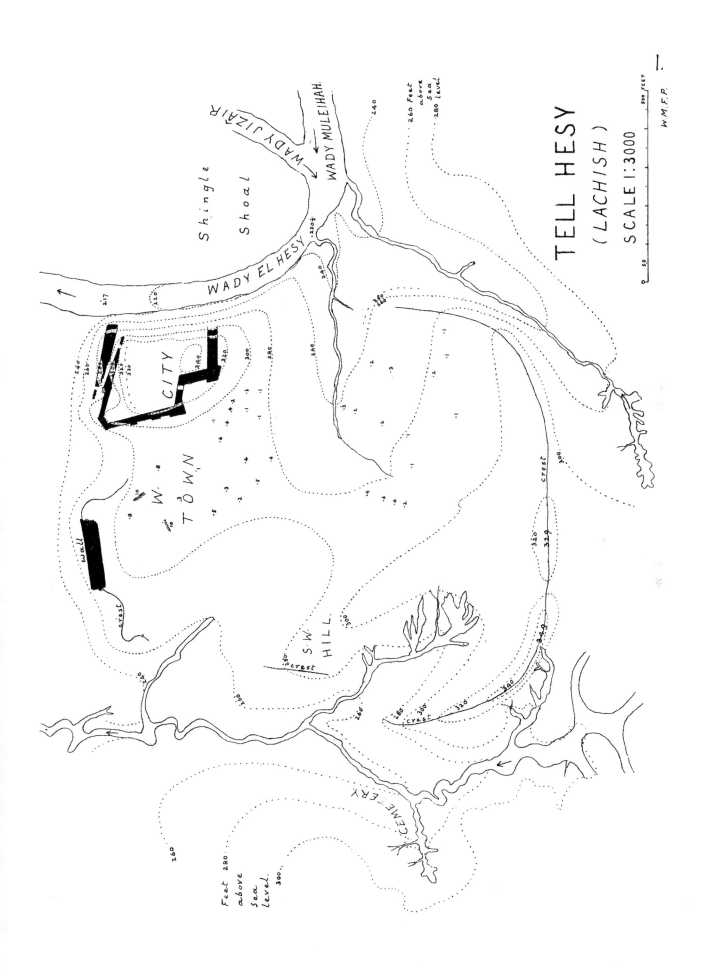

TELL HESY
(LACHISH)
SCALE 1:3000

W.M.F.P.

I.

Feet above sea level

WADY JIZAIR

WADY MULEIHAH.

Shingle Shoal

WADY EL HESY

CITY

W. TOWN

wall

crest

S.W. HILL

crest

crest

CEMETERY

which rises 120 feet above the stream. The east face is a steep slope at the angle of rest, ending below in a cliff about 20 feet high, where the marly earth is harder, and is cut away sharply by the scour of the winter torrents. None of the walls were visible when I began work, the whole surface being uniformly smoothed over by denudation. Next after the mound we notice the high rampart thrown up to form the S.W. side of the enclosure. This is made on a naturally high ground, and the artificial ridge being still as much as 7 feet high, it rises to 349 feet, or 9 feet higher than the mound. This ridge is very steep, as will be seen from the contours, and is furrowed on the outer side by water channels. The crest of the ground on the south side of the enclosure curves around on the east and the west. On the east it tails off near the little valley ; and there is no bank on the north of that, the edge of the ground to the stream being the natural boundary. On the west side the ridge tails down, and disappears at a small valley ; but a distinct edge to the ground is seen on the S.W. hill ; and, after another small valley, this edge can be seen again running on to the thick wall on the north side. This wall I could scarcely trace in the earth which surrounds it, and the inner side could only be seen at the west end because of the crops. It may therefore not be all as thick as at this end ; I measured it as 700 inches there, but have only drawn it as 500, in consideration of the uncertainty.

27. Outside of the city fortification, on the flat ground to the west is a small depth of earth, varying from a foot to 10 feet. There was no long occupation of this ground therefore ; and nearly all the pottery is Amorite. Some walls were found, of which the directions are marked on the plan. Wherever pits were made we went down to undisturbed clay, and the depth in feet is shown by the figures on the plan. The pottery found in the lower depths is not only Amorite in style, but more archaic than any found in the city. I believe that the earliest settlement was on the rise of hill in this west town ; and that the great Amorite wall on the north of the city perhaps runs through all in one with the thick wall which bounds the west town. The valley worn away on the N.W. of the city has apparently cut out all traces of this wall there. But certainly I did not see any wall like the great Amorite wall on the west of the city. It seems then that the Amorite town covered all the outer enclosure, as

pottery of that age was found wherever we dug, although only a few feet of soil remain.

The south-west hill is not striking, but is named here as we cleared over a good part of it, and found a good deal of Amorite and Phoenician pottery, in the foot or so of soil over the native clay.

28. The cemetery is outside of the town enclosure, on a slope of clean sandy ground, covered with short grass. It does not appear to have been for human remains; no bones that were found appeared human; and only a little wire circlet that might have been a child's bracelet would lead us to think of human burials. Among the fragments of bones found here is a part of the lower jaw of an ass, according to Prof. Boyd Dawkins. These bones were found in jars, which were all filled with sand; the filling sand was often white, and distinct from the light brown sand of the hill. The jars were generally large (Pl. VII, 123-4-5) and often contained smaller vessels such as figs. 138 to 146. Usually there was a bowl, figs. 106 to 112, inverted on the top of the jar, as a cover. The jars were upright in the ground. Small pottery was also found separately, particularly the common forms 138 and 144. I have named this place a cemetery, because bones are found there; but it may as likely have been a place of religious sacrifice and offerings. Such pottery as is found, belongs in the city mainly to the time of the Jewish kings; and that idolatrous worships should have occurred at that time is not surprising when we read the denunciation of Micah (1, 13) that Lachish was "the beginning of the sin to the daughter of Zion: for the transgressions of Israel were found in thee."

29. *Pl. II. Plan of Walls of Tell el Hesy.* On this plan the levels of the bases of the walls are marked upon them. Thus the north Amorite wall, the outermost, is 265 feet level at its base by the valley edge, and 270 level near the west. The intermediate wall of Rehoboam is 290 at the valley, and 292 level further along. The lesser walls are omitted. And the top wall, of Manasseh, is 311 at the valley, 303 further on, 289 at the N.W. tower; rises to 322 at the S.W. recess, and gateway (?), and then falls to 305 where it approaches the valley: but this latter level is out of proportion to the rest of the mound, as it is built on the lower part of the sloping glacis. The north side of the town near the west end is very difficult

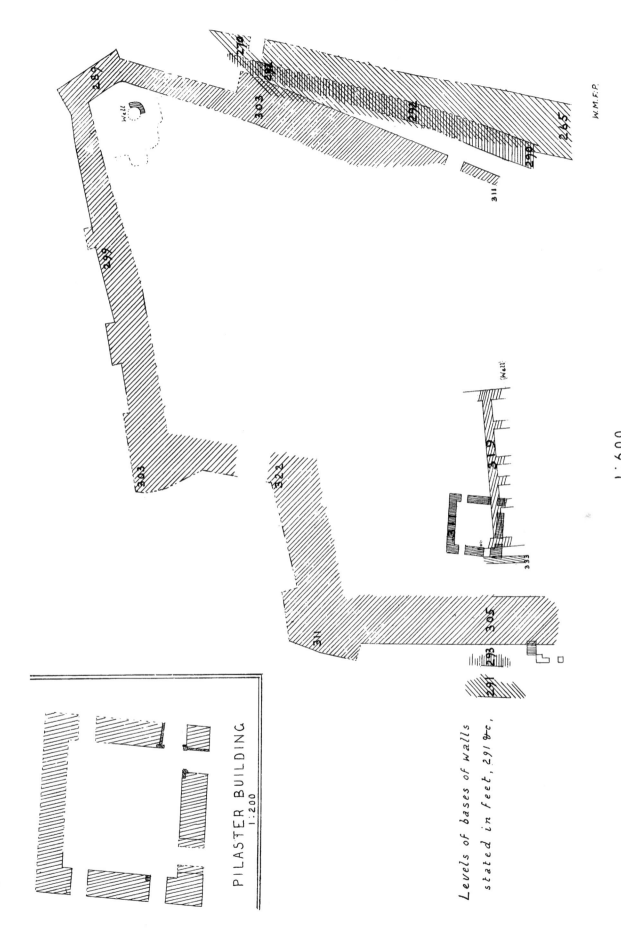

PILASTER BUILDING
1:200

Levels of bases of walls
stated in feet, 291 &c,

1:600

PLAN OF WALLS OF TELL HESY

W.M.F.P.

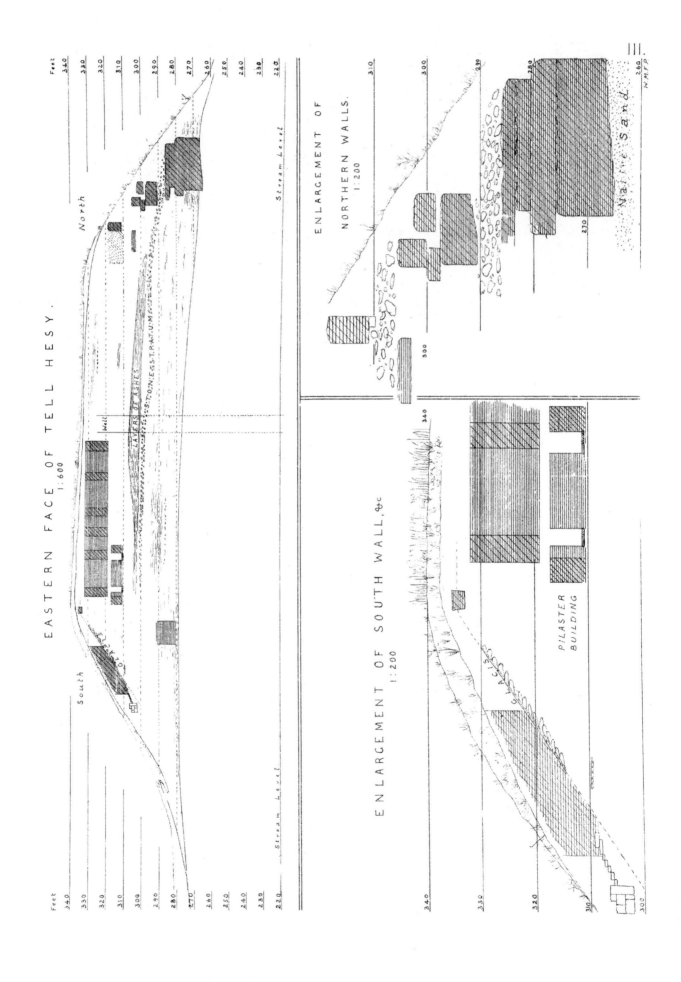

EASTERN FACE OF TELL HESY.
1:600

ENLARGEMENT OF NORTHERN WALLS.
1:200

ENLARGEMENT OF SOUTH WALL, &c.
1:200

to trace owing to the valley which has cut through all the walls of denudation. I could not even trace any of the upper wall across this; but as the portions on each side were exactly in one line, there could be no doubt of their original continuity. All the parts of walls actually traced are marked in full outline; those only inferred are in broken line. Most of these walls were found by making cross trenches through the sides of the mound.

The reasons for identifying the portions of walls with one another are, that the Rehoboam wall (290-292 level) is all one by the level of its base, and the parts being in a line: that the north and south parts of the top wall (Manasseh's) are one by the thickness; and that the N.W. tower and corner belongs to that, by its being so far inside the Rehoboam line, and being in the line of the Manasseh wall. What the west side was in the Rehoboam fort, seems quite uncertain; perhaps it was inside of the present west side, which may have been extended owing to the stream cutting away the east of the town. The N.W. corner looks as if it had been run out as far as possible, in order to include the well on as low a level as might be. This well is lined with blocks of rough Gaza sandstone; but strange to say one side of it has caved in, and the blocks lay filling the space. The shaft was 88 ins. across, and the courses from 10 to 14 ins. thick. The area of this corner was cleared as far as the dotted line, down to about 300; the top of the wall being about 305 level. And at the W.N.W. corner a large pit was sunk down to about 287, to find the base of the wall. In the re-entering angle at the S.W. I could not detect any trace of a wall at the part left blank, although I sank pits there and searched the earth very carefully. I could only conclude then that a gateway had existed here; though unfortunately I had not time to settle this, in the three days between the harvest here, and all my men deserting for harvesting at Bureir. At the east end of the south wall, a very large trench was cut inwards in the hill, and there were found to be two lower walls, below the glacis and that of Manasseh. These are marked on the plan, 293 and 291 level; but their age is uncertain, only 2 or 3 feet remains of either of them.

30. The pilaster building has been already described in general. Its length from N. to S. is 274 ins. inside; and from E. to W. about 260. The doorways all had limestone sills, laid on a bed of about 6 ins. of

E

clean yellow sand. The slabs with pilasters were set upside down against the lock sides of the doorways, but two had fallen over, and only the E.N.E. and N.N.E. remained in place. There was no stone lining to the sides of the S.S.W. doorway. At each doorway with a pilaster were found pieces of the stone lintel slab with the cavetto moulding fallen inside. The arrangement of this building is rough; the N.N.E. doorway is 50 ins. wide outside and 54 ins. inside, the stonework narrowing it 5·2 on the west and 7·0 on the east, so as to leave an opening only 42·0 wide. The adjoining doorway, E.N.E., is 48 wide, and the stonework only 39½ wide. So it is clear that there is no exactitude in the building. Two pairs of bowls, each pair being placed with one upright, and one inverted over it, were found inside the building near the south wall. The types are in Pl. VIII, 128 and 134. All the inside of the building was strewn with charcoal and ashes; and the conflagration had reddened the brick walls, and partly calcined the limestone slabs.

31. Above the pilaster building is a long range of chambers: these have been nearly destroyed by the falling away of the cliff; but very probably other chambers exist on the other side of the long wall, as a wall was found to run westwards at the south end of it. These chambers and walls measure, from the north end, 64 wall, 144 chamber, 48, 186, 49, 79, 57, 92, 56, 193, and 61 ins.; the long wall is 56 thick.

. At the extreme east edge of the S. wall, partly destroyed by the fall of the cliff, is a part of a building and a flight of steps (*see* Pl. IV). The plan of the remains will be seen to be the S.W. corner of a wall, which is 28 along the inside, and 84 long outside, with a thickness of 41 inches. On the east of this is a doorway 59 wide, and then a block of masonry of which two courses remained when discovered. The steps begin above the door-sill level, probably led up to by a slope of earth. They ran up outside of the building on the west. Their breadth is 65 ins.; the tread averaging 13 ins., and the rise 7 ins.: their work is very rough, being pieced together of several blocks to each step. From the position it seems as if these had been the steps leading up to the city gate; and that the building at the side was a guardhouse by the entrance.

Pl. III. Eastern face of Tell el Hesy.—This has been described in detail in the history of the place, where all the walls have been noticed, and their historical connection.

1:20

← Hole for lock
bolt. Fastening

In

Out

Section of doorway of pilaster building, restored. About 1000 B.C.

1:40

Flight of steps, and door of guardhouse. 700 B.C.

W.M.F.P.

32. The brickwork varies greatly in size, not only in different walls, but in the same wall. The sizes of the bricks are as follow :

Amorite wall, 265 ft. 22·8 × 12·6 × 4·2.
  (Alternate courses of headers and stretchers.)
Rehoboam's wall, 292 ft. 13·4 × 7·3 × 3·7.
Manasseh's wall, 310 ft. 15·9 × 15·9 ? × 5·7.
(Probably square tiles, as no narrow end was found.)
N.W. tower, 19·0 × 12·0 × 5·4 (4·0 to 6·3).
W. wall, 17·4 × 12·3 × 5·1 (15·5 to 19·0).
S.W. corner, 19·0 × 10·1 × 4·3.
Wall over glacis, 19·4 × 8·3 to 12·8 × 4·7.

This last is very variable; the lengths being 17·6 to 21·0, and the breadths commonly 11·5, and also 9·4 and 8·4 in other groups. It thus seems that little can be traced by the sizes of the bricks, and that there was no very fixed gauge for bricks at one period, as there was in Egypt.

33. *Pl. IV. Pilaster and lintel.*—These have been already fully described in the historical account of the remains. In this drawing I have ventured to restore the arrangement that seems most probable. The lintel was inside the building, as it was in each case found fallen within the walls. The pilaster backing up against the stop of the door, and with the dovetailed hole cut in it, to set in the metal holder of the lock-bolt, must have stood thus, facing over the thickness of the wall. The plain dado beneath is not only required to give the needful height to the doorway, but it also raises the lock-hole to a suitable height from the ground. The pilasters here are drawn from photographs or casts; and the lintels from photographs of the fragments built together in position. The additional outlines by the side of the restored doorway show the slight variations in form. Below this is an outline of the masonry of the guardhouse and steps, drawn from measurements and a photograph. This shows the raised bosses on the blocks, and the generally rough style of the building; much of it is made up with small stones and mud between the blocks. The steps are 65 ins. wide. The masonry 84, the doorway 59 ins. The height of the masonry is 58 ins., and the two courses on the right are 10·8 ins. each.

34. *The Styles of Masonry in Palestine.* Now that we have some
certain data for settling the styles of stone dressing, it is most desirable to
test in future such results as we may provisionally reach.

The first style, which we may call the Phoenician, is that of flaking
and pocking. The pilaster slabs, and the masonry of that building, is
flaked by heavy blows to give it the first dressing. This same flaking is
to be seen on the great monolith lying in the quarry in the Russian
quarter at Jerusalem. The flaking was reduced on the monolith by
pocking, or bruising down the surface at small points with a heavy
pointed hammer. The pilaster slabs I am not certain about, as the
dressed face has been scraped down by means of flint scrapers, or
"dragged"; and we only see now the long scratches of the scraping.
The later holes cut in the slabs are done with a chisel or pick of
metal, ½-inch wide. The pocked dressing I have seen on one reused
block in the galleries called Solomon's Stables under the Haram;
probably built in by Herod or Justinian. This same peculiar dressing
is that of the stone work of the temple at Hagir Kim in Malta; only
there it is developed into almost an ornamental arrangement of pocks.
This temple is called Phoenician; and what lends some support to
this, is that just the same system of stone tables, each on two blocks,
placed around the inside of an enclosure, is to be seen in the sacred
enclosures of the villages in Philistia to this day. The same pock
dressing is that of the wrought stones at Stonehenge; the best
examples of it are on the flat tops of the uprights of the great
trilithons. And another curious formation occurs there as well as at
Hagir Kim; the edge of an upright is somewhat raised, so as to
form a sort of tray, and a corresponding cutting is made in the cap
stone. This is of course in addition to the rough tenons at Stonehenge.

The second sort of dressing is the long-stroke picking. This is
done with an edge or point, without showing any breadth of cut;
the strokes are somewhat curved; and in groups of parallel cuts. This
is seen on the great blocks of the first building of the Beit el Khulil
near Hebron, which is almost certainly early work. Also it can just
be traced on the sandstone masonry of the gate-house, and steps at
Lachish, probably about 700 B.C. Also it is the dressing of the wall
at Tell Safi; this being surrounded by Amorite or early Jewish pottery,

and without any traces of Greek or later remains, is probably the old Philistine fortress of Gath.

The third style is the "claw-tool," or "comb-pick" as it is more clearly named. This is a heavy pick with a broad end, cut into teeth, forming a comb which was pounded slowly against the stone, leaving rows of narrow little parallel cuts. It is a very common tool now in Syria and Egypt. No certainly early example of this work is known. Not a trace of it was found at Lachish. In Egypt it is always a sign of the Ptolemaic times, and no earlier stone cutting I know of shows any trace of it. Prof. Hayter Lewis tells me that it occurs on the stones of the pre-Persian Parthenon at Athens. It is therefore known in Greece, two or three centuries before it appears in the east. And it is very unlikely that it should have been used in Egypt for centuries without leaving a trace, or that it should have been common in Syria without being known in Egypt. On the contrary, at Naukratis I found how much we are indebted to Greek invention for the forms of our modern tools, which occur there in iron during the VIth cent. B.C.; whereas no such forms were used in Egypt down to that time. It is most probable then that the comb-pick was invented in Greece, and thence introduced into Egypt and Syria. If so we must date the present dressing of all the stones of the Haram at Jerusalem to Herod; and thus confirm the statement of Josephus that Herod entirely rebuilt the great Temple wall from the foundation. The dressing of the stones of the Haram at Hebron is similar; the flat draft being comb-picked, and the face only slightly projecting and flattened. The great pool at Hebron is lined with precisely similar masonry. The relining of the Beit el Khulil, also bears the comb-pick marks; and this lining was put in probably by Herod, as there are inscriptions of the IInd cent. A.D. cut on the stones *in situ.* We have then now sufficient material to form a likely hypothesis of stone working; and in all future explorations there will be something for a guide on the subject, and something to be checked and tested whenever dated masonry can be found.

35. *Lachish on the Assyrian Monuments.*—Everyone who knows the Assyrian sculptures in the British Museum is familiar with one of

the largest compositions there—the Siege of Lachish, by Sennacherib. On looking at this, the truth of the geography of it is seen at once, when the site is known.   The city stands, on the sculpture, with a gentle slope up to it on the left hand, a steeper slope in front, and a vertical cliff directly down from the base of the wall on the right.   This corresponds to the view from the south.   The left side is the west, the only side on which the ground rises gently; the steep front is the south side; and the cliff on the right is the east side, which was always worn away steeply by the stream.   The gateway in front of the town must be that of which the steps were found on the south, leading up the glacis.   Thence the captives are led away to the king at his camp on the right; this was therefore on the tongue of land between the Wady Muleihah and Wady Jizair, where the wells above and wells below Lachish could both be reached, and where a great dam across the Wady Jizair probably retained a reservoir of water in those times.   The valley with palms, on the right, must be the Wady Muleihah.   This testing of a sculpture executed in Assyria, hundreds of miles distant from the place, is of great interest, as it shows that some sketches and notes were actually made, probably by a royal designer attached to the court, one of the secretaries.   The essential points of the relative steepness of the three contiguous sides, the gateway, and the likely position for the camp, all show that the view is not a mere fancy piece.

Another point of particular interest in this view is the decoration of the walls.   Along the top is a band of ornament, consisting of large discs with central knobs, divided one from the other by vertical bars. This might be set down as a fancy of the artist, were it not clearly the origin of the characteristic ornament of the Herodian Jewish tombs. On those the discs are placed between the triglyphs of a Greek architrave; or changed into rosettes.   But the motive is certainly the same, and the truth of the Assyrian artist is thus confirmed.   The origin of these discs along the parapet seems to have been a line of shields, held by soldiers, or hanging on the battlements.   And we may see here the purpose of the 300 shields of beaten gold, made by Solomon for the house of the forest of Lebanon; they were the external and prominent decorations which caught the eye, and were specially noted in the description.

36. Three weights were found in the excavations.   In the pilaster building was a small disc of limestone, with a dot mark on one side, weighing 378·1 grains ; this is evidently 3 Assyrian shekels of 126·0 grains each.   Low on the south side was a conoid rounded weight of haematite, with a groove around it, weighing 49·7 grains ; this is probably a quarter of the Aeginetan standard, which occurs in haematite weights in Syria ; or it may be a third of the Egyptian *kat*, which was also used in Syria,   In the N.W. tower, at about 295 level, was a cylinder of coarse dull red haematite, now weighing 142·3 grains, probably 144 originally ; this is the Egyptian *kat* weight.   Several scraps of bronze were found, wire armlets, hair-pins, a knife, and a sheep bell ; and some iron fragments, a knife, and arrow-heads.

CHAPTER VII.

The Pottery.

37. The excavations at Tell el Hesy proved to be an ideal place for determining the history of pottery in Palestine. And once settle the pottery of a country, and the key is in our hands for all future explorations. A single glance at a mound of ruins, even without dismounting, will show as much to anyone who knows the styles of the pottery, as weeks of work may reveal to a beginner. At Tell el Hesy

POTTERY FROM S.W. CEMETERY, XIITH CENTURY B.C.

there was a deep and stratified town to work on, and therefore good scope for dating by levels. And a clear section of the town had been cut open by the scouring of the torrent, so that any level could be worked

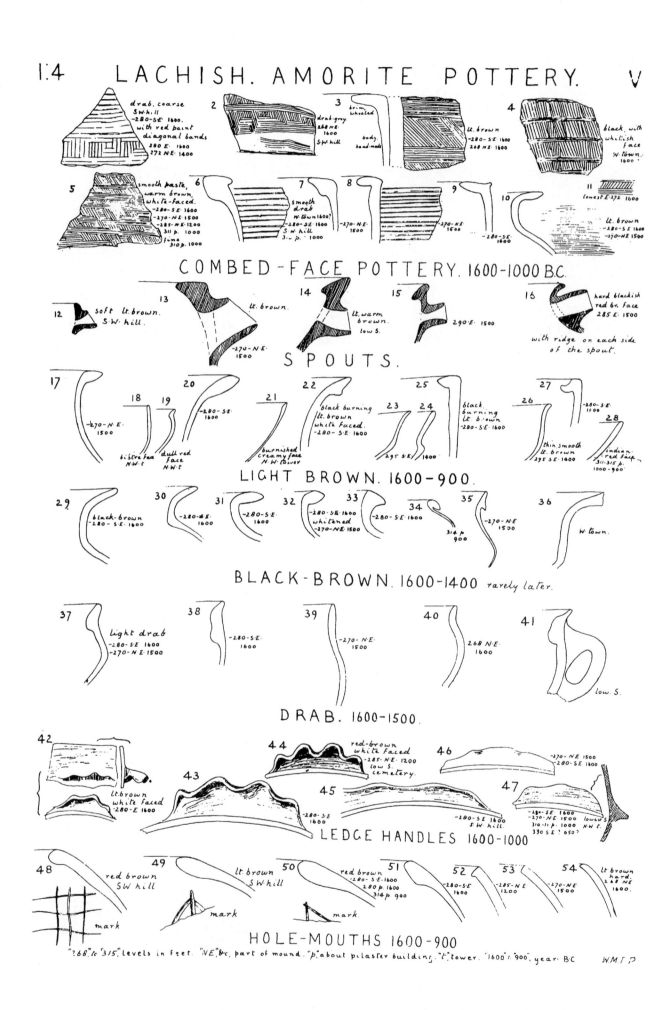

1 drab, coarse S.W.h.ll -280-S·E· 1600. with red paint diagonal bands 290 E. 1600 272 N·E· 1400

2

3 br.. wheeled 268·E· 1600 S.W. hill body hand·made

4 lt. brown -280-S·E· 1600 268 N·E· 1600

4 black, with whitish face W. town 1600

5 smooth paste, warm brown, white·faced. -280-S·E· 1600 -270-N·E· 1500 -285-N·E· 1200 311 p. 1000 fine 310 p. 1000

6

7 smooth drab W.town 1600? -280-S·E· 1600 S·W· hill 3·· p· 1000

8 -270·N·E· 1500

9 -270·N·E· 1500

10 -280·S·E· 1600

11 lowest E·272 1600
lt. brown -280-S·E· 1600 -270-N·E· 1500

COMBED-FACE POTTERY. 1600-1000 B.C.

12 soft lt.brown. S·W· hill.

13 lt. brown. -270-N·E· 1500

14 lt.warm brown. low S.

15 290·E· 1500

16 hard blackish red bv. face 285·E· 1500

with ridge on each side of the spout.

SPOUTS.

17 -270-N·E· 1500

18 bistre faa N·W·t

19 dull red face N·W·t

20 -280·S·E· 1600

21 burnished creamy face N·W· tower

22 black burning lt. brown white faced -280-S·E· 1600

23

24 295 S·E· 1400

25 black burning lt. brown -280-S·E· 1600

26 thin smooth lt. brown 295 S·E· 1400

27 -280·S·E· 1600

28 indian. red face 311-315 p· 1000-900

LIGHT BROWN. 1600-900.

29 black-brown -280-S·E· 1600

30 -280·S·E· 1600

31 -280·S·E· 1600

32 -280·S·E· 1600

33 -280·S·E· 1600 whitened -270-N·E· 1500

34 314 p· 900

35 -270-N·E· 1500

36 W. town.

BLACK-BROWN. 1600-1400 rarely later.

37 light drab -280-S·E· 1600 -270-N·E· 1500

38 -280·S·E· 1600

39 -270-N·E· 1500

40 268 N·E· 1600

41 low. S.

DRAB. 1600-1500.

42 lt.brown white faced -280-E· 1600

43

44 red-brown white faced -285-N·E· 1200 low S. cemetery.

45 -280·S·E· 1600 S·W· hill.

46 -270-N·E· 1500 -280-S·E· 1600

47 -280-S·E· 1600 -270-N·E· 1500 310-11 p· 1000 330 S·E·? 650? lowest S. N·W·t.

LEDGE HANDLES 1600-1000

48 mark

49 red brown S·W· hill

50 lt. brown S·W· hill mark

51 red brown -280-S·E· 1600 280 p. 1600 314 p. 900 mark

52 -280-S·E· 1600

53 -285-N·E· 1200

54 -270-N·E· 1500

54 lt. brown hard 268 N·E 1600.

HOLE-MOUTHS 1600-900

"268" to "315", levels in feet. "N·E" &c, part of mound. "p" about pilaster building. "t" tower. "1600" to "900", year· B·C   WMFP

in at once.   In these happy circumstances a few weeks sufficed to obtain pottery of each age, from the Amorite to the Greek times.   All of the pottery found was kept classified ; roughly at first, and then as I began to learn it, and to be able to understand the town, each piece was levelled to within a foot or two.   Every distinctive piece was kept, and is here drawn on Pls. V. to IX.   The nature of the pottery is stated ; the levels in feet, and the parts of the site, at which it has been found ; and the approximate dates corresponding to those levels, stated in years B.C. in upright figures, after the levels.   Where the level noted was only general, and not exact, the figures are put between two short dashes.   The letter *p.* refers to the pilaster building region ; and *t.* to the tower at the N.W. corner.   The cemetery and S.W. hill are not dated ; but in general I should assign them to about 900 or 1000 B.C , or possibly to pre-Israelite times.

38. The Amorite pottery (Pl. V.) is very distinctive and unlike any other in Syria, Egypt, or other countries that I know.

The combed-face pottery is usually hand made, though the brims are wheel turned.   It has been smoothed on the outside by scraping it down with a comb, or notched edge of wood, and then scraping it around. Perhaps the earliest example is Pl. V. 4, which has been scraped down, and then rubbed around with the finger.   No. 2 looks also rude and early.   The most usual is No. 5.   Another form of this is where the pot is all smoothed on the wheel, but the notched scraper has still been used, making concentric fine raised rings, as in Nos. 6 and 8.   This style is mostly found in the earliest period ; it extended in use but rarely down to the beginning of the Jewish Kings, and was soon entirely extinguished by the Phoenician styles.

The Spouts on the Amorite pottery are also peculiar ; they belong to both the upright sided vessels, such as were combed (No. 13) ; to the bowls (Nos. 14 and 15); and to the curved lip vases (No. 16).   The last is peculiar for having a ridge running around the vessel at the level of the spout and enclosing it.

The light-brown pottery is of the upright form (Nos. 25, 27), the open pan form (20, 22), the vase with lip (17) and the small bowls without thick edges (18, 19, 21, 23, 24, 26, 28).   These last come down to later times than the large pottery.

F

The black-brown pottery is all of the lipped vase form, except the very early bowl, 36.

The drab pottery is all of the deep bowl form, mostly with a thickening on the inner edge of the lip (37, 38, 41) which is not seen in other materials.

The ledge-handles are very striking and quite unknown elsewhere. They belonged to large vessels with upright sides; and it is very possible that they were parts of the combed-face vessels. The ledge is of various degrees. The most usual is figured in three positions (42); one of the finest examples is (43); sometimes it is very deeply and sharply waved as in (44); or else slightly curved, as (45); or merely nicked, as (46); or lastly a plain ledge (47), without ornament or hollow. On the whole this plain type (47) seems to be a degeneration, as it is the only form which survived into the Jewish times.

The hole-mouths are so called for lack of a better name. The opening is simply a hole cut in the vessel; without any lip, or turn, or decoration, beyond a slight thickening for strength in some cases. This type just survived into Jewish times; but it is as markedly Amorite as the combing, and ledge handles. Some of these vessels bear potter's marks.

Pl. VI. Thick brim bowls are essentially Amorite, though the type lasted in a debased form into Jewish times, both in form and burnished facing. The earliest style of burnishing on the red face is with wide open crossing lines (74); which yielded to closer patterns as (65); and in late times a mere spiral burnishing made on the wheel. The red face is very bright in early cases, evidently a haematite colour in the Amorite times, though a dull ochre was used in Jewish imitations; it is occasionally burnt black on the earliest pottery; or is yellow on the polished face pottery (78-92); this variety in burning being just what is seen on Greek vases. The forms are extravagant in some cases, as (56-57), but in general it is an excellent type for strength. The later forms may be seen in 119, 204, 218, but the dull rough Indian red facing and bad burnishing show the later work.

The polished facing is remarkable for the high surface attained in some cases, as (79). It is sometimes red, or light brown, or yellow. It seems to be solely of Amorite make. Sometimes a red face is found not polished.

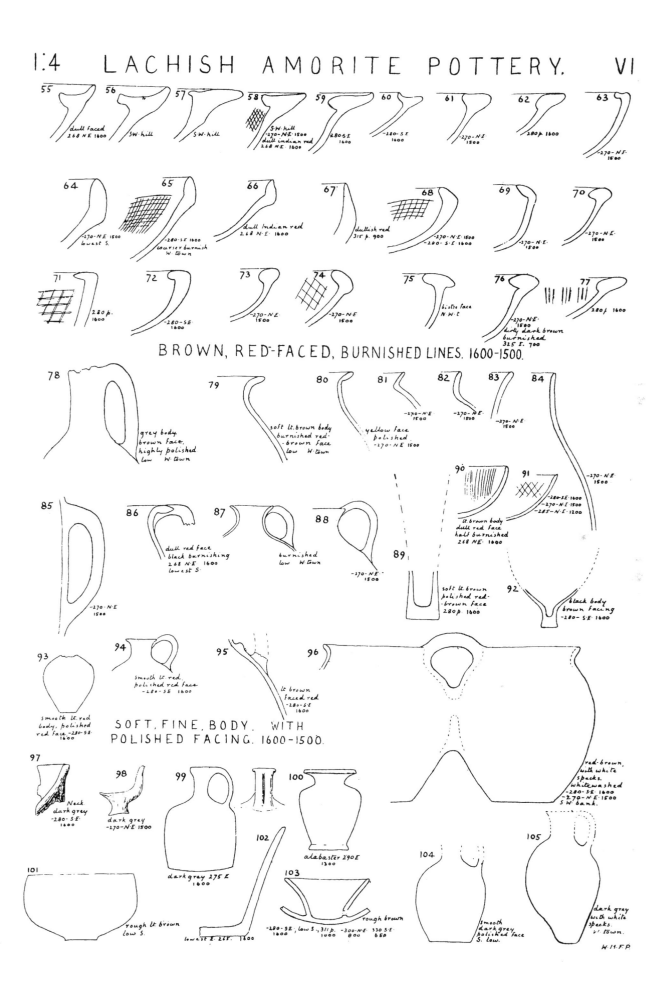

BROWN, RED-FACED, BURNISHED LINES. 1600-1500.

SOFT, FINE, BODY. WITH POLISHED FACING. 1600-1500.

Miscellanea.—A curious vessel is formed of two vases joined side by side, with a handle across the top (96); a small hole joins the two together inside, so that no different liquids could be kept in them.

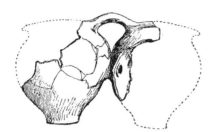

Fragments of this form were found in different places, but all of early Amorite time. It seems akin to the double vases of Phoenician pottery. A neck of a vessel (97) has a raised ridge curving on it, as if part of some ornament. The figure (98) seems to be intended for a bird. The vase (99) is of roughish grey pottery, with a double ridge handle ; such a handle is seen in (234) with a knob upon it of uncertain date, but probably early ; and such handles occur on pottery in Egypt, which comes apparently from foreign countries, before 1600 B.C. The alabaster vase (100) is the usual kohl vase of Egypt, but unusually large ; it is certainly imported. The cup in a dish (103) is strange, and occurs in very different periods. It seems to be probably intended to stand a porous water jar in, to allow of its evaporating, and to catch the filtered water which ran through. Similar stands, made of a ring of pottery set in an open dish, are found in Egypt of the XIIth dynasty. Vase (104) is of a very smooth polished grey ware, of close, fine, grain.

We now know that the varieties of Amorite pottery—the combed-face, spouts, ledge-handles, hole mouths, thick brimmed bowls, and patterned burnishing—are all peculiar to one period, that of that high civilisation, which we see portrayed on the Egyptian monuments, before the break up by the Israelite invasion. And, so far as we know, these styles are limited to Palestine. Neither Egypt on one hand, nor Phoenicia on the other, show any parallel to these peculiarities. Some of these characters lingered on in a debased form during the Jewish monarchy, but as a whole they were first overthrown by the introduction of a desert race, who cared little for pottery, and mainly used wood and skin ; and then the remnants were expelled by the Phoenician styles

39. *Pls. VII–VIII Phoenician Pottery.* We now come to a wholly different style, the rough, porous, light brown bowls and jars 106–114, 116–125, which are found with characteristic Phoenician pottery. The way in which these jars were buried has been described in mentioning the cemetery. This pottery also supplies the earliest form of lamp, an open bowl pinched up into a spout (137); ranging from 1000 to 600 B.C., and

POTTERY FROM S.W. CEMETERY, XIITH CENTURY B.C.

supplanted by the Greek form of the same type (227). *The thin black faced* is the most distinct Phoenician pottery (115), and (138, 141, 144, 149). This is sometimes made of a softish brown-red body, faced black, and sometimes of a hard homogeneous black paste of fine quality. The vases of this form (115, 138, 141, 144) are known to the Arabs by the name of *bilbil*, and it will be as well to use this for a name. They are common in all Phoenician places, both in Cyprus and on the mainland ; and are found in Egypt as far up as Thebes. I found a large group this last season in the tomb of Maket, of about 1100 B.C. (see "Illahun" 1891): and the range of them in Egypt is about from 1400 to 800 B.C. Two found separately, each with things of Amenhotep III, about 1450 B.C.,

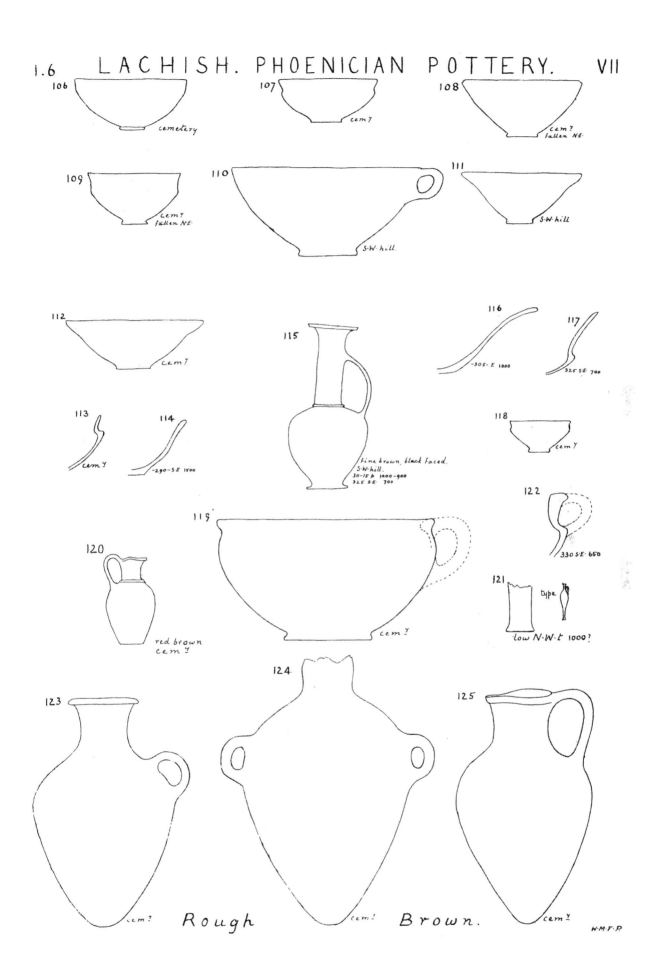

106 cemetery

107 cem?

108 cem? fallen N.E.

109 Cem? fallen N.E.

110 S.W. hill.

111 S.W. hill

112 cem?

113 cem?

114 -290-S.E. 1500

115 fine brown, black faced. S.W. hill. 311-15 b 1000-900 325 S.E. 700

116 -305-E. 1000

117 325 S.E. 700

118 cem?

119 cem?

120 red brown cem?

121 type low N.W. t 1000?

122 330 S.E. 650

123 cem?

124 cem?

125 cem?

Rough Brown.

W.M.F.P.

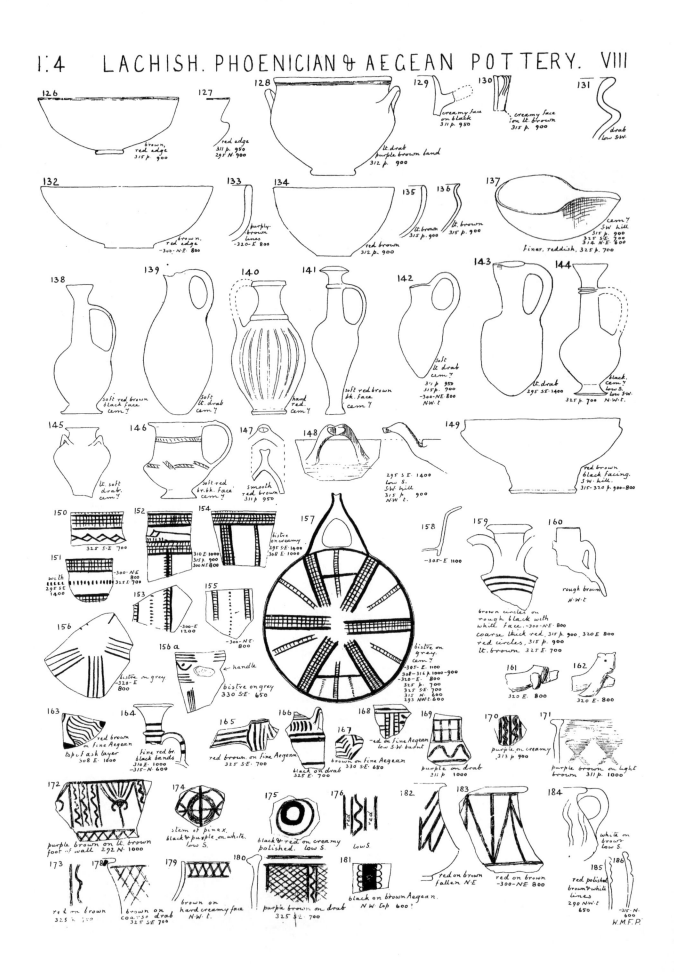

126 brown, red edge 315 p. 900

127 red edge 311 p. 950 295 N. 900

128 lt. drab purple brown band 312 p. 900

129 creamy face on black 311 p. 950

130 creamy face on lt. brown 315 p. 900

131 drab low S.W.

132 brown, red edge -300. N.E. 800

133 purply. brown lines -320-E 800

134 red brown 312 p. 900

135 lt. brown 315 p. 900

136 lt. brown 315 p. 900

137 cem? S.W. hill 315 p. 900 325 S.E. 700 314 N.E. 600 finer, reddish, 325 p. 700

138 soft red brown black face cem?

139 soft lt. drab cem?

140 hard red. cem?

141 soft red brown dk. face cem?

142 soft lt. drab cem? 311 950 315 p. 900 -300-NE 800 N.W. t

143 lt. drab 295 S.E. 1400

144 black. cem? low S. low S.W. N.W. t. 325 p. 700

145 lt. soft drab. cem?

146 soft red br. bk. face cem?

147 smooth red brown 311 p. 950

148

149 red brown black facing. S.W. hill. 315-320 p. 900-800

150 325 S.E. 700

151 with llll 295 S.E. 1400

152 -300-N.E 800 325 E. 700

154 bistre on creamy 295 S.E. 1400 308 E. 1000 310 E 1000 315 p. 900 300 NE 800

157 bistre on grey. cem? -305-E. 1100 308-314 p. 1000-900 -320-E. 800 325 p. 700 325 S.E. 700 315 N. 600 293 N.W. 600

158 -305-E 1100

159 brown circles on rough black with white face. -300-N.E. 800 coarse thick red, 315 p. 900, 320 E 800 red circles, 315 p. 900 lt. brown 325 E. 700

160 rough brown N.W. t

153 -300-E 1200

155 -300-N.E 800

156 bistre on grey -320-E 800

156a handle bistre on grey 330 S.E. 650

161 320 E. 800

162 320 E. 800

163 red brown on fine Aegean top of ash layer 308 E. 1000

164 fine red br. black bands 310 E. 1000 -315-N. 600

165 red brown on fine Aegean 325 S.E. 700

166 black on drab 325 E. 700

167 red brown on fine Aegean 330 S.E. 650

168 red on fine Aegean low S.W. burnt

169 purple on drab 311 p. 1000

170 purple on creamy 313 p. 900

171 purple brown on light brown 311 p. 1000

172 purple brown on lt. brown foot of wall 292 N. 1000

174 stem of pinax. black & purple on white low S.

175 black & red on creamy polished. low S.

176 red low S.

182

183 red on brown fallen N.E.

184 white on brown low S.

173 red on brown 325 p. 700

178 brown on coarse drab 325 S.E 700

179 brown on hard creamy face N.W. t.

180 purple brown on drab 325 S.E. 700

181 black on brown Aegean. N.W. top 600?

185 red polished brown & white lines 290 N.W. t 650

186 -315-N. 600

W.M.F.P.

at Illahun, have white strokes painted diagonally about them, as if to imitate basket work. Some pieces with white lines were found at Tell el Hesy, but apparently of a later age, as the levels were about 305 E., 313 p., 315 p., about 320 E., and 325 p. which correspond to 1,200, 900, 900, 800, and 700 B.C. These show that I have under rated rather than over rated the age of the Tell el Hesy levels.

The soft light drab pottery is peculiarly Phoenician being never found before or after. It is of a light yellow grey, or olive grey, and is almost always of the pointed bottom juglet, with one handle high up (139, 142, 143, 145). The three handles on (145) remind one of a similar form with three handles which was made in Egypt from about 1,200 B.C., for a short time. It occurs in late Ramessu II, in Seti II, in graves of that age at Tell Yehudiyeh; but not in the Maket tomb 1100 B.C., nor any later time, so far as I know.

The thin bowls are Phoenician, but not nearly so commonly exported as the *bilbils*. The outline (149) is more like a metal bowl, than one of pottery; and the *bilbils* show the same influence of metallurgy, especially in the bands on the neck, where the handle joins it. The handles are very peculiar (147, 148), but admirably formed to be held, and to give strength in the best way. They rise above the line of the brim, so as to enable the bowl to be hung on a wall.

40. *The painted Phoenician pottery.*—Many of the bowls are painted with bistre, in the style of No. (157). This painting is always on the outside; and with a broad band around the top edge (150–154), which is foreshortened on the whole bowl seen from below. This style is very well known in Phoenicia and Cyprus; but has not been found in Egypt as far as I know. It appears to have much the same range historically as the other Phoenician pottery, but perhaps it comes down later to the VIIth cent. B.C. If we may venture on a guess at the origin of this form, it would seem to be a loop of withy, the two ends brought together, forming the pointed handle and brim, and the double tip to the handle should be noticed; then a skin bowl was attached to it; the skin cut in flaps and turned down around the bowl and stitched round the brim; the edges of the flaps being imitated by the ladder pattern; and the skin which is turned between the fork of the handle, and opposite to that, being stitched on to the rest by lines of stitching, here marked with

a cross stroke and dots. The ornament is elaborate, and yet singularly pointless; if developed as pure ornament it would naturally concentrate in design on the middle, whereas that is the last and most unfinished part of it. This suggests that the ornament arises from imitation of some different thing; and the curious depth of these bowls, more than hemispherical, is like the proportion of a skin cup or baler. As an instance of such a style of vessel, I have seen the lower bill and pouch of a pelican used for baling by Egyptian boatmen of Menzaleh.

The Cypriote pottery.—The pilgrim bottle-type is usually credited to Cyprus in particular; and it does not seem to be Phoenician, as it is much rarer here than any of the Phoenician types. The examples are some painted (159) and some plain (160); they are late, ranging from 900 to 700 B.C. The curious little toys (161–2) are of the same age.

The painted Aegean pottery.—Not many fragments of the early Greek style were found; and these rather belong to the Aegean civilization, before the rise of the Greek race. The pottery is certainly foreign by its fine hard paste, and the painting is of the iron glaze. The pieces (163) and (168) are the earliest, about 1000 B.C. But it is unexpected to find the pieces (165) and (167) so late as 700 B.C. The black or drab (166) may well be of that age. The body of (164) is Greek, but the painting is flat black. Some pieces of Aegean pottery with plain iron bands were found: buff with red brown lines at about 305 E., or 1000 B.C.; red bands on creamy-white face at about 320 E., or 800 B.C.; a buff and black handle at 322 p., or 750 B.C.; and a bowl with a broad red band inside at 325 E., or 700 B.C. All of these dates are within the period for Aegean pottery shown in Egypt, as there the geometrical Mykenae style is of 1400 to 1200 B.C.

The painted rough pottery.—This is very various, but seems all to belong to one source, and is not, so far as I know, like that of other countries. So it is probably native, though perhaps Phoenician. Of plain bands of colour, red or purple-brown is the commonest. The bowls (126, 127, 132) all have red edges; and 128 has a purple band around it. These are of 900–800 B.C. Other examples of coloured bands, not drawn, are as follows :—

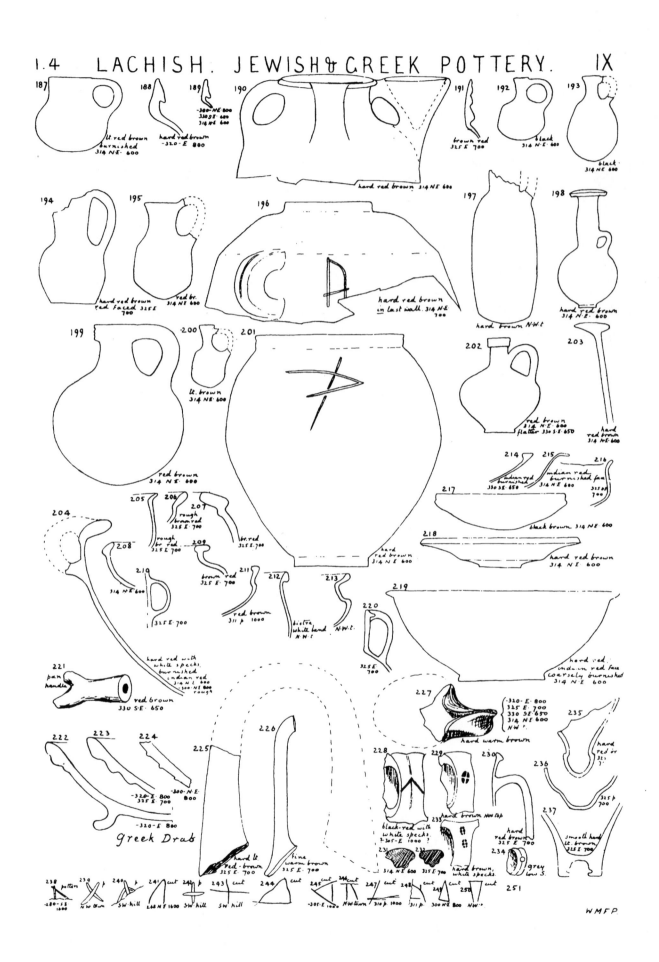

WMFP

Black on burnished red jar, 295 S.E. 1400 B.C.

   ,,   ,,   ,, bowl, abt. 320 E., 800 ; 330 S.E., 700.

   ,, ﹒ rough brown, 305 S.E., 1100.

Purple on white face, 311 p., 1000 ; 315 p., 900 ; 320 E., 800 ; 325 p., 700.

Red-brown on creamy face, 315 p., 900 ; abt. 300 N.E., 800 ; 290 N.W. t., 700.

Black edge to red or brown bowls, 315 p., 900.

Brown on dull drab, 320 p., 800 ; 325 p., 700,

And of double lines there are—

   Black and red on creamy, low S. ; 311 p., 1000.

   Black, red edges, low S.W.

   Brown and white, narrow, on neck, 315 p., 900.

   Bistre and white, about 300 N.E., 800.

   White between two red, lt. br. face, 325 S.E., 700.

   Creamy, red-brown edges, 325 S.E., 700.

Thus we see that these coloured bands on rough pottery belong mainly to 900 to 700 B.C. ; with a few earlier ones, mainly black.

The pottery with patterns is all drawn here. The simplest are the circles inside of flat *pinakes*, which remain on the thick stems (174, 175) ; these must have been much of the Rhodian or Naukratite form. Unluckily they cannot be dated, as they were found in the low S. ; probably early, but subject to the overflow of later material on that side. The details of the painted pottery are all stated on the plate (169 to 184) ; the range is just the same as that of the plain bands, 1000 to 700 B.C. The pattern on 172 seems to be a palm-tree. On the whole, this rough painted pottery belongs entirely to the period of the Phoenician predominance in pottery ; and similarly flat painting on a rough face, was found with the Phoenician pottery in the Egyptian tomb of Maket, 1100 B.C.

41. *Pl. IX., Jewish Pottery.*—By Jewish is here meant the styles which are neither pure Amorite nor Phoenician, but which consist of a mixture of characters ; they mostly have a uniform rough surface of red-brown pottery, belonging to these later times of the Jewish monarchy.

The descendants of the elegant pointed bottomed juglets (139, 142) of Phoenician ware, are more or less clumsy in form (192, 193, 194, 195, and 200); and the *bilbil* has equally deteriorated (198), or passes into a mongrel type (in 202), which borders on a globular vessel (199). The Amorite bowls are represented by poorly made vessels, with coarse rough faces (204, 207, 208, 211, 214, 215, 217, 219). The upright vessels with combed faces survive in a coarse type (203). And perhaps (187) is formed from a remembrance of the spirited Phoenician cup (146). Some large pottery jars were made; two of which have potters' marks upon them (196, 201). And one large vessel (190) has four handles; one of them being developed into a conical cup, which has no communication with the inside: possibly it was to stand a small dipping cup on.

The Greek pottery begins to appear as early as 700 or 800 B.C. The most important case is that of the thick drab bowls (222–224), with a smooth spherical inside and ribs outside. These are common at Naukratis, on the west of the Delta, being found among the early dedications of the Apollo temple about 650 to 550 B.C. But they are wholly unknown in the Greek town of Defenneh, on the Syrian road, at just the same period. It is clear then that their use in Syria did not arise from the Greek settlements in Egypt, as they are distinctly absent on the line of communication, while common at a town much further off. They must therefore have resulted from a maritime intercourse; and the Greeks must have been trading with Joppa or Gaza, if indeed they had not settled in Judaea, as early as 700 B.C. This is not at all surprising, as they were sufficiently strong to conquer Egypt under Psammetichos in 666 B.C. The massive loop handles (225) are common at both Naukratis and Defenneh in the VIIth and VIth cent. Also the lamps (227) are known there, but far more commonly at Naukratis. They result from the pinched bowl (137) of Phoenician type; but are worked with a wide flat brim, which is twisted in a strange way by the bending in, and forms contorted pieces—when broken up—which are unmistakeable. I would not place a stress on the date of 800 B.C. for the earliest of this Greek pottery; but it can hardly be later than 700 B.C. There is no impossibility in the Jews having used Greek mercenaries, as the Egyptians did at the same time.

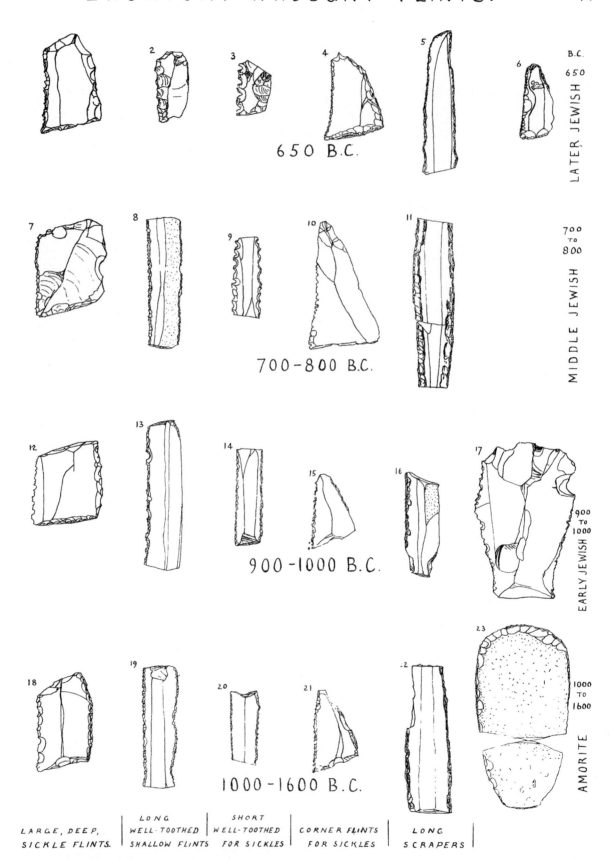

650 B.C.

700-800 B.C.

900-1000 B.C.

1000-1600 B.C.

B.C.
650

LATER JEWISH

700
TO
800

MIDDLE JEWISH

900
TO
1000

EARLY JEWISH

1000
TO
1600

AMORITE

| LARGE, DEEP, SICKLE FLINTS. | LONG WELL-TOOTHED SHALLOW FLINTS | SHORT WELL-TOOTHED FOR SICKLES | CORNER FLINTS FOR SICKLES | LONG SCRAPERS |

I had suggested the possibility, when writing on Defenneh in 1886, that Johanan the son of Kareah, the Jewish General, was a Greek, Yunani the Karian, in a Jewish dress. Probably the Jews were familiar with the Greeks in the frontier fortress of Tahpanhes (Defenneh) long before the fall of Jerusalem.

The handles (228 to 233) are all of late types, but before the rise of Seleucidan pottery. And the bottoms of vases (235-7) are also late, and (237) extended down to the Seleucidan period.

Of the latest pottery of Tell el Hesy I need say nothing; all that can be dated is the polished Greek black ware of the Vth cent. of which a few pieces were found, mainly about the middle of the E. side, and the W.N.W. region.

42. *Seleucidan and Roman Pottery.*—It only remains for me to complete this history of the pottery by describing the later styles which were *not* found at Tell el Hesy. The Seleucidan is generally of a hard warm light brown, smooth in texture, but without any colouring, facing, or polishing. The handles are very characteristic, small, rounded curve, streaked down by the fingers, and with a rough surface. The Roman pottery is ribbed around on the outside of the vessels, sometimes so fine as to be a combing, sometimes in wide waves; this ribbing began in Egypt about 150 A.D., and is universal in the later Roman pottery of Palestine. It survived into Arab times here, as well as in Egypt. The other characteristics of the Roman sites, which are the great majority in Palestine, are cubical white tesserae, glass of light green mainly, and of course Roman coins.

43. *The worked flints. Pl. X.*—These are found at every level of the site; and there is no great difference between those of the earlier and later periods, as may be seen from the drawings. They resemble the early Egyptian flints before the XVIIIth dynasty, but last in Palestine far later than in Egypt. The wooden sickles set with flint saws, which I have lately found in Egypt, explain what the purpose of a great part of these flints was. The broad notched flakes (column 1) were from large sickles; the corner pieces of such sickles being the triangular flakes (column 4). The narrower slips were fitted into smaller sickles. This use of the flints is not merely a conjecture from the sickles already found; but such flints show the characteristic polished edge, while the rest of their

G

surface is dull, having been protected by the setting. Other long flints were used as scrapers (column 5). And some large scrapers also appear (column 6) ; No. 23 is very early, having been found lying underneath the earliest Amorite part, the western town—upon the native clay. Hitherto we have seen very little of the use of flint in Palestine. We now see that it was very common, from the Amorite times down to the destruction of the Jewish monarchy : and the forms much resemble those made in the flint age in Egypt, before the Israelite bondage.

An unexpected use of flint has been revealed by the stonework of the pilasters. The surface of the limestone has been scraped down by some hard and irregularly notched scrapers. Certainly they were not of metal by the nature of the marks ; and one of the flint scrapers so common in the ruins produces exactly similar marking when used to scrape stone. Flints were then the regular finishing tools of the mason ; and what with corn sickles and stone scrapers we can account for the use of the greater part of the flints which we find.

INSCRIBED FRAGMENT OF POTTERY FROM TELL EL HESY.

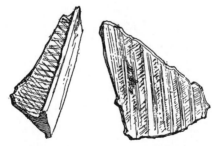

FRAGMENTS OF GLAZED POTTERY (AMORITE).

NOTES ON SITES VISITED IN SOUTHERN PALESTINE, 1890.

Jaffa.—About 1 mile S.　Roman pottery on ridge above the sea: many food shells, pieces of glass, cement, and chipped flints and glass.　Also about 1 mile N., a site with Roman pottery.

Jerusalem.—Details of tombs planned are given separately.　*Kh. el Khazuk*, Roman pottery and tesseræ.

Rameh near Hebron.　Beit el Khŭlîl.—Outsides of walls of flat dressed stones without any drafting.　Blocks large, courses remaining above ground 33 inches and 43½ inches.　Total length 216 feet 7 inches, breadth partly buried, but probably about 163 feet 6 inches, by the position of the end doorway.　Only visible entrance is by a wide doorway (17 feet 4 inches) in the west end.　Dressing of stones beautifully true, the error in flatness of the course joints being almost imperceptible in looking across the building.　The inner face has been relined in later times with smaller blocks, dressed by the comb pick; a large well in the S.W. corner has been made or relined at the same time.　From the lengths of some of the stones the cubit appears to be 22·1 inches; but by the courses and the size of the building 21·8 inches appears likely; probably there was a difference between the quarryman's and builder's cubits.　There is a large town site about this, rough stone walls and houses and pottery.　Also on the shoulder of the hill, about a quarter of a mile S. is a cistern of Roman age (probably), fed by several ducts from springs around, called Bir Ijideh.　A double flight of steps led into a double arched chamber, the two halves being separated by two very short columns, and from this a double arch led into the great cistern.

Yebnah.—Mounds entirely covered with modern houses and rubbish.

Esdûd.—I had not time to examine; but the present village seems to have been driven eastwards from the old site by sand encroachments; and those who have visited it agree that it would probably need deep sand clearances.

Kh Gheiyâdeh.—Rough stone walls (now mined for stones), Roman pottery and tesseræ; some columns are found.

Beit Durâs.—Roman pottery, white marble, and old mill centres of hard limestone.

Kh Ejjis er Râs.—Roman pottery, tesseræ, and glass, Strewn with rough stones.

Kaukabah.—Marble columns.

Bureir.—Marble columns by the well, brought from Askelon, as I was told: if so, this would account for many other such columns elsewhere. *Tell Mishnaga,*—¼ mile S.W. of Bureir (not on map); a long low tell, with Roman pottery. On the N.W. side of Bureir and under part of the village is Roman pottery, and building of concrete.

Gaza.—2¼ miles N.E. on S. side of road a large Roman site called Bab et Tokra, or Mahajarra (probably the Bab et Tokra is the gate, or octroi, of Gaza anciently, and Mahajarra is a trivial name referring to the pottery, *jarra*). Not on map.

Kh. Sh'aratâ.—All cultivated. Roman, and perhaps Arabic.

Kh Marashân.—Roman pottery widely scattered; well on the top, now dry, a piece of white marble column.

Kh Jelameh.—Roman pottery and glass.

Hûj—On N. side Roman pottery.

Kh. Lasan.—Very slight, scattered Roman pottery.

Kh. el Kôfkhah.—Much Roman and Arabic buildings, now being mined out for a new village settled from Gaza. Tesseræ, and a Cufic gravestone.

Kh. Umm Bâtieh.—Roman and probably Arabic pottery ; buildings and grey marble column.

Kh. Jemmâmeh.—Roman pottery and tesseræ, and late Roman marble capitals and columns.

Kh. Summeily.—Small amount of scattered pottery, pre-Roman.

Kh. el Hummam.—S.E. of the Kh. is Roman ruin, and white marble chips about a well.   The top of the well is now stripped of stone for a new well at Jemmameh, and will soon fall in.

Kh. Umm Tâbûn (near Nejed). — Much pottery, Seleucidan and Roman.

Kh. Nejed.—Roman pottery.

Kh. 'Amûdeh.—Much black pottery, probably late, also white marble. On sides of valley E. from that Seleucidan and Roman village. Cistern, just N. of road to Bureir, has marks hammered in roughly on the cement, after it was ruined ; some of these look like early

signs.   It would be interesting to know if the Egyptian ☥ has survived till modern times.

Kh. Umm Lâkis. — All Roman, pottery and glass.   Also another mound $\frac{1}{4}$ mile E., all Roman.

Kh. 'Ajlân.—No depth of earth, and only scattered Roman pottery.

Kh. el Hazzârah.—Roman pottery : no depth.

Kh. abu Shûkf.—Roman pottery ; but a high mound that might cover earlier levels.

Tell Idbîs.—Bare clay, and only one pottery handle seen, possibly of 8th century B.C.

Tell Nejîleh.—Large and important city ; pottery of Amorite type and of Jewish ; but no Seleucidan or Roman.   Mound about 30 feet high, and $\frac{1}{4}$ mile across.   All the top now covered with Arab tombs, and stone circle and pillar on the highest point.   In the valley at the foot of the tell are parts of a great concrete dam. 12 feet thick, to retain the spring water.

Kh. Umm Mu'arif.—Pottery Amorite and Jewish, 8 or 10 feet depth ? Not cultivated.   Caves in chalky soil just W. of it.

Kh. Kaneiterah.—Roman in parts ; but mostly of Persian period ?

Small Kh.—N. of Kh. Umm Bikâr, late Roman.

Tell el Hesy.—Separately described.   About 1 mile up the Wady Hesy from the tell are parts of a dam of masonry.

Kh. Resûm.—Many wells.   Pottery on surface all Roman and Arab.

Blocks of stone Roman and lintel, moulding, second century A.D. ?

Kh. Mejdeleh.—Wall of drafted stones, five courses remaining, large centre bosses, Herodian?   Large cistern with wide winding staircase around it.   Tombs like those near Jerusalem with court in front, Herodian?

Half mile N. of Mejdeleh a site *Rasm el 'Arus* not on map, not visited.

Kh. Abraka.—Roman pottery.   In a large artificial cavern are four rows of niche holes visible around it, 28 in the top line, about

8-9 inches deep, 1 foot high and wide, too sloping at the back to hold any large object.

Deir el 'Asl.—Roman pottery ; the hill hollowed all over with caverns. At Bir Asl just below it a capital, Arabic ?

Kh. Shuweikah.—All of late date, the main building being a mosque with kibla and projection outside with arch below it.

Deir esh Shems.—Roman pottery and tesserae.

Es Semû'a.—All buildings of Roman or later date.   The great tower attributed to *Mamun* by the inhabitants.

Râfât.—Large mosque, with barrel vault roof. A separate arch porch over the door, quite disconnected from the wall; Outside a

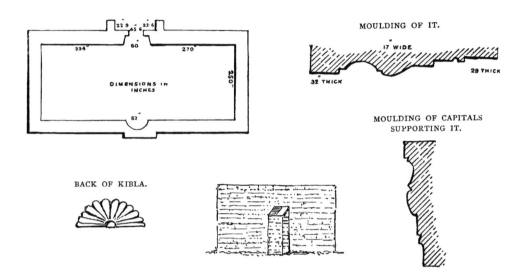

MOULDING OF IT.

MOULDING OF CAPITALS
SUPPORTING IT.

BACK OF KIBLA.

projection for the kibla with a piece of moulding upside down as part of the sloping top, and broken away below, but apparently not arched as at Shuweikeh.

Zânûta.—Main building a mosque, now half-ruined.

Somerah.—Roman pottery all over the side. Very debased mould-ing, grooved out of a flat face. Large circular mouth to cistern with holes in edge ring to let the surface water run in. Two

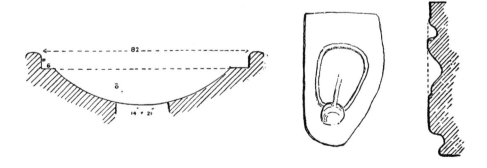

slabs with basins and grooves; 35 inches long, basin 7 inches

wide 9 inches deep, probably for clothes washing with small
water supply.

Anâb.—Main building a mosque, with barrel roof length E.–W., kibla
built with columns from the church.   A block about 15 inches

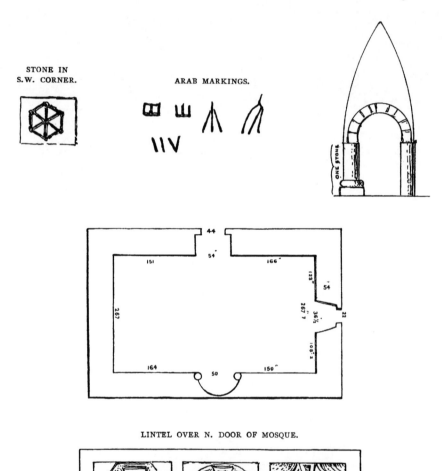

STONE IN
S.W. CORNER.

ARAB MARKINGS.

LINTEL OVER N. DOOR OF MOSQUE.

square projects 3 feet from the N. wall high up, between the door
and E. end; and another 5 inches thick projects 1 foot at top
of wall, more to E.

On the ridge to the E. of the mosque, foundations of a church.

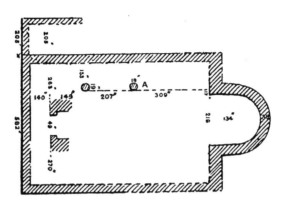

W. end measures 582.

Apse to wall   12 line of columns outside of apse.

                19 columns.

            153 aisle.

            ——

            184

Other side   184

Apse   216

            ——

E. end   584—584

    Total length by sum 978.

The column A stands complete, and may be seen for miles around, Probably the plan was, making an intercolumniation of $4\frac{1}{2}$ diams.

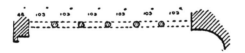

There is no drafting, and the stones are dressed with the comb pick.   About $\frac{1}{4}$ mile S. of this is a ruin called Abu 'Ora, apparently Roman.

Resm el Mukatat.—Half mile S.S.E. of "Aseilah" on map, in line with the Western Anab, (mosque) and Shekh Abn Kharrubeh.   A building of drafted stones with central bosses; one portion of it is $231\frac{1}{2}$ inches on W., 244 inches on S.

H

'Aseilah.—Only loose stone ruins.

'Umm Deimneh. — Large building of Christian date, drafted stones and comb-pick dressing.   On two lintel slabs, 17 diameter.

Slabs 26·3 × 61·0, 28·0 × 67·5.

W. Dômeh.—Greek and Roman pottery, mostly late.   On a lintel.

A washing stone (?) 28 × 20 inches, along with columns near the walled entrance to a large cave.

Dômeh Mosque.—On a block in the kibla a pattern of drilled holes, also a circle of drilled holes on an arch stone of the door.

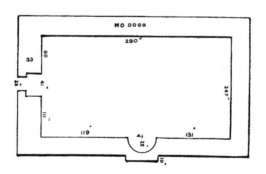

ON A LINTEL.

A BLOCK INSIDE.

PATTERN OF HOLES.

Remains of a church, with a column, close by the mosque.

E. Dômeh.—Some building with tesserae, Roman.

Kh. Kûrza.—Much ruined building, comb-picked work, Roman. An arched chamber of good work 140½ N. to S., 136 E. to W.

Kh. Rabûd.—W. part Roman pottery. On main hill pottery about 500 B.C. ? One piece of late burnished about 800 ? B.C. Space cultivated on top, with late Jewish pottery about 800–600 B.C. But no Seleucidan or Roman.

Kh. er Rabîyeh.—Pottery all Roman. Rough stone walls.

Es Sîmia. — Streets of building with drafted stone walls. Stones

generally with two bosses, sometimes one, or three. Tesserae and Roman pottery. S.S.E. of it about ½ mile on opposite side of valley apparently a tomb of Herodian age with a court, and two columns to the porch. On the N. of Edh Dhaheriyeh are Roman tesserae and pottery. Between Khurbet Bism and El Hadab Roman pottery.

Khurbet Kan'an.—Roman pottery.

Additional notes on *Beit el Khŭlîl.*—The dressed faces of the first period, where lately exposed, are very flat, in and out about $\frac{1}{25}$ inch, but with some wind, about ¼ inch. The dressing is *long*

stroke. The blocks are laid with mortar. The W. end bows out

about 1 inch in the length of it.   The S. side is hollowed about
1 inch in the length of it.   The N. side is nearly buried, but some
parts of a fourth course project from the ground.   In the latter
relining of the W. end the original lintel and door-sill have been
built in on edge.

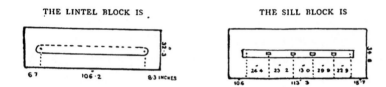

THE LINTEL BLOCK IS   THE SILL BLOCK IS

with four bolt holes, the centres of the rounded socket hollows
being estimated by eye.   Thus the doorway was 7·1 narrower at the
top than below.   If the height was 1½ × the width (or each door
height 3 × its width), the door foot would therefore rise 1·2 when
the door was opened.   There is an average of about 7 feet depth
of earth inside probably; and this is not cultivated.   On the S.

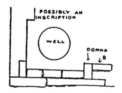

side of the well in the S.W. corner are two inscriptions, on the edge

of the block marked " Domna " is  on the

next block marked " B " is

Hebron. — The pilasters of the Haram have sloping tops, mostly hidden
by the Muslim wall.   The large pool is all of small blocks dressed
exactly like the Haram wall.

Ballûtet Sebta.—Seleucidan and Roman pottery.

Khurbet B'arneh.—Roman pottery.

      On the N. side of the hill at the head of the Wady as Suwed a large Khurbeh all Roman.

Kh. Abu ed Duba.—Roman pottery, columns, and tesserae.

Tŭffuh.—A building in the village of regular courses of stones, not later than early Muslim, perhaps Roman.

Khurbet Fir'ah. — Very little pottery, but Roman. In the Wady Afranj much Roman pottery opposite mouth of wady, N.W. of Khurbet Jemrurah.

Khurbet el Heshsheh.—Roman pottery and building.

Khurbet el 'Atr.—Roman pottery and building.

Khurbet Mer'ash.—All Roman pottery and building.

Tell Sandahannah.—At N.W. foot, joining to Khurbet Merash ridge, is Jewish pottery, both early and late. On the tell is Seleucidan and Rhodian pottery, with only occasional scraps of Roman. The S.E. spur is all Seleucidan. Buildings show all over the tell level with the ground. *There are no crops.*

Khurbet Hamdeh.—Foundations of masonry and Roman pottery.

Khurbet el 'Arab.—Rough stone work, and Roman pottery.

Khurbet Kŭka.—Roman pottery. On the east foot of Sandahannah much rough stone building and late Roman pottery.

Tell Bornat.—Late Jewish pottery, no Greek (?) or Roman. Top is in crops, the sides half barren. About 200 feet square, with long slopes.

Kh. Dhikerin.—Piece of a bowl red burnished (Jewish or Amorite) on the top. Some Roman and Arabic pottery about. Large bottle pit.

Tell es Safi.—All Jewish or Amorite pottery, at least to 30 feet from
top. Walling of shallow-drafted blocks with flat faces, long-stroke
dressing. On E. spur also early pottery and some Seleucidan.

Khurbet el Mekenna.—A large place, later Jewish and Persian period ?
No Roman, and probably no Seleucidan.

Kh. Umm Kelkah. — Very little pottery. Some lamps and Roman
pottery.

Akir.—No mound or pottery. By the well a trachyte mortar.

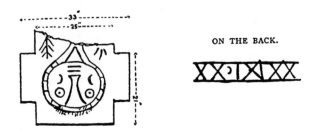

Kh Dajun —Only about 3 feet of soil, and that all Roman.

THE END

London : Harrison and Sons, Printers in Ordinary to Her Majesty, St. Martin's Lane, W.C

BRITISH SCHOOL OF ARCHAEOLOGY
IN EGYPT, AND
EGYPTIAN RESEARCH ACCOUNT
TWELFTH YEAR, 1906

HYKSOS AND ISRAELITE CITIES

BY

W. M. FLINDERS PETRIE

Hon. D.C.L., LL.D., Litt.D., Ph.D.
F.R.S., F.B.A., Hon. F.S.A. (Scot.)
MEMBER OF THE ROYAL IRISH ACADEMY
MEMBER OF THE IMPERIAL GERMAN ARCHAEOLOGICAL INSTITUTE
CORRESPONDING MEMBER OF THE SOCIETY OF ANTHROPOLOGY, BERLIN
MEMBER OF THE ROMAN SOCIETY OF ANTHROPOLOGY
MEMBER OF THE SOCIETY OF NORTHERN ANTIQUARIES
MEMBER OF THE AMERICAN PHILOSOPHICAL SOCIETY
EDWARDS PROFESSOR OF EGYPTOLOGY, UNIVERSITY COLLEGE, LONDON

WITH CHAPTERS BY

J. GARROW DUNCAN, B.D.

LONDON
OFFICE OF SCHOOL OF ARCHAEOLOGY
UNIVERSITY COLLEGE, GOWER STREET, W.C.
AND
BERNARD QUARITCH, 15 PICCADILLY, W.
1906

PRINTED BY
HAZELL, WATSON AND VINEY, LD.,
LONDON AND AYLESBURY.

BRITISH SCHOOL OF ARCHAEOLOGY IN EGYPT, AND EGYPTIAN RESEARCH ACCOUNT

The need of providing for the training of students is even greater in Egypt than it is in Greece and Italy; and the relation of England to Egypt at present makes it the more suitable that support should be given to a British school in that land. This body is the only such agency, and is also the basis of the excavations of Prof. Flinders Petrie, who has had many students associated with his work in past years. The large results of this centre of work in the subjects of the prehistoric ages, the early dynasties, the relations of prehistoric Greece with Egypt, the papyri, and the classical paintings, have shown how much need there is of maintaining these excavations in full action. The present year's work on the Temple of Onias, a Hyksos cemetery and fort, the cemetery of Goshen, and the town of Raamses in Succoth, has carried on the course of historical discovery. Active support is required to ensure the continuance of such work, which depends entirely on personal contributions, and each subscriber receives the annual volume. The antiquities not retained by the Egyptian Government are presented to Public Museums, after the Annual Exhibition, during July, at University College. The accounts are audited by a Chartered Accountant, and published in the Annual Report. Treasurer: F. G. HILTON PRICE, Child's Bank, 1, Fleet Street, E.C.

ADDRESS THE HON. SECRETARY,
BRITISH SCHOOL, UNIVERSITY COLLEGE,
GOWER STREET, LONDON, W.C.

CONTENTS

CHAPTER VI

THE CEMETERY OF GOSHEN

BY J. GARROW DUNCAN, B.D.

CHAPTER VII

THE CEMETERY OF SUWA

BY J. GARROW DUNCAN, B.D.

LIST OF PLATES

WITH PAGE REFERENCES TO THE DESCRIPTIONS

(Plates with lettered numbers are only issued in the larger edition.)

HYKSOS AND ISRAELITE CITIES

INTRODUCTION

1. THIS volume marks a new departure in the course of British excavations in Egypt. Hitherto the Egyptian Research Account has been a small resource for the promotion of the work of students; and, as such, it has enabled several to obtain that footing in the subject from which they have gone on to more important positions. It has been for eleven years a basis for the new men who have been entering upon work in Egypt. Now it has been largely expanded, and with the support of most of the British authorities in archaeology and history, it has taken the more permanent position of the British School of Archaeology in Egypt. Such it has long been *de facto*; but *de facto* in Egyptian affairs is not always *de jure*. It is well at last to adapt the name to the facts, and place this beside the schools at Athens and Rome, as the basis for British students. My best thanks personally are due to those who have helped this change with their counsel and names: to the Earl of Cromer for so cordially accepting the position of Patron of the School; to our Treasurer, the Director of the Society of Antiquaries, for continuing his support; and to none more than to Prof. Ernest Gardner, whose long experience at the British School at Athens adds weight to his opinions. The heavy work of the organizing and correspondence, which was undertaken by my wife, has been much lightened by the kind co-operation of Dr. J. H. Walker, to whom we owe many thanks. This expansion of public interest has enabled me to continue my excavations in Egypt, and the direction of students, on a larger scale than in the past two years. The limitations of the Exploration Fund, with which I had worked, led to that basis being withdrawn, greatly to my regret; such a break was entirely contrary to my wishes. Yet, when changes thus came about, it seemed fitting that a broader width of interests should be connected with the present position of Egyptology in England, which has developed so much in the last quarter of a century.

In the work of the past winter our party consisted of five. Part of the excavations were directed by my old friend the Rev. J. Garrow Duncan, who, many years ago, had worked very carefully at Naqada; and another student, Mr. C. Gilbart-Smith, after some experience in managing the workmen, also took charge of a site. My own part was the surveying, and unravelling the history, of the important structures that we found, as well as directing workmen during most of the season, and obtaining the photographs here published. The greater part of the drawings were made by my wife; and most of those from Mr. Duncan's excavations were made by Mr. T. Butler-Stoney, who kindly offered his artistic help.

We all began work at Tell el Yehudiyeh, which lies about twenty miles north of Cairo, and after leaving there I returned again later, when the water level was lower; altogether my wife and I spent about 8 weeks there, 9 weeks at Tell er Retābeh in the Wady Tūmilāt, and a week at Saft el Henneh a short distance east of Zagazig. Mr. Duncan spent 10 weeks at Belbeys and Sharañba, and 7 weeks at Saft. Mr. Butler-Stoney and Mr. Gilbart-Smith divided their time between the two camps, according to the requirements of the work.

2. It is perhaps desirable to give here an historical outline of the results of the season, so that those who are only interested in some one part, may better see where to look for their subjects in the following pages.

The earliest piece of history found was the settlement of the Wady Tumilat in the XIIth, and probably as far back as the IXth dynasty. A few objects at Tell el Yehudiyeh show that it also was occupied in the XIIth dynasty. The main interest of that place was the discovery of the original form of the great camp. This proves to have been an earthwork intended for a system of defence entirely foreign to the Egyptians. The high outside slope, 60 feet up

1

the face of it, proves that archery was the protection of the occupiers; and the curious long ascent, to enter over the bank, shows that neither gateways nor any constructions in brick or timber entered into their defensive system. The rapid change to the use of brickwork, and later to stonework on a great scale, shows how the barbaric ideas of these invaders became altered by contact with the Egyptians. The whole evidence of the scarabs and the pottery, found in and near this camp, proves that we here have for the first time a great work of the mysterious Shepherd Kings or Hyksos. The graves of this age have supplied the means of tracing the changes that went on between the XIIth and XVIIIth dynasties, in the styles of scarabs, of the black foreign pottery, and of the Egyptian pottery. For the first time we can assign objects to their relative positions, throughout what has hitherto been one of the dark ages of Egyptian history. Whether this site be the celebrated camp of Avaris, as seems probable, or whether it be a parallel site, its history is in accord with the outline of this age as stated by Manetho.

The next period, the XVIIIth dynasty, showed at Tell el Yehudiyeh the later stages of burials following those of the earlier cemetery. And at Saft, the ancient city of Goshen, a large cemetery begun in this age has given us a considerable quantity of beads and amulets. To the XIXth dynasty belongs the temple of Ramessu II at Tell er Retàbeh. This site thus occupied by him is now seen to fulfil in every way the accounts of the city of Raamses, where, with the sister city of Pithom, the Israelites are stated to have been employed. The site of the temple founded by Ramessu has been found, and also much of the temple sculpture. Thus we can now identify another of the fixed points in the narrative of the Exodus. Of this same age is a large forti-fied town in the plain of the Delta, discovered by Mr. Duncan. This place seems to have been "the fountain of Horus," and is now known as Sharanba. As there seems no likely purpose in thus planting a stronghold out of touch with the roads on the edges of the desert, we are led to look for its purpose in the time when the Hyksos camp at Yehudiyeh was being girdled by the Egyptians, in order to cut off its supplies and eject the hated invaders. Thus the erection of this fortress may probably be taken back to the beginning of the XVIIIth dynasty.

Of the XXth dynasty we have the fortification of Tell er Retabeh, where Ramessu III left his founda-tion deposits beneath the corners. A careful gleaning of the site of his palace at Tell el Yehudiyeh has produced some dozens of pieces of the glazed tiles with figures, and shown that nothing more is to be hoped for from that ground. The XXIInd and XXIIIrd dynasties have left several interesting objects for us in the cemeteries of Tell er Retabeh and Saft. The later branch of the Goshen cemetery at Suwa represents the XXVIth dynasty; and the cemetery of Tell el Yehudiyeh has supplied some of the beautiful green glazed bottles of that age.

Within our concession for work lay the pieces of the great granite stele of Darius at Pithom, which was published in transcription by M. Golenischeff. From the remains of the stele I made paper squeezes, from which my wife has drawn the facsimile here issued. This is the most complete of the great monuments put up by the Persian king, to com-memorate his cutting again the canal from the Nile to the Red Sea.

Another of the main results of the season belonged to the Ptolemaic age. The curious return of the Jews to the protection of Egypt, from the persecutions of Epiphanes, is known to us from the pages of Josephus; and it had always been supposed that the site of the town granted to the High Priest Onias lay at Tell el Yehudiyeh. The discovery of the Jewish tombstones there by Dr. Naville confirmed this; but yet the site of the new temple and town was unfixed. Mr. Griffith came very near to the mark when he wrote about the great mound, "The most probable site for the temple of Onias, if it stood here at all, is on the top of the mound." But he then adds, "I believe that the temple of Onias must be sought for not here, but in one of the neighbouring Tells" (*Mound of the Jew*, p. 53). Our work this season has, however, shown that this is Leontopolis, and that the great mound agrees in every detail with the site of Onias. The outer walls of a powerful fortification can be traced around it, constructed of great stones hewn like those at Jerusalem. The site of the temple courts, and of the sanctuary itself, is now bared and measured. The proportions of this temple were copied from that at Jerusalem. And the whole site was formed in imita-tion of the shape of the Temple hill of the Holy City. It was, in short, a New Jerusalem in Egypt.

Of the later ages the cemetery at Saft yielded many graves of Roman times, with beautiful glass vessels and strings of coloured beads; and the cemetery at Gheyta has shown how Syrian influence was coming into Egypt in the later centuries of the Roman occupation. Thus the way was paved for the Arab conquest, much as the Saxon conquest of England was preceded by the settlements on the "Saxon shore" of Roman Britain. Of the Arab age some houses were cleared at Belbeys, in course of a search for earlier remains. Thus every age of Egypt after the Old Kingdom has been touched this year; and in two periods results of the first importance have been ascertained.

In issuing the great number of plates needed to record such an extensive course of work, it was not practicable to publish the less important portions in so large an edition. Therefore the ordinary subscribers receive a complete work giving all the material of general interest, while the larger contributors will receive the extra plates with lettered numbers, IV A, VIII A, VIII B, etc., inserted in their volumes. Thus the requirements of a full record can be kept up without undue expense or troubling the general reader with less interesting details.

3. I have alluded above to previous work at Tell el Yehudiyeh. In 1886-7 Dr. Naville and Mr. Griffith found the cemetery with the Jewish tombstones, but did not otherwise clear up the history of the place. Dr. Naville revisited the site this year when we were at work, and was much interested with the great sloping face of the camp. At Tell er Retabeh the same explorer had made some trials in 1885-6, but left that site with the conclusion that it was only a Roman camp, and not of historic value. And at Saft el Henneh it is to Dr. Naville that we owe the first notice of the place in 1885-6, when he found monuments there. The cemetery was, however, not attempted at that time. After a lapse of twenty years passing without any further researches in this district, it seemed desirable to try to clear up its history, especially in continuing those researches bearing on the Israelite questions on which I touched last year in Sinai (see *Researches in Sinai*). The archaeological results now reached carry us in many respects much beyond the topographical work of the earlier explorers.

CHAPTER I

THE HYKSOS CAMP

4. ON first viewing Tell el Yehudiyeh there seemed hardly any possibility of recovering details of the ancient structures of the place. The accumulations of brick ruins of the ancient town, some twenty miles north of Cairo, had almost entirely disappeared; the site of the palace of Ramessu III was high in air, and amid the heaps of potsherds strewn over the enclosure the bare desert floor appeared in many parts. The sandy masses of the great square camp, and of the mound on the north-east of it, were cut away on all sides, so that not a fragment of original face appeared to be left. The stone wall has vanished, leaving only a long trench to mark its site; the earth and bricks have all been elaborately cut away to put on the land around; the sand is being carted away every day to use in building; and even the very potsherds are collected to place in foundations of houses. Every fragment and product of the ancient site is being removed, so that before long no trace will be left of this great city.

5. Yet as a continual flow of scarabs of the age of the Hyksos had come from this region, and the supply had not ceased, it seemed needful to try to rescue some history if possible from this site. Our first venture was the turning over of an area marked "Chips" on the plan (Pl. II), where a large mass of limestone chips showed that a building had been there destroyed. From this part northward, along the nearer half of the "Sand Foundations," I opened a trench down to the native desert. In some parts four or five feet of black earth yet remained, in other parts there was none left. This trench from north to south was moved westward across the ground to beyond the "Granite Base," thus completely turning over about an acre of ground. Parts which had rubbish descending below the water level in December, were cleared to lower levels in March. That a temple had existed here is shown by the long line of sand foundation of the walls, by the column of the XIIth dynasty usurped by Merenptah, by the large black granite base for a statue, and by a life-size kneeling figure of which we found the lower part to the west of the chip ground. But it seems that the building, and all the other monuments which it formerly contained, had stood at higher levels which have been entirely swept away by the diggers of earth.

This clearance of ours was, however, fruitful in another way. Five graves were found, all containing scarabs of the Hyksos period, with pottery copied from the earlier Egyptian types, and imported pottery of the black incised ware (Pl. V). From graves which had been already dug over by the natives we found many other examples of this pottery left behind, and a gold-mounted scarab of King Khyan, with a plain band of gold, perhaps a head fillet. That such graves of the Hyksos might well have been dug inside their camp, we see from the example of graves inside the town of Ehnasya under the later temple, and the graves of the Ist dynasty inside the town of Abydos.

While this work was going on I observed, in walking round the great bank of sand, that on the eastern side a thin white line ran through the ground inclined at about 45°. I traced this again and again at other points, and at last found it on every side of the camp. I dug down the slope of it, and bared a wide plane of sloping white plaster or stucco (Pls. IV, IV A), extending as wide as the earth was left remaining, and as deep as the present water level below it. This was evidently a great sloping face to the sand bank, and therefore gave the position of the outer surface as originally finished. As the present outside of the sand bank had been cut back in many parts to as much as fifty feet inside this stucco slope, the recognition of the original face greatly restored our view of the site.

The outside being thus identified, the inside needed fixing. This was more difficult as there was no white stucco, and the brickwork lining wall had been systematically dug away. Traces of it were remaining against the sand face, mainly in the north-east corner. But only one piece of the north face, one piece of the east face, and the line of the south face could be recovered. These suffice to show the position and the thickness of the great sand bank, which even at the top was 80 to 140 feet wide.

The entrance to this camp was the next point to be studied. On the eastern side the sand bank is much lower in the middle, and it was natural to suppose that a gateway had been destroyed there. Also there was no trace of the stucco slope in the middle of the side. I cleared this part therefore to find the gateway. To my surprise the stucco slopes on both sides of the middle turned into walls running outwards to the east, and no trace of a gateway could be found. We dug on, but only uncovered a long slope of brickwork pointing up to the top of the sand bank (Pl. III), with lesser lines of sloping brick in the sand below. At last it was clear that there had never been any gateway, but that the entrance was by a long sloping roadway, leading over the top of the sand bank.

The western half of this region was occupied by walls of a different character, evidently associated with the remains of Ramessu III. Whether this part was ever included in the original camp was

for some time a problem. On the south side a sloping face of brickwork was found (Pl. II, see A) cutting across the main bank, and at first it seemed as if this were an original corner. But it was traced outward to a sharp bend with the outer stucco face of the bank, and it became clear that it was only a revetment to hold up the end of the bank, when cut through and replaced by the walls of Ramessu. The later discovery of the stucco slope, complete on the west side, proved that the camp was almost equilateral. Having now described the order of examination of the site, we may proceed to the details that were discovered.

6. FOUNDATIONS. The first question in dealing with a sloping structure is the position of its original base level. Any building that was founded within a few yards of water-level in Egypt, is now submerged at its base by the steady rise of the Nile deposits, and of the general water-level of the country. This rise amounts to about 4 inches in a century : therefore since the Hyksos times, over 4,000 years ago, the rise of level must have been about 160 inches or more. As even now much of the inside of the camp shows the desert ground almost up to high Nile level, it seems that the highest part of the ground was about 12 or 13 feet over high Nile. Naturally the site fell away on most sides, but we cannot suppose that the earthwork extended below old Nile level, as the general plain was covered with Nile deposits up to that. I have sounded the face of the wall down to 20 inches below the present level of water in March ; and the level of that season is marked on the sections, both for the present time and for the period of construction.

The best guide as to the starting point of the slope is given by the stone wall which was added around it, as shown in the sections on Pl. III. It is not likely that in adding such a wall any large amount of the slope would be cut away ; the base breadth of the wall might very likely be removed ; but more than that is not so probable. Therefore the slope is not likely to have continued lower than the level marked "old ground?" Indeed it cannot have gone more than a couple of feet lower, as the general level of the alluvial plain (even if there were no desert footing here) would be about two or three feet over the "old water" level of the spring-time. Nor is it likely that the slope ended higher than we have marked it, as the stone wall would naturally be cut a little into the foot of it. We have therefore adopted the level marked as "old ground," as an approximation. It happens to be the theoretical zero of all my levelling, which was started by taking a signal on the top of the bank as 500 inches level. Hence all levels named here are in inches above the probable original ground.

On the plan the outline of the slope was fixed by taking as high a portion as could be found in each part, and measuring the angle of it, or angles if it varied. This angle was then carried upward to 500 inches level and downward to zero, or old ground. The horizontal distances from the point fixed were plotted on the plan, and so the outline of the top and foot of the bank were determined at each part, as shown in the plan. Each point which was thus fixed is marked by a short cross stroke on the outline. Where the top and bottom of the bank come closest together, as at the north-east corner, the slope is at its steepest.

The width of the bank as laid out varies from 1580 inches on the south side to 2360 on the east, at its base, roughly 130 to 200 feet. This irregularity is similar to the want of parallelism and of squareness between the sides. The whole outside varied—

N. to S. . 17600 to 18430 inches, 1467 to 1536 feet.
E. „ W. . 17650 „ 18750 „ 1471 „ 1562½ „

Hence it was more nearly equal in length and breadth than the skewness of the sides would lead us to expect.

The inside dimensions are less certain, as I have not uncovered the original inner face of the west side. It is here restored from the north side. But a piece of wall just within the remaining heap of sand at the north-west may be part of the lining wall ; and, if so, the bank was thicker than it is marked. The inside was about 400 yards square. We may perhaps allow two square yards of house room for each man in a closely packed camp ; and the roads and walls might occupy as much as the floor space. The whole camp might then hold 40,000 men ; or if they were put together as closely as English soldiers in tenting, there might be 80,000 men.

7. BANK AND STUCCO SLOPE. The great bank is in most parts pure sand (see views, Pl. IV). Along the eastern side it consists largely of marly lumps ; and on the south-east corner much of it is of yellow lumps of decomposed basalt, collected from the surface of the basalt flow, which is now found a mile or two to the east on the desert. In most parts there are embedded in the bank scattered bricks, and irregular short walls of loosely piled bricks. Such seem to have been marks for limits of working gangs, or possibly shelters for the men employed. These bricks are 14·0 to 15·4 inches long, 6·5 to 7·8 wide, 3·2 to 3·8 thick ; the details of sizes of bricks will be given in Section 8.

The angle of the stucco slope outside of the bank is by no means constant, as is shown in the base of Pl. III. The variations of it are from 27° to 55°, and these limits are found in a single slope on the south-east. But four-fifths of the cases fall between 36° and 43°, the mid example being 41°. From this amount of variation it does not seem that any measurement was followed in setting out the face, any more than there was in laying out the direction of the sides. The height of the slope was from 50 to 70 feet, according to the varying angle. The stucco face is plastered over with hard white plaster, about ⅛ to ¼ inch thick. This was spread by the hands, as may be seen by the finger-sweeps showing upon it, where well preserved at the south side of the sloping ascent. It is laid on in bands about 30 inches high, leaving a slight ledge at the top of each band (see view, Plate IV A). This evidently marks the breadth which was covered at once in the plastering, the ledge being the slight foothold left by the workmen as they went round the plasterings. Such slight ledges greatly detract from the inaccessibility of the slope, and they are another mark of the untrained and badly organized character of the whole work.

Behind the stucco slope there is a steeper retaining wall, seen on the north and the south-east, as shown in the sectional view of variations of slope, Pl. III, base. This wall is in ledges, each course stepped back, and the appearance of it where bared on the south-east is shown in the photograph, Pl. IV. This wall has been nearly all removed, as it was a source of brick-earth to the modern diggers ; and in some parts a deep trench runs between the stucco slope and the sand bank core. Where preserved, this wall has an angle of 58°, and is built of bricks 14·5 to 14·8 ins. long. Why the face of this wall itself was not smoothed and stuccoed we cannot understand. To add more earth to the lower part, and so make a flatter slope for the final face, seems to throw away the defensibility of the bank. Perhaps this wall was originally intended for the face ; but, if so, it may not have proved strong enough, and have bulged with the pressure behind it, as it was fifty feet in height. This would account for the lower part being banked over, and a flatter slope substituted. Such seems to be the only explanation of this inner sloping wall.

The inside wall of the bank towards the town was almost vertical, as seen along the south side, where it is best preserved. The traces of the backs of the bricks can be seen all round the north-east corner. The inner face was traced for some way inside the north side, and on the east it was identified at one spot where it is preserved.

There is no trace of any brick wall on the top of the sand bank; and though in other positions brick-work has been diligently cut away, yet in all such places some fragments have been casually left. The top where best preserved is flat, and strewn with weather-stained flints and potsherds, while there is no trace of any trench or space where a brick wall has been dug away from the top. Mr. Griffith, who saw the place when it was much less disturbed, also considered that there was no trace of a defensive wall on the top. It seems therefore that at first the earth-work alone was the defence; and later, when walls were valued, the great stone wall outside rendered any brick wall needless.

8. ENTRANCE. There does not seem originally to have been any gateway through the bank into the camp. Certainly there was none on the east; on the south the bank is continuous beyond the middle; on the west the line of the stone wall continued across the middle; and it is only on the north that the destruction leaves us in doubt as to the continuity of the bank, though the sand is certainly continuous to ten or fifteen feet above the old ground level, and therefore probably no opening existed. The only original entrance that we can trace is the sloping ascent on the east side. This was a gentle slope about 225 feet long; but the lower part of it became covered with a great mound of town rubbish in the Ptolemaic time, and hence I have not cleared or planned it further out than the upper half. Near the bank it has been entirely cut away in removing the inner retaining wall of the bank, hence only a part of the upper half can be seen. The outline of the entrance given on the plan, Pl. II, is certain in the upper part; but the lower end is conjectural, as it is still deeply buried. At first there was only a con-tinuous ascent 35 feet wide, as shown on the plan, Pl. III; this ran up over the slope of the bank, pointing towards the top. The actual breadth of this ascent is still well preserved, with vertical walls on each side of it. The stucco slope outside of the bank bends irregularly to meet this, and turns round in the corner where the wall joins it. The foot of this ascent would perhaps not be as wide as the upper part, as there was good reason to limit the rush of an enemy at the beginning. The fact that the stucco slope turns out to join this ascent proves that this approach is the original roadway, and not a siege-work or an alteration of later times.

After this raised sloping ascent was thus made, a remodelling of the defensive system was soon adopted. The plaster on the stucco slope on either side of the roadway was perfectly fresh, and had not been exposed for even a few years, when it was covered over with new works. It seems to have been perceived that the ascent was too far from the archery defence. The long slope withdrew the bowmen from the beginning of the ascent, so that the flank attack was at 300 to 400 feet distance. This led to a change in which the Egyptian system of vertical walls began to be utilised. A flanking wall was thrown forward, out to the edge of the great slope, for more than 200 feet along (see the model, Pl. IV). This shortened the diagonal attack on the approach by 80 feet. Then the flank wall was continued along the sides of the approach itself (see "Outer retaining wall" in the plan, Pl. III), the inner retaining wall being that at the sides of the road. This gave standing room of over forty feet on either side of the actual gangway; and this fresh space could hold a large body of archers commanding the gangway from above. The defence then consisted of not only distant flank attack on the approach, but a sunk causeway leading through a body of archers, and so forming a complete trap; thus the defence was far superior to the attack on the vulnerable point.

The place of this flanking wall on the north of the ascent was later occupied by the stone wall shown on Pl. III, in "Section north of sloping ascent." On the south side of the ascent, in the next section, the flank wall of brick occupies the same alignment as on the north, but it was raised on a bank of sand. Where the later flank wall of stone joined the ascent on the north (Pl. III, plan), it fell into just the same place over the foot of the slope; but it has all been removed for stone, leaving only the brick flank wall along the side of the ascent, marked "Outer retaining wall." On the south side the flank wall was not only based on a sand heap, but it curved round irregularly to the side of the ascent. The whole of it has been removed, and only the lumps of marl in the backing show where it stood. The sizes of the bricks vary a good deal. They may be summed up as follows:

In the sand bank :

14ᐧ0—15ᐧ4 × 6ᐧ5—7ᐧ7 × 3ᐧ2—3ᐧ8 inches.

In the gangway :

14ᐧ3—16ᐧ1 × 7ᐧ3—8ᐧ2 × 3ᐧ4—4ᐧ7.

In the flanking walls are three different classes :

14ᐧ5—15ᐧ1 × 7ᐧ1—7ᐧ4 × 3ᐧ2—3ᐧ5 ; also

15ᐧ4—16ᐧ2 × 7ᐧ2—7ᐧ4 × 4ᐧ4—4ᐧ5 ; also

17ᐧ5—18ᐧ1 × 6ᐧ5—8ᐧ5 × 4ᐧ2—4ᐧ4.

9. STONE WALL. On all sides of the camp may be seen a deep trench in the ground, which is filled with water early in the season, and the natives all agree that they have in recent years removed from that ground a great stone wall, three blocks in width. In 1887 the remains of the wall were in course of rapid destruction ; but now none could be reached except at low water in March, and even then only a few stones were found in the less-disturbed parts. I was anxious to examine this wall, owing to the previous description of it (*Mound of the Jew*, p. 49) as a stone-lined ditch 32 feet wide. Mr. Griffith informs me that he intended by this a dry ditch— that is, two walls at 32 feet apart over all. This appearance which he saw was doubtless due to the relation of the wall around the camp, to the wall facing the western side of the hill of Onias, as these would be about that distant apart where running parallel at the north-east. And I could not hear, or see any traces, of a second wall around the camp. The position of the stone wall in relation to the stucco slope of the bank, depends upon the original ground level ; but it seems that the most likely arrangement, already discussed (that is, the slope being cut away three or four feet for it), accords very well with the probabilities of the levels. On the north of the ascent (Pl. III) there was no stone remaining as low as we could reach in March. But the sand and marl backing came to a vertical edge ; and against that there was only recent loose earth, which had evidently fallen into a hollow dug during the last few years. This was then the position of the wall. Farther north of this, at the north-east corner, I made a large excavation down the slope, and also advancing from outside ; we found much broken stone in large flakes, evidently from the destruction of great blocks of fine white limestone. This destruction seemed to be ancient, and was doubtless due to the removal of materials by Onias.

To the south of the ascent I carried down a pit at the place marked " Wall," and found two blocks in place above water-level. A second pit north of this was dug, outward from the lower courses of the flanking wall, and again two blocks were found, one on the other. One block was 56 inches wide, 33 high, the length not seen ; another was over 56 long and 45 wide. Both were of the finest white limestone. Their relation to the retaining wall is shown in the section " South of the Ascent." On the north of the ascent the stone wall replaced the brick flanking wall ; on the south it was about nine feet in advance of the flanking wall. This difference will be seen in the plan, Pl. II. I had selected the above places as having apparently not been dug out recently ; most of the circuit has only a deep modern ditch in the line of the wall.

On the west a long trench appeared, cutting through higher ground on the edge of the Arab cemetery. This trench ended in high ground, so there again I tried for the wall, and found two stones of the outer face in position. The upper of these blocks was 81 inches long, 40 high, and 25 thick. An excellent section was bared here, showing the relation of the stone wall to the stucco slope, and the nature of the filling between them. The slope had lost all its stucco in some parts, and in others it was weathered and rotted, before the stone wall was added. This points to the slope having been used for two or three generations before the system of defence was altered. On looking at this section, the lowest on Pl. III., " On west face," it will be seen that the filling is mainly of sand in layers, sometimes with potsherds, and one stratum is of yellow lumps of decomposed basalt, such as is usual in the filling behind the slope on the south-east. The upper bed of sand sloped steeply back at 120 inches over the water ; and I was told that the stones that were removed had been found up to this higher level. The history of the place then was that the upper part of the stone wall had been anciently removed, and the sand backing had run out over the lower part. Then it was entirely buried with earth of decomposed bricks, from the great Ramesside wall inside it. Recently the lower courses had been also removed, and when I went there I found only two stones left.

This great stone wall was about 6 feet thick, as shown by the bed on the west side. It must have been somewhat higher than the sand bank, which was 41 feet high, so we cannot reckon it at less than 45 to 50 feet in height. The length was 5,450 feet, or over a mile. It contained therefore about 80,000 tons of stone. The quality of the stone where seen in building or chips was of the finest white Mokattam limestone, which has no grain, and which flakes evenly in all directions. It was equal in quality to the best casing stone of the pyramids.

10. LATER HISTORY. Of the XVIIIth dynasty we find no trace. Ramessu II appears to have favoured a temple here. A group of two seated figures in red granite shows the king and a god, doubtless Ra according to the references on the back. The back of the group, as it lies on its side, is photographed on Pl. XIV B, and copied on Pl. XV. The inscription has been translated by Dr. Naville thus: "(1) I am thy venerable father, the lord of thy beauties; (2) . . . Rameses thou art prosperous like Tum in the great hall; (3) . . . like Khepra every morning crowned on the throne of Ra in the vestibule of Tum. (4) I am protecting thy limbs every day: thy might and the power of thy sword is above all lands. (5) Thy head is never opposed in all countries, Rameses, friend of Harmachis, the great god." The position is shown as "Granite Dyad" on Pl. II. Another block probably of the same reign is the large black granite base for a statue. It did not belong to the dyad, as the front of it was the narrower dimension. Though the granite is much weathered I could still trace the symmetrical inscription on either side of the axis, *Ankh Hor Ka nekht*. The block is 37 inches wide and 69 long. The position is marked on the plan.

The next piece that can be dated here is the red granite column with the names of Merenptah. The original work is doubtless older than this king, probably of the XIIth dynasty. It may have been brought by him from another site, and is not therefore an evidence of a temple being here before the Hyksos. The photograph is on Pl. XIV B, and the copy on Pl. XV. The two pieces of column are 76 and 96 inches long; the whole height therefore was 172 inches, or a sixth less than the granite columns of Ehnasya. This shows that a temple with a portico had existed here.

The great work of later times was the rearrangement of the place by Ramessu III. He cut away the great bank of the camp over the western half, and built a new town, with thick brick walls, and a long front facing the old town. In the middle of this front was a portico, of which the square basement of brickwork remains, with the red granite base of a column lying upon it. The mass of brick is 605 E. to W., by 590 inches N. to S. The granite base is 63 inches across; its inscription is given in Pl. XV. West of this are the blocks of alabaster pavement of the great hall; this was long since dug away, thus

letting down the blocks to a level far lower than the original pavement. The present view is given on Pl. XIV B. To the west and north-west of the portico were found most of the remaining fragments of the celebrated glazed tiles with figures, shown in Pl. XIV B. The sad history of the destruction of this place may be seen in the *Transactions of the Society of Biblical Archaeology*, vii, 177. The remaining pieces of the wreckage are in the Cairo and British Museums.

On digging deeper in this ground we found at a little above the water-level, a thin drinking cup of the form usual in the XIIth dynasty; this type may very probably have continued rather later, so it does not prove any occupation before the Hyksos time.

The removal of the bank of the camp was not completed on the western half. One block of the sand and marl was left outside of the Ramesside wall, near the north-west corner. It is shown on the plan, Pl. II, and also appears at the left hand of the view of the great bank on Pl. IV. And on digging for the western wall we uncovered the stucco slope to ten feet above water-level, outside the line of the Ramesside wall; and a further portion near by was bared by the *sebakh* diggers. Probably most of the stucco slope could be yet found along this side. It seems then that Ramessu III cut down the upper part of the bank, and doubtless used the sand to mix with Nile mud in making the bricks, for all his great constructions here. Where he cut off the bank at the south side a sloping wall was built across it to hold up the sand, at A, Pl. II.

In the XXVIth dynasty some temple existed here, as otherwise the life-size figure of the admiral Hor (Pl. XIX) would not have been placed in the town. And at that time the worship seems to have been directed to the lion-headed goddess, the *Bubastis Agria* named by Josephus.

In Ptolemaic times also there was a temple, as is shown by many fragments of Greek architectural features found near the other sculptures. The house ruins of the town had so much increased that the ground had risen to the top of the great bank. The remains of this condition were seen in 1871 and 1887, but now only a few high walls are left in the south-east corner.

11. ORIGIN OF THE CAMP. Having now described the actual remains, and what can be gathered from them, we may sum up the results of the facts, and consider the origin and meaning of the camp.

The most obvious point is the entirely un-Egyptian

nature of the camp, and of the mode of defence which it implies. Instead of the high massive brick walls which were used from the IInd dynasty onward, as at the Abydos forts and city, at Semneh and Kummeh, at El Kab, and every other Egyptian town that has been preserved, we have here a very thick bank of sand with a slope sixty feet long, and no trace of a wall on the top of it. Instead of the elaborate gateway traps that the Egyptian reckoned on for his defence, there is here no gateway but the exposed sloping ascent over two hundred feet in length.

It is evident therefore that the people who made the fort were not accustomed to the hand-to-hand fighting, such as the Egyptian found profitable owing to his superior weapons; for a fine illustration of early Egyptian fighting we may refer to the spirited siege of Nedaa, sculptured at Deshasheh (*Deshasheh*, Pl. V). On the contrary, by trusting their defence to a protracted approach of the enemy these people must have depended on projectiles. A barbed wire tangle in the present day, or a long glacis, is expressly for use with gun fire; and a slope sixty feet long, with an entrance approach two hundred feet long, would be useless without good archery. It is clear therefore that the type of fighting of the settlers was archery, combined with a long exposure of the enemy.

In describing the entrance, and the changes in its form (Section 8), I have explained them as adapted for archery. At first it was solely made to agree with plain earth-bank defences. Then after a year or two it was modified by the use of walls for flanking defences. And when, after two or three generations, the old system of fighting was abandoned, then a stone wall was substituted for the sloping bank.

That the camp is older than the XXth dynasty is certain, from its having been cut down and altered at that age. What people before that age were using a defensive system entirely different to that of the Egyptians? We can only look to the foreign invasions which broke up the XIVth, the VIth, and the IInd dynasties. Among these the choice is absolutely decided by the profusion of scarabs of the Hyksos age in the camp and the region around it, while there is no trace of the earlier periods. No conclusion is possible but that the camp was due to invaders between the XIVth and XVIIIth dynasties.

The position of the camp is excellent. It lies between Memphis and the Wady Tumilat, by which any eastern people must advance into Egypt. It is on a low rise of desert which here projects into the cultivation. Probably this was connected with the eastern desert in the earlier history, and it has since been separated by the rise of Nile mud, which now occupies about a mile width between the desert and the camp. The desert edge at present projects into the Delta, this region having been largely protected from denudation by a flow of basalt which covers the soft marls and limestone. Hence the position of the camp was surrounded on three sides with cultivation, while yet belonging to the desert. It commands a fine view into the desert for many miles; and an invader would need to make a wide detour to avoid touch with a fortress so placed. The distance from Memphis rendered this position the key to the capital, in the days of foot-marching or small horses. Thirty miles was then, what the fifty miles from Tell el Kebir to Cairo is now with large horses. This camp was the limit of striking distance from the capital, the point which must be secured before any advance from the east into Egypt was possible.

That such fortified camps were made by the Hyksos is shown by the passages of Manetho quoted by Josephus. He states that the invaders after a barbaric period, equivalent to the age of the earthwork camp here, became more civilised, and that their first king, Salatis, made the city of Avaris "very strong by the walls he built about it," and that they "built a wall round all this place, which was a large and strong wall." Thus the history that we have traced here of an earthwork camp constructed by nomads, who later placed a great wall around it, exactly accords with the account of the Hyksos.

12. POSITION OF AVARIS. A further question indeed arises as to whether this camp was itself the celebrated stronghold Avaris, which has been generally supposed to have been down by the coast in the north-east of the Delta. In favour of such a site as Tell el Yehudiyeh there are the following connections:

(1) Avaris was built to defend Egypt against eastern invaders (*Josephus c. Ap.* i, 14). This implies that it was on the eastern road which went by the Wady Tumilat; for it would be absurd to put a fortress for this purpose near the coast and far to the north of that road.

(2) Avaris was upon the Bubastite channel (*Jos. c. Ap.* i, 14). This implies that it was between Memphis and Bubastis; were it near the coast it would be referred to the Pelusiac, Tanitic, Mendesian, or Pathmetic channels, and not to Bubastis, north of which the channel branched in two.

(3) The only monument known which belongs to Avaris (*Hatuart*) is the altar of Apepa II (PETRIE, *Hist.* i, 243), which states that Apepa made monuments for his father Set, lord of Hatuart. This was found in Cairo, and must have been brought from the region whence stone was collected for Cairo building. Memphis and Heliopolis were thus plundered, and perhaps our camp; but certainly a town in the marshes of Menzaleh would not supply material to Cairo.

In favour of the northern site near the coast we must consider :

(4) Avaris is said to have been in the Saite nome (*Jos. c. Ap.* i, 14); and as this is recognised as absurd in relation to its eastern position, an emendation of Sethroite for Saite has been accepted. This is supported by Africanus' excerpt from Manetho, " The shepherds founded a city in the Sethroite nome." But there is no proof that this is the same as the city named by Josephus in the Saite nome. On the contrary, a corruption of Saite from Sethroite is unlikely. The more probable origin of the reading may be in some place ending in ——polis, as ....OΛITHC might well be read as CAITHC if the earlier part of the name were defaced. This would be therefore an easy corruption from the words " Heliopolite nome."

(5) There is a mention of Set of Hatuart by Merenptah upon a statue at Tanis (PETRIE, *Tanis*, i, II, 5 A); but this is only an addition to an earlier monument, and it merely states that the king was loved by Set, and does not refer to making monuments to Set as on the Cairo altar.

(6) Avaris is stated to have been garrisoned by 240,000 men, and to have occupied 10,000 arouras (*Jos. c. Ap.* i, 14); this would be a camp of nearly 3½ miles square. But it is very unlikely that any single fortified camp would be of this size, owing to difficulties of health and management; nor is it likely that a " large and strong wall " would be of 14 miles in length to surround it. Rather must we suppose a stronghold of practicable size, surrounded with encampments covering altogether 12 square miles, the whole group holding quarter of a million men beside their families.

The only serious reason for seeking Avaris near the coast is its supposed identity with the " city in the Sethroite nome " of Manetho ; while in favour of the Yehudiyeh camp being Avaris there is the position on the road to Syria, the relation to the Bubastite channel, and the altar of Avaris found near Cairo.

It seems therefore probable that the camp which we have described is the Hyksos capital of Avaris, and that we have before us here the " large and strong wall " of Salatis.

CHAPTER II

THE HYKSOS CEMETERY

13. THE principal cemetery of Tell el Yehudiyeh lies on a sandy rise of desert ground stretching out to about half a mile on the east of the town. Beside this there is a cemetery on the edge of the desert a mile and a half to the east, and there are isolated graves beneath the black-earth ruins in the camp itself. We shall here deal with the graves in their probable order historically. The numbers applied to them, and marked on their contents when found, have no relation to their chronological order, being necessarily applied in the order of discovery. The consecutive numbers extend to over a hundred, but higher hundreds were begun on other occasions to avoid any possible overlapping of numbers.

We will first describe those graves which had pottery and scarabs distinctively between the XIIth and XVIIIth dynasties. These were partly inside the camp and partly in the eastern cemetery. Those in the camp had suffered by crushing, owing to the great height of town ruins that had accumulated over them, and the wetness of the soil. Those in the cemetery had suffered by plundering, and none were complete, as they had been broken into when digging later graves. Unhappily, not a single skull could be saved from this class : in the camp they were in fragments as soft as putty ; in the cemetery nearly all were destroyed anciently, and others were rotted by damp.

The important question of the general age of these tombs is proved by the scarabs found with them. All of these were of the style which is always recognised as a degradation of that of the XIIth dynasty. And three scarabs found by us, and one bought here, gave four names of kings who are believed to belong to the age of the XIIIth to XVIIth dynasties. These are of Merneferra, 116, Pl. IX, Khyan 124, Sekhanra 143, and Apepa I 144. The photographs in Pl. IV A show these as A. 3, B. 3, B. 4, F. 3. It may therefore be accepted that this class of graves covers the period of the Hyksos kings, a few centuries before and after 2000 B.C.

On comparing the contents of these graves we

find some variety in style; and as the scarabs are the most varied and distinctive of the contents, and are linked to the known forms of the XIIth dynasty, it is best to begin the distinguishing of ages by means of them. Accordingly, the scarabs and the black pottery, which are the most clearly variable contents, are published here together, in groups as discovered, on Pls. VII, VIII. The metal work is on Pl. VI. The black and foreign pottery found without other dating material is on Pls. VIII A, VIII B, as it is not of historical use, but only shows undated varieties. And the plain red pottery is on Pl. X.

The remainder of the early scarabs found singly, or bought at the site, are on Pl. IX, and photographed on Pl. IV A; while on Pl. V are photographs of the daggers, of the most complete tomb which we found, and of the types of red pottery and black incised vases. Finally, in reading the following descriptions, the plans of the graves on Pl. XII should be used. Thus the whole material is fully placed at the disposition of the student.

14. The order of sequence which appears most likely, has been followed in arranging these grave-groups on the plates VII and VIII. The scarab of the most regular work, no. 1, is probably the earliest, and so dates grave 2; with it was a buff vase, no. 2, with red lines, clearly of foreign origin, and four black vases, of which the types are given, nos. 3, 4, 5.

The grave 407 appears to be the next in age. The scarabs nos. 6 and 7 seem to be variants of Kheper·ka·ra, the name of Senusert (or Usertesen) I of the XIIth dynasty. The substitution of *nefer* or *neferui* for *ra* is pretty well established by many other instances; and the coil patterns have their finest development in the reign of Senusert. The signs of coarseness in these, however, preclude their being of the age of Senusert, but they are good copies of his. With them are two others, nos. 8 and 9, which are clearly of debased style; and the eight uraei on no. 10 are similar in idea to the uraei on scarabs of Antef Nub-kheper-ra. With these were five black vases, of the types nos. 11, 12, 13, and one red one of the type no. 93.

The next in date appears to be grave 3. There are no good copies of older scarabs, but only ignorant and clumsy groupings of signs. No. 20 is senseless, but of fairly good cutting. The nos. 14, 15, are clearly like 8 and 9, but ruder. Nos. 16 and 17 begin the series of animal figures; but this sphinx and this hawk show how far removed they were from the good work of the XIIth dynasty. And we see

here the hawk-headed man holding a palm-branch, which is fairly clear, but which became far ruder subsequently. The kohl vase, no. 21, is departing from the good forms of the XIIth dynasty, and approaching the type of the XVIIIth dynasty. The black vases show a change: no. 22 being exaggerated, and no. 25 more elaborate than the earlier nos. 3 and 11; while no. 26 is less graceful than nos. 5 and 13, and this type here ends.

In grave 5 there are only two scarabs, nos. 27 and 28, for dating. They have the coarse figures later than no. 18. A plain amethyst scarab in gold setting, no. 29, was with these. The tomb chamber had certainly been disturbed, and the two eyes were doubtless a later introduction of the XXIInd dynasty.

We now reach the scarabs with concentric circles. No. 33 is clearly earlier than no. 47; and also, having two hieroglyphs, may claim precedence of 34, which is senseless.

In graves 16 and 20 there were no scarabs; but the black vases nos. 36 to 41 may be classed in this place. Nos. 39 and 40 have the more acute lines of pricks, like nos. 35 and 48; while in earlier times, as in no. 4, the lines are flatter. The outline in no. 38 is fuller and less shapely than in 24 and 25, and approaches the coarse forms of nos. 49 and 50. No. 41, widening below, approaches the late form no. 57.

The fine grave 37 contained a late group of scarabs. No. 43 is coarser than 27 and 28; no. 44 is ruder than 17; no. 45 is much worse than no. 18; and no. 47 is coarser than any others here. The types of the black pottery are also fuller and more clumsy than any before this, while the combing round the pot no. 52 is a cheapening of work, on the road to the plain surface of no. 57.

In grave 1 there was no black pottery, and no construction of a tomb. But by the types of the scarabs Pl. VI, 4, 5, they seem to be quite as late as as nos. 43 and 44.

Later still is grave 6, as we must date scarab no. 53 later than 43, and no. 55 later than 42. The pottery here is plain black without any incised pattern, and of a later form than any which have been noticed here.

The subsequent stages are outside of this group of graves with scarabs. But it is clear that the form of no. 57 passes on to a flat-bottomed shape, no. 103 (Pl. VIII B); and that again to a globular flask of black ware, nos. 107, 108, which is already known to belong to the XVIIIth dynasty. Thus the changes of type of the black pottery are now continuous from those with well-made scarabs of the XIIth dynasty style, down to those of the XVIIIth dynasty. Having dealt with the relative ages of the graves, we will next consider them in detail, with their plans and contents altogether.

15. Turning to the plans of the graves, Pl. XII, it will be seen that of these Hyksos graves six have the head to the east, and three (graves 2, 5, 43) have the head to the south. This seems to be a true mixture of usage, as those to the east are both early and late; we cannot, therefore, suppose a change of custom, such as was traced between the VIth and XIIth dynasties (*Diospolis Parva*, pp. 42-3).

Grave 2. The body was all broken up, but the vases and pan seemed to be in original positions; the line of vases suggests that the length was N—S, and therefore the head may be also in place. There was a blade-bone in true relation to the head; and on it a copper pin, shown at the base of Pl. VI. These pins were used to fasten garments, being secured to one edge by a string through the hole in the middle, and then passed through an eyelet in the other edge. Such pins are known in Cyprus, and so were probably introduced here along with the painted buff pottery nos. 2, 51, 58, 98-102 (MYRES, *Cyprus Museum Catalogue*, nos. 591-8; see also pottery no. 368, black incised ware nos. 281-8). They were also found down to the XVIIIth dynasty at Gurob, one being of gold (*Illahun*, XXII, 1, 2, 3). The position of the pin upon the blade-bone shows that it held the garment at the throat. Just before that was the scarab, which was probably on a hand placed in front of the face. In the pan at the head were animal bones and a fish, and the ring-stand near it had a jar upright upon it. This was a disturbed group in the mud of the camp, and no sides of the grave were noticed. The red pottery is shown in Pl. X, 1, 36, 52.

Grave 407. This grave in the camp had been broken up at the west end; but the trunk of one skeleton remained, and the whole of another. This was the only instance of two bodies being found together; though the two skulls in no. 5 may have belonged to simultaneous burials. The general appearance of the grave, cleaned from mud so far as practicable, is given in Pl. V, which should be compared with the plan, noting that the right-hand end is much foreshortened. The sex of the two bodies could not be determined, as the skull and pelvis were too much crushed and decayed in both. But the western

body had the dagger on the thigh, and would therefore be a man. The scarabs are nearer to this one, but strangely placed; two (nos. 6, 10) were far in front, while three (nos. 7, 8, 9) were on the bones of a hand which lay detached, with the wrist to the north-west. This cannot have belonged to a third body buried here, as the hands of the others are on the north of the grave. It seems then to have been a hand buried alone. The bones of the western body are difficult to understand: the left arm was bent, and the hand by the dagger; but the right arm was stretched out in front, and apparently the ulna turned upwards in front of the knees of the other figure. This seems an impossible distance from the body. It may be that these persons were slain in a battle. This would account for there being two bodies together and part of a third; also for the apparently separated arm, and for the certainly superfluous loose hand. There were six black incised vases, and an unusual amount of the red pottery (Pl. X, 2, 3, 4, 5, 28, 29, 53, 54, 55), including a tall stand (Pl. X, 30) and a large globular vase (Pl. XIV A) of the XIIth dynasty style. The dagger is shown on Pls. V and VI, 1; the ring is a very thin casting of bronze over an ash core, and was the pommel of the handle, judging by its position.

Grave 3 was a burial in a wooden coffin in the camp. The thigh was very small, being only 14 inches, instead of about 18 as usual; but the humerus was normal, 12 inches, and the height of the trunk from the thigh ball to the vertex was 29 inches, which is not small. In the whole body of grave 407 the trunk similarly was 31 inches. Both of these heights should be increased a couple of inches to allow for curves and decline of the head, if making comparison with the living. Three scarabs (nos. 15, 16, 17) were placed on the stomach, and two others (nos. 14, 20) among the black incised vases at the feet of the coffin. The knees rode up over the coffin edge, as if it were too narrow for them. The coffin was of thin boards, the traces of which remained running through the mud as straight black planes about ¼ inch thick.

Grave 5. This grave was the most ancient found in the cemetery east of the town. The chamber was 90 inches long, and 38 wide; and adjoining it on the west was an annex 37 long and 25 wide. Two skulls were in the chamber; but whether of the same period, or one due to secondary burial, could not be settled, as the bodies were entirely broken up anciently. In the annex were only sheep and lamb bones. This annex seems to have been for funeral sacrifices; yet a pile of lambs' bones were also in the south-east corner of the chamber. By being built on against the chamber, the annex certainly seems contemporary. Bones lay in the two pans (Pl. X, 5), a skull and a blade-bone in the middle, and a bronze knife had been thrown in with the sacrifice ; this is drawn in Pl. VI, 9, and photographed on Pl. V. The annex had a roofing of bricks covering it. The tomb had also a complete barrel roofing. The red pottery is usual (see Pl. X, 5, 6, 7, 19, 31, 32, 34, 58, 59, 62), and there were no black vases. The three scarabs were all probably in front of the body by the hands, judging by the rank of pottery on the opposite side, which is like that behind the body in grave 407. The bronze dagger lay by the head ; it is figured in Pls. V and VI, 7. Two bronze toggle-pins (VI, 10, 11) were found in moving the earth, but their position is uncertain. These suggest two burials of the same age. In the corner at the south-west lay a curious mud figure very rudely formed (Pl. VI, 8). It might be supposed to belong to a later age, and as late eye beads (Pl. VII, 31, 32) were found here, a secondary burial seems probable. But the position of this mud figure, in a corner behind the early pottery, seems to show that it also is early. The thickness of the tomb side was not measured, but the door was 12 inches through.

Grave 19. This burial in the cemetery was much broken up, the trunk being entirely wrecked. A few red vases remained in the east end (Pl. X, 5, 10, 11, 36, 38, 66, 67), and lambs' bones in the north-east corner, analogous to those in the corner of no. 5. Only one scarab remained here. The section of the tomb is shown at the end of the plan.

Grave 4. The plan of this is shown below no. 5. The body was complete, but the lower jaw was set upright at right angles to the head. It was a child, as the thigh was only 10 inches long, and the shin 8 inches long, in place of 17 and 14 inches as usual. One scarab lay near the wrist, and the pottery was in front and above the head—two pans (Pl. X, 8, 9) and two jars (X, 63) upon ring-stands (X, 41, 45). This burial was in the town, the only one found there later than the first three.

Grave 16 is not drawn among the plans. The bones were all scattered, and two pans (Pl. X, 10, 12), two jars (X, 68, 69), and a ring-stand (X, 40), lay with the broken skull at the east end. The black incised vases were found scattered (Pl. VIII, 36-40). Cemetery.

Grave 17 was a circular pit with only animal bones. In it were four pans (Pl. X, 1), four jars (X, 62), and four ring-stands in a heap (X, 32, 33, 35, 36). Cemetery.

Grave 20 was a disturbed grave, with one black vase (VIII, 41) and one pan (Pl. X, 13), a ring-stand (X, 43), two jars (X, 72, 73), and a cup (X, 24). Cemetery.

Grave 37 was a fine tomb, cut away in later times along the south-west corner, and the body entirely broken up. Only the humeri were left. The section of the arching is shown at the end of the plan. There were four black incised vases of the later style, and a buff one with red lines, Pl. VIII, 48-52. Five scarabs were placed near one humerus, as if the body had faced the south. The positions of all these, and the red pottery (Pl. X, 41, 45, 47, 49), are shown on the plan. The bronze pin was found near the place of the neck, as in grave 2. Between the black pots on the north was a goose's egg, and under it a bead necklace, and a rough scarab, no. 47. The beads were small white discs, probably blue originally, and small black globular beads coloured with manganese. A small slate rubber, 2 inches long, lay under the right humerus. One amethyst bead lay near the legs ; probably there had been a string of amethysts taken by the plunderers. The floor of the grave was of brick, as well as the barrel roof.

Grave 1 was a curious deposit in the camp, the first burial that we found. It was a heap of bones stacked closely together ; most of them were of animals, but among them I found a piece of human jaw and patella. On the north of the heap lay the dagger, Pl. VI, 3 ; and two scarabs (4, 5), with an amethyst bead (6), were in the heap of bones. Perhaps this may have been a burial of portions of a man killed at a distance in battle, placed with sacrifices beneath his own dwelling to appease the spirit. The burial of a knife along with the sacrifice at the side of grave 5 should be compared with this. Also the following burials in the cemetery :

Grave 9. A pit 76 inches by 66 contained a large quantity of loose bones, of both oxen and sheep, irregularly thrown together. With these was the broken upper end of a human thigh-bone, and four of the usual red pans.

Grave 17. A circular pit containing entirely animal bones, irregularly heaped together. With them were 4 jars, 4 ring-stands, and 4 pans.

Grave 6 was entirely broken away at the head (plan, Pl. XII). Two pans (X, 14) were placed, one each side of the stomach, and two scarabs (Pl. VII,

53, 55) were on the body between them. These show that this is one of the latest burials of this age. An amethyst scarab (54) lay by the left hand, and a black vase without any incised pattern (57).

Grave 43 is also a late grave, 70 inches by 28. In it were two jars (X, 75, 76), two ring-stands (X, 49, 51), a pan (X, 15), a cup (X, 26), and one buff vase with black pattern (Pl. VIII, 58).

Grave 45 appears from the type to be of a yet later age. The body lay with head to the south. Upon it were two portions of globular jars (Pl. XIV A), and by the head two red jars (Pl. XII A), and the black vase VIII B, 103. Two blocks of basalt were placed by the legs.

The later stages of such pottery are seen in nos. 106 and 107, 108. The latter belong to the XVIIIth dynasty, as such were found at Gurob. Of other burials not figured here we may mention of this age:—Grave 8, body broken up, head east: 2 pans (X, 10, 11), jar (X, 71), and stand (X, 44), and a fragment of black incised pottery. Grave 16, bones all scattered, head to east: 2 pans (X, 10, 12), 2 jars (X, 68, 69), and a stand (X, 40). Grave 22, no bones left, head probably south-east: pan, jar (X, 64), and stand (X, 42), with one other vase (X, 23). Grave 33, with second interment of a child: the older pans (X, 15) were inverted over the child's skull, and a jar and ring-stand were also left.

16. We may here notice the changes traceable in the red pottery. This class is much less variable than the scarabs and the black pottery, and it is therefore on these classes (already discussed) that we must depend for the history of the red pottery. On Pl. X are shown the forms, classified according to the order of the graves already described. A few singular forms are given on Pl. XIV A. In the pans, 1-17, there is no apparent change; and, as in the prehistoric age, the plain pan seems to have been the most stable type. The bowls and cups, 18-27, are not so common as the other forms, and there are hardly enough examples to show definite changes. The ring-stands are tall at the beginning, as in the XIIth dynasty (*Dendereh*, XVIII, 153), but show little variation until they become rather taller at the end, nos. 47, 50, 51. The jars are the only distinctive class. The bottom is rounded at first, as in the XIIth dynasty (*Dend.* XVIII, 162), in graves 2, 407 and 5. Then a pointed form comes in, beginning in 5 and continuing in 19 to the end; while the sides become more parallel. By the time of grave 20 the red tops begin to appear, which are usual in the early XVIIIth dynasty, Pl. XII A.

Thus some differences of age can be shown by the red pottery, though not nearly so decisively as by the other objects.

17. Having now described all the burials of Hyksos age, it will be well to refer to the other objects of early period in the order of the plates.

PL. I. The fragment of a black and white porphyry vase, no. 1, is of the pre-pyramid age, and by the poor hollowing of the interior it is probably of the IIIrd dynasty. A cup, no. 2, of black and white syenite, and a cup of black porphyry, no. 3, may be also of the IIIrd dynasty. The bowl of white felsite, no. 4, is of the style and material of the IInd to IVth dynasties. There seems therefore to be fair evidence of some settlement in the region of the later temple as far back as the early historic times.

Of the XIIth dynasty are the pieces of rubbing dishes in quartzite sandstone, nos. 5, 6; such are well known at that age (*Diospolis Parva*, XXX, Y. 448). The fragment of the front of a seated figure of the time of Amenemhat III belonged to a "*ka* prince, chief of the prophets A(meny ?)." The incised pottery dishes, nos. 8-10, 14, are well known to belong to this same age at Kahun (*Kahun*, XIII; *Illahun*, V), but they are not found in the south of Egypt; and being of more vigorous designs at Yehudiyeh than they are at Kahun, this suggests that they originate in a northern influence. A small group of two beads of blue paste, no. 11, a cylinder of Amenemhat III, "beloved by Sebek of the Fayum," no. 12, and a plain cylinder, no. 13, were found together on the temple site. It is certain therefore that in the XIIth dynasty there was here a town, and probably a temple. The granite column may well have belonged to such a temple.

PL. IV A. The two busts here photographed have been broken from seated figures, such as were dedicated in temples or tombs. They were both found in the temple ground; and they appear to be of the XIIth or XIIIth dynasty. The scarabs shown here will be annotated in describing Pls. IX and XI.

PL. VIII A. The many fragments of fish (59-63) made in black incised pottery show that such figures must have been common. The lobate vases, 64, 65, were both found in the camp; they probably belong to the earlier age of this ware. The fragment 70 was found on the top of the sand bank of the fortification. The bowls 73-5 were from the camp, none such were found in the graves. The flask 84 was found in grave 120, with the types of pottery given in Pl. X, 8, 36, 63. The lemon-vase, 78, 81, was only found in the camp, and not in graves.

PL. VIII B (read pottery scale 1 : 2). This is all foreign pottery, 88, 90, 91, black, and 89 red ; 92 to 97 are of light red or buff ware. 98 is red with black stripes ; it was found with a full length female body, lying with head to east, and wearing copper earrings. But as this burial had cut through and disturbed an earlier burial with jars (Pl. X, 68, 69), and ring-stands (X, 40), it is possible that the vase was also of the earlier period. The red flasks with black stripes, 99-101, and buff with red stripes, are certainly foreign, akin to the Cypriote pottery, but not quite of the same fashion. The little pale drab flasks, 104, 105, are probably of the XVIIIth dynasty, like the black ware 107, 108.

Regarding these foreign fabrics, Mr. J. L. Myres, who is the principal authority on the Cypriote and Eastern Mediterranean pottery, informs me that the black incised ware of these shapes is limited to Egypt, Palestine, and Eastern Cyprus ; and it has never been found in the west of Cyprus, Asia Minor, or Greece. We must therefore look on it as probably Syrian in origin. The bowls Pl. VIII A, 73-5, are hitherto unknown. Regarding its date, all examples agree in the pre-Mykenaean age. Those published with Mykenaean tombs by MURRAY, *Excavations in Cyprus*, fig. 9, were not found in the tombs, but were loose, and doubtless belong to an earlier denuded cemetery, as in other Cypriote instances. That in GARSTANG, *Arabah*, XVII, tomb 10, was with an ivory wand and alabaster kohl pots of the XIIth—XVth dynasty, but mixed with pottery of a later burial of the XVIIIth dynasty. These are the only instances which might seem to be of a later age than that we have here fixed. The painted buff pottery here Mr. Myres looks on as akin to that of Cyprus, but of probably some neighbouring source.

18. PL. IX. The scarabs are here arranged, so far as practicable, in what appears to be their most probable order of age. The column at the left hand is of those found singly in our excavations, the remainder were all bought from the natives at the place. Nos. 109 to 113 may be purely of the XIIth dynasty. 113 belonged to the "*Uartu* of the city Senaa." 114 is of the age of Apepa I (see NEWBERRY, *Scarabs*, XXIV, 34) ; the inscription must be compared with 115. Possibly we may understand these as belonging to officials of the *uza* canal or embankment, one named Met-desher, the other Ankhs. 116 is of the well-known king Mer·nefer·ra

Ay. 124 is of the great king Khyan, whose scarabs are nearly always of fine work, and several are mounted in gold like this ; it was found along with a strip of gold in the camp. The symmetrical scarabs, 125-30, come in as early as grave 407. 143 is one of the king Se·kha·n·ra, whose scarabs are often found. 144 is of Apepa I, and ruder than most of his ; I bought it from men who had just found it in the fields north of the camp. The scarabs 152 to 161 seem to belong to the age of grave 5. Nos. 162 to 173 are like those of grave 37. It should be noted that on Pl. VIII, nos. 44 and 46 show the beginning of two parallel side lines with cross strokes at right angles. The two side lines begin under Khyan and Yaqeb-her, but no cross strokes appear on their scarabs. It seems then that those kings precede grave 37 ; and so 162 to 173 are of a later time contemporary with Se·kha·n·ra, Ymu, Yaqeb, and others whose scarabs are of the ruder type.

PL. XI ; here F, or a grave number, is placed against those found in the work. Nos. 190-1 may be before or after the XVIIIth dynasty. 192 is a bright green scarab of Tahutmes III, found in the small pottery cist (Pl. XIV A, XV) with a cup, but no bones. 193 is of the age of Tahutmes III (see *Illahun*, XXVI, 13). 195 is probably of the reign of Amenhotep II. 196 is in a silver mount, the reign is not certain. 197-8 are of Amenhotep III ; the latter is of gold (bought), but as likely as not it is modern, as it resembles others that I know to be forgeries. 199-201, 203 are probably posthumous uses of the name of Tahutmes III. 202 is an interesting jar-handle stamp, naming Sety I, "Men·maat·ra builder of Thebes," doubtless referring to the great hall of Karnak. 204-5 are of Sety I. 206-8 are of Ramessu II, the latter showing the king sacrificing a gazelle to Ptah. 209 has a very interesting figure of Sutekh, with the horned cap and long streamer (see PETRIE, *Researches in Sinai*, fig. 134), winged like Baal-zebub of Ekron, and standing on a lion in the manner of a Syrian god. 210-12 are figures of a throned king, probably rude copies of Ramessu II. 213 is the type of Ramessu II (?) between Set and Horus, here modified to two Horus figures. 216 is a plaster cap of a jar sealed by Ramessu III, probably from one of the wine-jars of his palace here. 218 is a clay mould, also of Ramessu III. 220 is probably a debased copy of one of Siptah. 221 is of Ramessu VI. 227 is of blue paste, with Ptah and Sekhet. 230 is probably of the XXVth dynasty. 236 bears a monkey eating a bunch of grapes, in relief on the back. 238, bearing the name of Pedu-ast, was found with the iron spear photographed in Pl. XIX D. 241 is a blundered copy of the name of Shabataka, XXVth dynasty. 247 may be modern (bought). 248 seems to be of the same name as another with Ab'ra (PETRIE, *Hist. Scarabs*, 2141). 251 is a gnostic charm in dark brown steatite; the back bears curious imitations of cartouches of Ramessu II and Merenptah, doubtless copied from large monuments; this is one of the very rare cases of cartouches being noticed after their meaning was forgotten.

CHAPTER III

THE LATER REMAINS

19. THE XVIIIth dynasty has left many graves in the Gezireh cemetery, which carry on the customs of the earlier age in a modified form. The large brick vaulted grave has disappeared; and instead we find the small brick grave with pottery inside, grave 31 (Pl. XII), or shrunk so that the pottery is stacked outside, grave 41; or the open sand graves, 23 and 34 (Pl. XII); or a pot coffin with the pottery placed outside it, as in the grave of Men (Pls. XIV, XV), and graves 24 and 30 (both on Pl. XII); lastly there are jar-burials of children probably beginning as early as XVIIIth or XIXth dynasty. The plans already referred to will show the arrangement of the pottery in the graves. The variations which can be traced in the pottery have been taken into account in the classifying and dating of it in the plates here given, and we may best follow this order in considering it.

PL. XII A. The pottery with red edges, or black edges, is well known in Upper Egypt, always of the early XVIIIth dynasty period. On referring to the Maket tomb (*Illahun*, XXVI—VII), it will be seen that there is no example of this edging; and subsequent discoveries show that this tomb is entirely of the date of the scarabs in it, Tahutmes III. This edged pottery may therefore be dated to about the first four reigns of the XVIIIth dynasty, though it touches the reign of Tahutmes III (see GARSTANG, *Arabah*, XXVIII, E. 259, dated by a scarab). The large group of contemporary pottery, grave 54, is useful for showing relative ages.

PL. XII B. This whole group was found in a basket, covered by a mat, buried in clean sand in the cemetery. The two ivory arms were placed one on the other. The blue glazed bust should be compared with the later mould (PETRIE, *Tell el Amarna*, XVII, 278) and other instances in stone. This group is probably of about the reign of Tahutmes III.

PL. XII C. Here we reach the well-dated pottery of Tahutmes III. The foreign bottles imitating leather-ware are of the early type, showing the ridges of stitching. A puzzling case is that of the bowl found in grave 23: it is of Ptolemaic style, but the other three pots of this grave are all of the Tahutmes age. The skeleton of a man lay at full length, on the back, head to east; the leather-ware flask was at the left of the skull, the bowl inverted at the left of the jaw, the little jug at the side of the left humerus. We must suppose that the burial is late, and that the pottery was robbed from an earlier tomb. The pottery coffin face also seems certainly late in style.

PL. XII D. Here some of the pottery is from the same grave as the foreign flasks in the previous plate, grave 24. The burial was in a pottery coffin; one flask was inside at the west, head end; the two long jars were lying at the south of the coffin, the rest of the pottery along the north, as shown on Pl. XII. The blue glazed eye is probably later; it may have been loose in the filling of the grave. I did not mark it in my notes where every vase is entered. The strips of ivory, 411, were from a broken-up toilet box in the painted pottery coffin of Men, Pl. XIV. The long jars of graves 24, 100, 404, 406, are all of the type of Tahutmes III, as in the Maket tomb, fig. 42.

The changes in the forms of the jars should be compared. On Pl. X they are at first swelling to the base and rounded below, next somewhat pointed below. On Pl. XII A they are moderately rounded below. On Pl. XII D they are larger, pointed below and swelling out from the neck. On Pl. XIII, in grave 403, this type is associated with others flattened below.

PL. XIII. The pottery here is probably of about the age of Amenhotep II. The foreign flask, grave 55, is stumpy and awkward, and in grave 414 bulging and degraded. The jars have two or three incised lines around the necks, never found under Tahutmes III, but under his successors, Amenhotep II (*Six Temples*, V, 1) and Tahutmes IV (*S. T.* VII, 12). The little *repoussé* bronze ornament is akin to similar rosettes of Amenhotep II (*S. T.* III, 17).

PL. XIV. This painted pottery coffin was found in the cemetery, with the head to the north-west. On the right side stood a jar, the top broken; on the left a jar like that from grave 404 (Pl. XII D) with black bands. This must be assigned to the time of Tahutmes III. The top of the coffin had been smashed in by plunderers, and dozens of pieces lay in the sand within it. I collected these entirely, and built up the remains as shewn. The photographs of parts of it are in Pl. XV. At each side of the head are figures, one probably of Isis, the other of Nebhat, here written Nebt-hat; Isis is holding the *shennu* rings, and Nebhat is pouring out vases of water. Then follows the speech of Nebhat and of Osiris, the latter blundered and continuing "for the *ka* of Men, *maa kheru.*" After this come blundered speeches of the four genii and of Anubis, whose figures are shown. At the foot and down the middle band are funeral formulae for the deceased Men. On the end is a figure of Isis given on Pl. XIV A. It will be seen that some of the drawings have a straight red line through the length of the figure. These lines give the clue to the Egyptian system of posing a figure truly upright. The points which should fall on a vertical line were (1) the front of the wig lappet, (2) the middle of the shoulders, (3) the middle of the trunk, (4) the front of the backward knee, (5) the middle between the backs of the two heels. Similar vertical lines may be seen in drawings in the Tombs of the Kings.

PL. XIV A. Beside the base of the painted coffin there are here three views of a small pottery cist found in the cemetery, and see also the photograph on Pl. XV. On the east side of it stood a jar (XII A, no. 413), on the west a pan, much like the arrangement by a coffin. But on removing the lid, and carefully scraping out the sand in thin layers by hand, I found nothing inside except a small cup (XII A, 413) and a fine scarab of Tahutmes III, Pl. XI, 192. It cannot be supposed that bones would entirely dissolve where protected in a cist, when they remain distinct in the open sand; so the purpose of this curious ceremonial cist is yet unknown.

20. PL. XV. The kneeling figure will be described later on, under the XXVIth dynasty. The coffin and cist have been noticed already. The corn-grinders are usual in Egyptian sites, but have perhaps never been illustrated before.

PL. XVI. The inscription on the back of the granite dyad of Ramessu II and Ra has been described in the history of the site, Section 10. The view of the inscription, as it lies in a hole, is given on Pl. XVI A. The granite column, which probably was part of a temple of the XIIth dynasty, had an inscription added by Merenptah; the photograph of it is also on the next plate.

PL. XVI A. Beside the above-named subjects there are here the fragments of the beautiful glazed figure tiles of Ramessu III, the last remains of the wreck of his palace at this place. The subjects are figures of foreign captives, in decorated dresses which are of much interest; pieces of a frieze of *rekhyt* birds; pieces of cartouches; and some alabaster inlays. It would be most desirable to have a complete photographic publication in colour of all the unique work of this kind now scattered in Cairo, London, and other museums.

PL. XVII. The larger pieces here are fragments of great jars painted with a buff ground, and decorated in dark red and black. These were found amid the rubbish of the palace of Ramessu III, and this suggests that they were imported there in his reign, or shortly after. At the bottom, figs. 18-22, are pieces of rough red pottery with incised patterns imitating network.

PL. XVII A. From the XIXth to about the XXIIIrd dynasty very large jars were in use. They were doubtless made for domestic purposes, but we have recovered them from their use as coffins for infants in the cemetery. Probably no. 6 is the earliest of them, perhaps of the XIXth dynasty; 2, 3, 5, 7 are supposed to be of the XXth to XXIInd dynasties, and no. 1 probably later. The coffin no. 4 shows the degraded form copied from the painted coffins of the XVIIIth dynasty.

21. We now reach the later class of burials of the XXIInd to XXVIth dynasties; and though the objects are all well known, yet as these burials were the most numerous in the cemetery, the series may enable us to trace their order, and to place these common amulets in a more definite position. They are here placed in the following classes, which seem clearly to succeed each other:—(1) The groups without *uza* eyes, and with inscribed amulets, about the XXth to XXIInd dynasties, Pl. XVIII, top. (2) The smooth, well-made, *uza* eyes with black brows, Pl. XVIII, lower part. (3) The badly made *uza* eyes, with which appear glass beads with blue spots surrounded by brown lines in white, and the beginning of incised *uza* eyes, Pl. XIX. (4) The predominance of incised *uza* eyes, and the small bronze bells with bracelets; the glass beads degrading to mere spots in a small bead, without lines around, see Pl. XIX A. (5) The rise of quadruple eye beads, and of coloured glass heads as Pl. XIX B in group E, next to E, and the ram's head in 301. (6) The degraded quadruple eye beads framed in a square or circle, and very degraded

figures of gods. It does not seem possible to invert the order of any of these classes, though very likely there was a gradual change and overlapping from one class to another. Unfortunately it is so rarely that any cartouche scarabs are found with such later burials that we are at a loss to state the exact periods of the classes. But on reaching the period of the pottery which is well dated to the XXVIth dynasty (at Defenneh), as on Pl. XX A, the whole of the small amulets and eyes have disappeared, and none are found with the alabastra, which also are of the XXVIth dynasty (group 320, Pl. XX A). Hence it seems that all these amulets must be earlier than the XXVIth dynasty. We now turn to note a few details of these classes.

PL. XVIII. The groups marked by numbers were mostly recorded, but those with letters were merely found loose, usually in a child's burial, and were picked out by the diggers. Grave 101, the scarab reads *Khet neb nefer*, "all good things"; the square plaques are rude copies of those of Tahutmes III. From having a jar of the late XVIIIth dynasty type it is possible that this group is of the XIXth dynasty. Grave 307 seems to be about the XXIInd dynasty by the style of the frog amulet. The small bronze figure and earring in grave 105 seem to be not later than the XXIInd dynasty by the disc of black and yellow glass and the little rosette; this appears to be the earliest of the *uza* eyes, and of the bronze bracelets.

PL. XIX. The earlier of the glass spot beads are associated with these eyes, in graves 66, 71, 307 and A. In grave 310 the figure coffin is seen in a simplified stage. The style of this might even be as early as the XXth dynasty (see *Mound of the Jew*, pls. 13, 14), but the glass beads and other objects seem to be later than that. In group C we have an indication of the XXIIIrd dynasty, or later, in the name Pedu-ast on a scarab, associated with a fine spot bead. In group E another such bead with a rude aegis of Bast points to the same date.

PL. XIX A. Here in group A the figure of Nefertum is probably of the XXIIIrd dynasty, as he rose into fashion about then. The jar in grave 108 is inclining toward the style of the XXVIth dynasty. The little bells which come in at this time were probably worn for amulets, as in Italy at present.

PL. XIX B. The cats in grave 306 show the Bubastite influence of the XXIInd—XXIIIrd dynasties. The crocodile in group D is the earliest forerunner of the common crocodile amulet in the XXVIth dynasty.

PL. XIX C. Here the style of the figures has become as bad as any that are known, and the eyes are almost unrecognisable, as in group L. The rude eye with raised lines of brown slip in group O is more akin to the Roman figures with raised detail in yellow.

22. On reaching the XXVIth dynasty we should here notice the kneeling figure of the admiral Hor-Psamthek, which was found in the temple. It is of yellow quartzite sandstone, and unfortunately the upper part is lost. Perhaps some bust in a museum will prove to belong to it; and any possible fit should be tried by comparison with the back pier in Pl. XX. The photographs in Pl. XV. will show the general character, and the figure of Bast in the shrine. This evidence that Bast was the goddess of the place, connects it with the lion-city, Leontopolis, where Josephus states that Bubastis Agria was worshipped. Down the edge of the front of the shrine is the inscription, . . . *mer suten ahau ne aha em mu uaz ur, Hor, ran f nefer Psamthek*—"Chief of the royal fighting ships in the great green sea, Hor, whose good name is Psamthek." On the opposite edge is, . . . *ma ar nebt per Ra·ne·pa·ua*—". . . ma born of the heiress Ra·ne·pa·ua." Along the top of the base is, *kherp khastu Hanebu, Hor, ran f nefer Psamthek*—"Commander of the lands of the Hanebu (Greeks), Hor, whose good name is Psamthek." Down the back is, *sah, her ab ne neb taui Hor Menkh·ab, benen er nebu her . . .? nezem f*—"(Acceptable in the) council chamber in the heart of the lord of both lands Hor Menkh·ab, sweeter than all upon his throne of sweet wood"; and, *udu ne neter nefer Ra·nefer·ab, kherp khastu Hanebu (Hor ra)n f Psamthek*—"(Doing the) commands of the good god Nefer·ab·ra (Psamthek II), commander of the lands of the Hanebu Hor, his name is Psamthek." Around the base is, to the right, *Erpa ha, baty khetmu, | semer uati ne mer, meh ab ne suten em khastu Hanebu, rekht ne neb taui aqer f Hor ran f nefer Psamthek*—"The peer, the royal seal-bearer, the chiefly companion in love, satisfying the heart of the king in the lands of the Greeks; known to the lord of both lands was his excellency, Hor, his good name is Psamthek." Around the base to the left, *Erpa ha, baty khetmu, | semer uati ne mer, met er ab f her sekher du em her f, seau ab ne neb f em uzut neb ne khast, Hor*—"The peer, the royal seal-bearer, the chiefly companion in love, direct of heart is his plans that were entrusted to him, widening the heart of his lord in all his expeditions abroad, Hor."

I am indebted to Dr. Walker for clearing some

difficulties in this inscription. The sign rendered as "throne" is clearly an animal's skin; this may be used for the seat, or (as Miss Murray suggests) may be the *nes* throne with stroke below, misread by the scribe and turned. The sign read as Ra, in Ranepaua, appears to be *ra* in the name oval, somewhat misengraved. This official was thus the principal personage for dealing with the Greeks in this reign, 594–588 B.C., as Admiral of the Mediterranean fleet and Governor of Cyprus.

23. The graves of the XXVIth dynasty had better be noticed in the order of the objects on the plates.

Grave 320, Pl. XX A. The style of the alabastra shows the age of this grave, and serves to date the mirror, and the four-handled slate dish.

Grave 321 was perhaps of a foreigner, judging by the fibula, and the little steatite pendant.

Grave 18 has a similar fibula, but not ornamented. The body was in a narrow brick tomb of the size of a coffin; it lay at full length, on the back, with head to the east. The fibula was on the right breast; the alabastron and bronze kohl-stick were on the right side of the head; the ring upon the finger. The cup was placed upon the brick coffin. The body was of a female; thigh 17·8, humerus 12·7 inches: the jaw had only one molar on each side, and was peculiarly wide and short, being 2·4 inches wide and only 1·2 from back to front—in fact, a semicircle.

Below 321 is a fragment of a thick early Greek bowl, as in *Naukratis*, i, IV, 2, with part of a Karian inscription, read by Prof. Sayce as *l* or *s e z a*. I picked this up in the north-east corner of the camp; and though I completely turned over all the heaps of potsherds for some yards around not another scrap of such pottery could be found.

Grave 410 was a brick tomb, body on the back, head south. The jars were placed at the left humerus and right of the pelvis. There was a network of coloured glazed beads on the body; and many such were found on other bodies in this cemetery, but all too much broken up in the earth for the patterns to be traceable.

Grave 44 was a brick tomb, 81 by 40 inches, the body entirely broken up, but many beads in the earth. The head was probably east, and so the jar would be on the right of the head, and the saucer in the corner to the left.

Below is a small bronze chisel; a group of bracelets, pendants, earrings, and red glazed beads found together; and at the right a bronze point from the butt of a spear.

PL. XXI. Two green glazed bottles, nos. 1, 3, were found with a scarab, no. 2, which has the name of Psamthek blundered. In other graves were found the two other bottles, 4 and 5. The iron strigil 8 was found with a fragment of a similar bottle no. 7. These bottles were made for new year presents from maid-servants to their masters. The inscriptions are, on 3, "Tahuti open a good year for her lord," "Horus the good give life for her lord." On 4, "Amen open a good year for her lord," "Ptah and Sekhet open a good year for her lord." On 5, "Ptah and Sekhet" "open a good year for her lord."

PL. XXI A. The pottery here is probably Ptolemaic from 1 to 46, and Roman from 47 to 56. The iron bracelets, 57, 58, are Roman; as also the necklace of blue, green and yellow glass beads, and earrings, 59, and the amber necklace 60. The glass bottle 61 is probably Arabic.

24. PL. XXI B. The rough stone implements of various kinds have scarcely ever been published, and it seemed well to give some examples of them. 1 to 5 are stone caps for holding a drill-head in working. 6 to 12 are probably all loom weights. The reels 27-34 are common about the XIXth dynasty, and were probably used in net-making. The fragment of a cartouche, 37, cannot be identified, as most of the Ptolemies end with "living forever, loved by Ptah." 38 is an iron hoe. 39 are two anklets of massive copper, also shown in Pl. XIX D. These were on the ankles of a female, aged about 25; the skull very thin and moderately prognathous. The whole length was 58 inches, thigh 14·8 long, humerus 11, ulna 7 inches long. The body was on the back, with arms at the sides, head to the west. It lay in a shallow grave, cut 9 to 12 inches into the soft marly rock, just beneath the houses in the gezireh cemetery.

A strange burial of animal bones thrown together was in a pit in the cemetery; I counted 46 ox teeth, and five copper rings of the form in fig. 40. Perhaps these were the nose-rings of the oxen.

CHAPTER IV

THE TEMPLE OF ONIAS

25. THE curious episode of the return of the Jews to Egypt, as a refuge from the tyranny of Antiochos Epiphanes, and their establishment of a new centre of worship there at about 154 B.C., is well known from the accounts preserved by Josephus. The site of this new Temple had so far not been identified,

although it was generally recognised as having been about Tell el Yehudiyeh. The treatment of the statement of Josephus, crediting him with having "mixed together and applied to one settlement circumstances which refer to several Jewish establishments" (NAVILLE, *Mound of the Jew*, p. 20) is not generally conducive to settling questions. In this, and other cases, when we ascertain the facts, it is seen that we do best to stick closely to our authorities. As the passages of Josephus can easily be referred to at length, it will be best here to give a summary of them, and then to discuss the data which they afford.

The earlier account in the *Wars of the Jews* (VII, x, 3, 4) states that the whole region of the Jewish settlements on the east of the Delta was called Oneion, from Onias, see also *Ant.* XIV, viii, 1, where a large district is implied. It is also said that this Onias fled from Antiochos, was well received by Ptolemy (Philometor), and offered to form a corps of Jewish mercenaries, if a new centre of worship for the community were granted to him. Onias appears as the general of Ptolemy, in *contra Apion*, ii, 5. So Ptolemy gave him a place 180 stadia from Memphis, in "the nome of Heliopolis, where Onias built a fortress and a temple, not like to that at Jerusalem, but such as resembled a tower. He built it of large stones to the height of 60 cubits." The altar was correctly made, but a hanging lamp of gold was substituted for the seven-branched candlestick. "The entire temple was encompassed with a wall of burnt brick, though it had gates of stone." Lupus, the Prefect of Egypt, in 71 A.D., closed the temple and took away some of the gifts. Paulinus, his successor, stripped the place, shut up the gates, and made it entirely inaccessible. From the building to the closing of the temple was 343 years. (This is certainly incorrect.) In the *Antiquities of the Jews* (XIII, iii) are given two letters, that from Onias to Ptolemy, and the reply. Whether these are original, altered, or invented, does not much affect the indications which they give about the place, though they are generally considered to have been composed by Josephus. Onias is said to have come to Leontopolis, and to have found a fit place in a fortress that is called from Bubastis of the fields (the goddess Sekhet written with the field sign, N. *M.J.* 23); it was full of materials of several sorts. He asked leave to purify this place, which belonged to no master, and was fallen down, and to build there a temple after the pattern of that in Jerusalem, and of the same dimensions. Ptolemy granted him the

fallen temple at Leontopolis in the nome of Heliopolis, named from Bubastis of the fields. So Onias took it and built a temple and altar, like that at Jerusalem, but smaller and poorer. Such are the essentials of the accounts in Josephus.

26. First let us see how far these indications can be followed. The site was Leontopolis where a form of Bast was worshipped, in the Heliopolite nome, and 180 stadia from Memphis; and a high mass of ruin should remain from a structure 60 cubits high. The distance from Memphis would preclude our looking very much beyond Heliopolis itself, certainly not as far as Belbeys. Moreover Belbeys belonged to the nome of Bubastis (N. *M.J.* 22). There is no centre for the worship of Bast between Belbeys and Memphis, except Yehudiyeh, where the figure of admiral Hor holding the shrine of Bast has now been found. And this would agree with the name Leontopolis, which is otherwise unknown south of the city of Bubastis. On considering what the stadia may more exactly mean, we must look to some Egyptian measure. The nearest to the Greek stadion is the itinerary length of 500 cubits, such as is marked off by a row of way-marks along the Fayum road (*Season in Egypt*, p. 35): this was a third longer than the stadion, but distances stated in it would easily be called stadia in the loose use of itinerary measures which prevailed. From Tell el Yehudiyeh to the north gate of Memphis would be about 186 of these stadia, and so we now see that this site will completely agree with the distance which is stated. Here also there is the greatest mound of any for a day's journey around—a mound which was all thrown up at one time, and which indicates that the buildings on it rose to a height of at least 59 cubits from the plain below, in one great face of walling. The locality therefore agrees to all the indications left to us, and no other place can possibly agree so closely. Moreover the cemetery with Jewish tombstones, found here by Dr. Naville, is proof that a wealthy Jewish community occupied the place; and finding now the name of Abram in the builders' accounts shows that Jews were concerned in building on the great mound.

These essentials being settled, we are at liberty to look at details. The place of Onias was built with stone, and he built a tower-like temple of large stones to a height of 60 cubits. The greatest supply of material for such masonry lay to hand in the immense stone wall of the Hyksos camp, which would supply all the masonry that Onias could require, and which was close to the new settlement, see Pl. II. There was a temple fallen to ruin at Leontopolis, and we know that a temple existed in this camp in the XIIth, XIXth, and XXVIth dynasties. Such temples were only built in nome capitals and important cities, and we do not know of any other between Heliopolis and Belbeys. Though the temple of Onias was built of large stones, like a tower to a height of 60 cubits, yet it is said that the entire temple was encompassed with a wall of burnt brick. This brick probably refers to the northern side and the inner wall round the crest of the temple hill. Burnt brick was unknown for building in Egypt before Roman times; but the northern wall has been burnt in a conflagration, probably in the civil war when the place was besieged, which must have been in Ptolemaic times. Hence may have arisen the statement in the time of Josephus that the wall was of burnt brick. Onias asked to be allowed to build a temple like that in Jerusalem, and of the same dimensions; and he is stated to have actually built it like that at Jerusalem, but smaller and poorer. His attainments may very likely not have come up to his expectations. The temple is said further to have not been like that at Jerusalem because it was like a tower. There is no difficulty about these statements when read in view of the place itself. The plan of the whole hill is strikingly modelled on that of Jerusalem; the temple had inner and outer courts, like that of Zion, but it was smaller and poorer in size; and while the hill of Jerusalem was natural, and the temple was built on the top of the rock, here the artificial hill had to be revetted with a great stone wall, which made the temple like a tower 60 cubits high, as seen in the model, Pl. XXIV. There is not any point of difficulty or discrepancy left in the accounts of Josephus, so soon as we find the true site.

27. OUTER FORTIFICATION. Having shown that no other site can fulfil the conditions, and that this site not only fulfils all the requirements but also reconciles apparent contradictions, we may now enter on the details of the structure. First of all the actual remains of the buildings should be stated. On the north side of the site (see Pl. XXII) there is the lower part of a massive brick retaining-wall along the whole length. It is from 180 to 220 inches thick; and on the inner side it has a slope of 58°, the courses being laid tilted to correspond. This inside slope was covered by the filling in of marl and sand forming the northern edge of the great mound. At the west end this wall ended flat, where the stone face

of the gateways joined it. The other side of the gateway can only be projected from the fragments shown in Pl. XXII, as drawn in Pl. XXIII. It appears that the whole breadth at the gateway was 1780 inches, or 148 feet. The length of the north wall was 716 feet up to the turn of the bastion. The north-east corner (see inset in Pl. XXII) is entirely destroyed by a road, a light railway, and cultivation of fields. But as the north wall turns outward, it must have turned east again before long, as the width between that and the east wall is not very great. This leads us to an end very nearly symmetrical with the southern bastion of the east face, the great stairway being the axis of the face. It is therefore only reasonable to restore this as symmetrical on the eastern front.

On the east side there remains a trench filled with fallen top-rubbish at the northern part of it; near the stairway some stones of a wall remain in place. At the stairway itself is a pier of brick, the south side of which is in line with the face now destroyed, and which was therefore built against the stone wall. South of the stairway there is a long distance with a face of sand filling, where the wall is destroyed. Beyond that is a large piece of the great wall in good condition, see photographs, Pl. XXV, and elevation, Pl. XXVI. The base of the wall is at 106 inches level, the present top 231, and the original sand mound inside probably 300; with about 80 inches of walling this would be 380 level, or 23 feet high along the front, which was 688 feet long between the corner towers. The detail of this wall will be noted further on. Beyond this are two more parts where the stones of lower courses remain in place. Then the direct line turns at right angles, where a mass of marl and sand projects forward. Round this mass is a brick foundation on the north, one stone left on the east, and three or four stones on the south. The southern end wall has been less deep than elsewhere, and recent digging has removed all trace, excepting a shallow trench in the black earth filled with sand, which is fixed on the plan.

The western side can only show a single piece of brickwork. At the south end of it is another trench in the black earth filled with sand, marking the foundation. Then at six places along the west side there can be traced a flat face to the broken mass of marl and sand; one place has a short piece of brickwork against it still; all six places are in the line of a smooth curve, as shown on the plan. This is then the plane of the inner face of the great brick revetment-wall, which upheld the great mound, until stripped away in modern times (see Pl. XXIV, west face). This revetment is 247 ins. thick up to the core, where it exists south of the entrance ; and as the higher wall cannot have been thinner, we must take this as a *minimum* for the west face.

28. FORMATION OF THE MOUND. The mound is based on a shallow bed of earth derived from brick ruins ; the earlier town had evidently spread out here, and had thus left a few feet of earth with potsherds in it. This is highest opposite to the entrance to the Hyksos camp ; it is seen all along the west side, above the present water-level, but it was not found along the north and east sides, perhaps because we did not dig below the foundation. This rise of ground was, however, immaterial in view of the great elevation which was demanded. The position was doubtless chosen as being just outside of the heathen temple site, yet as close as possible to the great stone wall which should supply all the masonry, see Pl. II.

The mound is formed of varied earth, but the pieces of amphorae of the IInd century B.C. found in it are exactly alike at the base and at the top, showing that it was all thrown up at one time. The date of occupation is given by the coins found on the top, which were all small Ptolemaic copper with two eagles apparently of Ptolemy Soter II, beginning 117 B.C. The date of Onias is placed a generation earlier, at 154 B.C. The widely spread beds of earth that run across the area, the sloping stratification of the tip-heaps by which the mass was accumulated, the absence of town rubbish, and the use of clean sand in many parts, all show that the whole elevation was due to intentional construction, and not to accidental accumulation. In this respect it differs from all other mounds of such a size that I have seen in Egypt. It is unique, for an entirely different system was followed by the Egyptians ; they constructed their high fortresses with a great cellular substructure of brickwork, as at Pithom, Daphnae, and Naukratis.

The northern and lower part of the western sides show large masses of brown marl, up to one or two cubic feet in size, loosely tumbled together, with sand to fill up the interstices. Here and there a scraping of town ruin can be seen with pieces of pottery in it, but such sources form but a small fraction of the whole. On the eastern side and south end the material is white limey concretion of sand, in similar lumps with loose sand between. On the top (see West Face, Pl. XXIV) is a deep bed of sand, with enough lime in it to compact the whole, so that it never runs loose, but will stand in vertical faces, when the outer surface falls away by undermining.

In the base of the mound are found cylinders of pottery containing burnt offerings. Such are exposed to view at intervals along the whole of the west side, and were also found at the east end of the north side. One complete cylinder was measured as 23 to 25 inches across inside, and 29 inches high. The forms of the cylinders are shown in the section Pl. XXVII, and the general appearance in the photograph Pl. XXIV. I cleared out some of the cylinders, and always found a bed of white ashes of wood one to three inches thick; bones of lambs lay upon the ashes, usually burnt, sometimes unburnt. Pieces of pottery are sometimes included, and in one case there was the bowl which had been used in the sacrificial feast, shown on the left in Pl. XXVII. The cylinders had no lids, but were filled with the lumps of marl, loosely fallen in when the ground was heaped over, and sometimes burnt red below. In some cases the cylinder had been sunk in the ground before the fire was burnt in it, as the earth touching the outside was reddened by heat for an inch or so in thickness. In other cases the cylinder was left visible, as it was carefully bricked around, and the bricking was mud-plastered by hand quite smoothly so as to cover all the joints; this plastering was picked away by me in order to make the bricks visible, before taking the upper photograph of the cylinder on Pl. XXIV. After removing the bricks the lower photograph was taken. These cylinders were grouped together, and in these views part of the inside of a cylinder may be seen on either side of the perfect one. Mr. Griffith in 1887 saw a double row of the cylinders together, and these had " a base formed of two or three small slabs of limestone or bricks." We must then picture to ourselves the great dedication ceremony of the site. All over the area were groups of these offering pits, some sunk in the ground, others standing up, bricked around. Probably each group belonged to a tribe, and each pit to one family who had " a lamb for an house " (Ex. xii, 3), as in the Passover feast. Assembled from all the Diaspora in Egypt, to the founding of the New Jerusalem, each family lit its fire, probably cooked and ate the sacrificial lamb " roast with fire," and then the bones, " that which remained of it, they burnt with fire." Lastly the fires were smothered by casting in earth ; this was a form of the lamp and bowl burial, usual in Palestine under new buildings, whereby the flame was extinguished as the life of a child had been extinguished in the earlier infant-sacrifice at a foundation.

29. APPROACHES TO THE TEMPLE. There were two approaches leading up to the Temple site. One ran through the area of three or four acres, which was certainly covered with houses (Pls. XXII, XXIII); heaps of potsherds still lie about this ground, though the natives have carried away every fragment of brickwork. The upper part of the approach from the town still remains for about thirty feet length, and 10 feet 8 inches width. On the upper end of it are two blocks of nummulitic limestone, greatly polished by the tread of feet, which have evidently been part of the threshold of the Temple.

The other approach was a great stairway which led up the eastern slope from the plain, see the views Pl. XXV. This stair rested on two brick walls 46 inches thick, between which was a space 79 inches wide filled with sand. Thus, over all, the way was in the middle part 174 at base, and 170 at top; and at the upper end 175 inches wide at the base. It formed a high wall running up the slope of the hill, plastered white on both sides. The highest part of the ruin is 131 inches, shown in the first view Pl. XXV. At this point there is no trace of the mass of brick which must have formed the basis of the steps; hence we must add at least 30 inches for the actual height of the steps, making 160 inches above the hill slope. A parapet must have existed along the sides, at least 40 inches high, and therefore the side wall must have been at least 200 inches, or 17 feet, above the ground.

This great stairway ceased at the stone wall, which ran along the face unbroken. A large pier of brickwork remains on the outside of the wall line, the same width as the side wall of the stair, 46 inches, and 103 inches out from the wall face. This was entirely burnt by a great conflagration, which suggests that there was only a wooden structure to carry the stairway outside of the great wall. This stair is restored as a block without details in the model, Pl. XXIV, as the arrangement of it is uncertain.

The sides of the stairway were plastered three times. After the second coat the ground-level was raised 47 inches by heaping more sand on the mound; this protected the plastering below, as may be seen where it is still preserved white in the first view, Pl. XXV. The new sand bed is quite distinct at the base of the later ruins which overlie it. The stairway has also been repaired, as the upper triangular piece of the brick wall may be seen in Pl. XXV to be different in character from the older wall below.

This stairway was not only the main feature of the eastern side, but it agreed with the direction of the approach to the place across the plain, see inset on Pl. XXII. In the view of the north side of the stair, Pl. XXV, will be seen a long clear line of ground amid the ruins on the plain. This was the old roadway, the houses of the town being all laid out square with it; and as it was clear of obstruction it has continued to be used to this day. It led out to the desert, where a modern village may be seen in the distance; and the Jewish cemetery was excavated at the desert edge, a little to the right of this. This road was, then, the approach to the cemetery, and the way to the eastern desert and Syria. The opposite view is shown at the base of Pl. XXIV, which is taken from this roadway; the road appears smooth between the ruins, leading straight to the great stair, which can be seen on the mound by the trenches which we cleared up each side of it, below the letters D, E.

The slope of the great stair carried upward (at its *minimum* height as stated) produces the result that its top end was at least at 990 inches level, and this gives the *minimum* height of the platform which has now disappeared. The foot of the wall being at 106 level, the platform was 74 feet above the plain.

30. THE TEMPLE. On the top level there are various portions of the basements of the walls yet remaining, as on Pl. XXII, sufficient to show the form of the buildings as restored on Pl. XXIII.

The outer enclosure wall, along the east side of the platform, is very broad in its foundation. The base level varies from 775 inches at inner edge to 744 on outer edge. A small piece of it, which turns diagonally, at the south end is at 784 at inner edge, and 768 further out, but not reaching now to the outer edge; by the levels this was evidently all one with the larger piece. Further to the north this outer enclosure did not reach as far as the great stairway, for the white plaster is continued on that to the upper end without interruption. The wall therefore turned to the west, and we cannot doubt that it turned along the north front of the temple enclosure. To what point this ran after passing the axis is not certain; it may have joined the tower, or may have run separate from that to join the western wall.

The outer court had a thick basement to the walls; but we cannot suppose that the whole wall was continued upwards of this thickness, or it would be disproportionate to the width of the court. Probably the brick basement of 8 feet wide was required to give a firm footing on the artificial sand mound, for a wall about twenty inches thick. If we allow

10 inches footing outside of the wall (as is the case in the temple) the interior of the outer court would be about 32 feet wide at the front and 27 feet at the back. The length of it would be about 44 feet. That this court was the principal feature seen on reaching the top of the mound, is shown by the ascent from the town having the same axis as the court, within a small variation of only 14 inches.

The division between the two courts is shown by a trench in the sand which is filled up with rubbish, apparently where a stone wall has been extracted. This trench is 36 inches wide. The interior of the inner court had a breadth of 27 feet in front and 21 feet at the back, with a length inside of 63 feet. It is probable that these courts were of brickwork stuccoed. A great quantity of pieces of stucco lay about the ruins here; it is hard, white, and smoothly faced, with a black dado and a line of red as a border to the white.

At the end of these open courts we find a mass of brick foundation; this is solid, with the exception of a narrow space of a foot up the axis of it. It measures, at the smallest dimensions above the footing, 201 inches wide and 658 inches long. This is so nearly the proportion of Solomon's Temple, 20 by 70 cubits, that we are justified in supposing that the measures had the same relation. If so, though the amount of the footing of the brick basement outside of the stone wall is now unknown, yet if it were alike all round the difference of the two dimensions must be 50 of the units employed. This difference is 457 inches, yielding a unit of 9·14 inches. Now such a unit is so very closely half a Greek cubit, 9·12 inches, that we are justified in taking the original dimensions of the temple here to have been, in Greek cubits, half of the numbers used for Solomon's temple—that is to say, 10 by 35 cubits. This would be 182 inches by 638 inches; leaving a footing of 10 inches all round the stone walls. Herod in his address to the Jews on his rebuilding of the temple of Jerusalem (*Ant. J.* XV, xi, 1) dwells on the fact that the temple of Zerubabel was much lower than Solomon's, and that its measures were determined by Cyrus and Darius, as an excuse for the Jews not having been able "to follow the original model." This suggests, what is indeed most likely, that Zerubabel at the return of the exiles in poverty, could not succeed in building as large a temple as Solomon. That he should take a span for a cubit, and so keep the same numbers, is very probable. And as we find this copy of the temple of

Zerubabel to have had the scale of it reduced in this manner, we may well accept it as a copy of the dimensions of that at Jerusalem.

The positions of these various structures may be seen in the views on Pl. XXIV. On the East Face at A is the turn of the end of the temple enclosure. From B to C is the block of basement of the Temple itself. From C to D is the position of the courts, and from D to E is the great stairway. In the view of the West Face, from B to C is the tower which we shall describe, and at A is a terrace of earth against which the houses were built. Thus D on the upper view is about the position of C in the lower.

Of the divisions of the temple, into the Porch, Holy Place, and Most Holy Place, there is no trace left, as the whole was founded on one mass of brickwork, which is all that remains. There was however a part of a marble column found, lying near the foot of the town mound on the north, now in the Mocatta Museum, University College, London. It had doubtless been rolled down the hill from the top. Now a marble column would not be in place in the defensive work of the outer enclosure of the temple; nor would so large a column be used for cloisters in the comparatively small courts. The diameters of this column are 19·6 and 20·5 inches at the broken ends, 67 inches apart. This would agree well enough with the size of the two pillars of the porch of the temple, and it is difficult to see any other position where such a marble column would have been in place. The temple as we have seen was 182 inches wide. The side walls may be assumed at about 20 inches thick, leaving 142 for the inner width, about 12 feet. Two columns like the above would occupy 41 inches, and the 100 inches may well have been divided into a middle opening of 40 and two side openings of 35 inches each. As the height of the temple was equal to its width, it was 182 outside height; or let us say 162 inside, and so about 145 under the architrave, for the whole column and capital. Thus the column would be 7 diameters in height.

The breadth of the whole platform on the top was at least as wide as is shown in the plan Pl. XXIII, and the model Pl. XXIV, as this much is proved by the existing top of the mound. In every case we have only adopted the *minimum* dimensions that are shown, where any doubt exists—the least height of stairway, the lowest level of platform, the least breadth of platform, the least height of the eastern front wall.

31. THE CASTLE. At the head of the stairways are seen several foundations, still showing as trenches

or steps in the sand core of the hill, see Pl. XXII. These indicate that there was a square building here, of about 52 × 73 feet, see Pl. XXIII. Such a position was perfectly adapted for the citadel of the whole place; it rises sheer up over the ascent from the town; it rakes down the whole length of the great stairway; it rakes the whole of the western wall; it commands the entrance to the temple, which is just below it; and it also commands the temple courts and the space outside of them. It gives the entire mastery of the place. The position is seen on the view of the west face, Pl. XXIV, between B and C. At B is a steep face about 12 feet high which was evidently upheld by some wall now removed; this would be the north wall of the castle. The ground below was made up in a broad terrace to give a firm foundation, and then it fell again at A to the general level of the town. The position of the castle, placed diagonally to the outer wall, is a very strong one, as the faces cannot be weakened by direct attack.

The total height of the whole place may be reckoned thus. The platform was at least 992 level, or 886 inches over the plain on the east, and 845 over the ground on the west. Taking 845 as the *minimum*, we must add the temple height which was 182, so that its top was at least 1027 inches, and the top of the protecting fortification would be at least 1040 inches, and therefore very probably 1060 or 1080 inches (90 feet) over the west ground. The statement of Josephus that the building was 60 cubits high, gives 1094 inches, and this accords with the original form of the buildings as closely as we can trace them.

The detail of the restoration of the western wall is curiously involved in the curve of the base of it, and the slopes of the core ground which it must have followed. When these are taken together no other result seems possible beside that here followed in the plan and model. It is hardly needful to enter on all the minute reasons for this at length, as in any case a variation would not be important. But this much should be stated to show that there is a *minimum* of uncertainty, or mere imagination, in this restoration. The only piece of guesswork is the detail of the wall across the entrance; the place of it is known, but the gateways are only what may be presumed on, as likely for such a situation. Doubtless there were many details of the finishing off of the parapets, gangways, and entrances. But as we have no evidences about these, no attempt is here made to restore them in the model.

32. We may now notice the stone-work and fragments of decoration that remain. The external wall-surfaces are shown by the fine piece of the great eastern wall which we dug out. The elevation of it is given in Pl. XXVI, and in Pl. XXV is a view looking down into the excavation, and another view of part of it at close quarters. The courses at the two ends of the wall are as follows:

Top .	. 21·6 to 21·0	inches.
„ .	. 21·3 „ 21·5	„
„ .	. 20·8 „ 20·7	„
„ .	. 20·8 „ 20·7	„
Base .	. 21·8 „ 21·0	„

Thus they average 21·1 inches, and the variations of the stones from that size have been sorted into each course, so as to get them to rank more evenly together. The lengths are not uniform, varying thus:— 38, 43, 46, 47, 48, 49, 49, 50, 50, 50, 51, and 53 inches, The breadths are 21, 21, 21, 21, 23, 24, 24, 24, 24, 25, 25, 25, 27, 29, 37, the latter three being in the lowest course, which is a less regular foundation. It seems then that the standard size for the blocks was 50 × 25 inches and 21 inches thick. The surface is the original quarry face with pick-marks on it; but round the edge is a draft about 4 inches wide, slightly sloping down to the joint line. The drafting is seen to be cut with a claw tool where the marks are visible (shown in the elevation, Pl. XXVI), such as is very plainly seen in the dressing of the piece of cornice photographed above the view of the wall. The quality of the stone is not so good as that of the Hyksos wall, or the chips of the upper structures; it is full yellow, and inclined to powder away if exposed. At the base the lowest course rests in part on the desert *gezireh* surface, which is supplemented by lower blocks in some places.

The finish of this wall above was with a cornice of white limestone. A piece of this was found in digging to trace the north-east corner. The profile of the fragment is on Pl. XXVII, scale 2 : 3, and the photograph of it on Pl. XXV. The use of it was evidently for eaves to shoot off rain, clear of the wall face, as is shown by the under-cut slope and drip edge below. Now such a feature is quite needless at Tell el Yehudiyeh, and would never be invented there; it is copied from some original in the rainy climate of Palestine. Moreover the drafting of the masonry of the wall is not known in Egypt, or only rarely as an exotic copy; whereas it is the regular dressing of the masonry of the temple revetment-wall at

Jerusalem. These points are good evidence as to the origination of the design of this place.

Another piece of moulding was found, at the west side of the block of brickwork which formed the basement of the Temple; it is shown also on Pl. XXVII. It is imperfect above and below, and clumsy in form; but it is doubtless a part of the top cornice of the sanctuary itself.

Other fragments of limestone were found by turning over the heaps of chips and earth, to the north of the tower and the ascent from the town. Here the columns and blocks had been rolled down to be trimmed into shape, and some fragments were left, shown on Pl. XXV. The important piece in the middle is carefully restored, from a series of sectional measurements, on Pl. XXVI. It was a semicircular battlement, like those on the top of the tower at Medinet Habu, which was copied from a Syrian original. On the face of the battlements was a band of at least five ribs, which seems to have run along the top of the wall, rising up into each battlement, and then descending again. Probably the space in the middle of the square pattern was occupied with some ornamental boss. The rosette is suggested here on the strength of six-lobed rosettes as centre bosses in Palestinian decoration.

The fragments of capitals show that the architecture of the temple was Corinthian. They could not belong to the marble column as they are of limestone, and so they prove that there were other ornamental columns here, besides those which we have considered above to belong to the temple porch.

33. The history of the site was not peaceful. On all sides, and especially about the great stairway, there are limestone balls thrown by the *balista* in a siege. They are usually about three inches across, but some are of double that size. The siege to which these belong was very possibly during the war between Cleopatra II and Ptolemy Physkon in 146 B.C., when we read that Onias acted as the general of Cleopatra (*c. Apion*, ii, 5), and therefore the opposite party would have special reason to attack the town of Onias. That the same man should be high priest and general was familiar to the Egyptians, as we see in the XXIst dynasty, and the Asmonean rulers were also high priests (*Ant.* XV, xi, 4).

At the same siege, or more probably later, the place was burnt on the east side. A great quantity of burnt brick has been recently thrown out in heaps along the east wall. This seems to have been the remains of brick and timber houses built inside the

wall; and when the stone wall was quarried away in recent times, this mass of ruin had to be removed, and was thrown further down the slope. The brick pier built outside the wall to carry the stairway is also thoroughly burnt, showing that probably a wooden stair led down from the wall to the plain. On the north side the thick wall is burnt through in the middle part; and so low down that the conflagration must have been due to wooden houses built against the outside of it, rather than to any burning on the platform of earth inside.

Of the final destruction of the buildings the traces have nearly all been removed by the modern denudation. There is however a small patch still left on the east face, showing the layer of chips of white limestone which were thrown down in cutting the masonry to pieces; next above these followed the pieces of bricks from the destruction of the walls and platform; and over all are some feet of sand from the overthrow of the upper layers of the sand platform. This patch of ruin serves to prove that we have the original face of the sand hill preserved here, and hence we can identify several other parts of the face amid the modern cuttings. These pieces of the hill-face were all carefully surveyed, and form the data for the contours shown along the south-eastern part of the hill. On the northern side, and the north-eastern part, the soil has been greatly cut away; the present contours of this part are given on Pl. XXII, and the presumable ancient contours on Pl. XXIII.

34. Only a few objects were found on the top of the hill, besides the architectural features; a clay jar seal with a monogram stamp (Pl. XXVII), perhaps reading *pin* or *pen*; an earring of glass beads on bronze wire (Pl. XXVII); a ram's horn (cut off the skull), which lay at the side of the Temple platform, probably from a sacrifice. With this should be noted the great mass of burnt bones of calf and lamb, which were found and removed many years ago from the north of the town, as recorded by Mr. Griffith (*M. J.* 53). The only piece of inscription found here was an ostrakon, which lay with other pieces of similar brown amphorae, as part of the foundation of the courts. This is shown in Pls. XXIV and XXVII. Mr. Griffith agrees that it may be as late as Ptolemy Philometor, though he would have been inclined to date it rather earlier. The last line, and the third above it, read Harkhêb son of Zeho; and the last line but one reads Abrm, followed by the foreign determinative. After the names follows the word

"bricks," but the numbers of bricks are lost. Thus we learn that both Egyptians and Jews were employed in the supplying of bricks for this temple. The coins found on the top of the mound were all of the later Ptolemies after Philometor.

In the cemetery on the edge of the desert a few tombs were opened by us, and in these were found the handled bowl and jugs on Pl. XXVII, also the bronze lock-plate and ornaments from a box. The plan of one of the most typical tombs is shown as the last on Pl. XII. There is no doubt that this was the Jewish cemetery; but the form of the tombs belongs to the age, and not only to the people. The rock-tombs of Alexandria are very similar, and the Ptolemaic tombs of Denderah are alike in the entrance and the chamber, though one broad loculus there occupies the back of the chamber.

Outside of the town there are also other remains of this age to the east of the mound, see inset Pl. XXII. The banks around the Egyptian cemetery contain potsherds between the IInd century B.C. and the Ist century A.D.; and the broad bank to the north-east by the Arab cemetery is dated by pottery of the IInd century B.C. It seems then that much enclosure here was done during this Jewish occupation. This may have been in order to preclude settlements of houses upon the ground defiled by the graves. The town through which the road runs, as seen in the view Pl. XXV, is strictly limited by the bank to the south of the cemetery.

35. We may now summarise the conclusions about the site of the Temple of Onias. The indications about its position,—Leontopolis, the distance from Memphis, in the Heliopolite nome, the existence of a temple and a great mass of building material, and the Jewish names in the cemetery,—all these agree with what we find at Tell el Yehudiyeh, and cannot be all assigned to any other site. The statements about the height of the place, and the copying of the temple of Jerusalem on a poorer scale, exactly agree with the great mound and its buildings, and this place reconciles the apparent contradictions of Josephus. The nature of the site agrees with the requirements of the structure of Onias, and with no other purpose. An immense mound was constructed all at once, with a great number of sacrifices at its foundation, pointing to a concourse of a people. This mound was strongly fortified, but differs from any Egyptian fortification in its nature. It comprised

a town, and an isolated building higher than the rest, and even more strongly protected, the precious part of the whole place. This building had just the proportions of Solomon's temple, and had an inner and outer court before it. The bricks were partly supplied by Jews. And outside of the town on the north was thrown a great quantity of burnt bones of the sacrificial animals, as from the burnt sacrifices. The external connections, or the structural evidence, would either of them be sufficient to make the purpose of this place almost certain. Together, they seem to leave no possibility of question that we have here the New Jerusalem and Temple of the rightful High Priest Onias.

We may now draw attention to another matter, which might seem fanciful, were we not certain of the nature of the place. This New Jerusalem copied the form as well as the character of the Holy City. On the west side of Mt. Moriah was the deep ravine of the Tyropoion valley, on the other side of which lay the town. So here the steep revetment 90 feet high on the west stood over against the wall of the town 50 feet high, with in one part a space of only a few yards between them. On the east a natural slope led down to the Kedron valley; and here the sloping side of the mound descended eastward to the plain. From the Kedron there led up to the north end of the Temple area the great ceremonial stairway whose lower rock-cut steps I found in 1891; this ran up on a high ridge of wall to the great platform. So here there is the great high stairway on the east side leading to the north entrance of the temple courts. On the north of the Temple lay the quarter of Bezetha, which was the main new region of Jerusalem in the later history. So here the new town lay on the north of the temple. At Jerusalem the great citadel was the castle of Antonia, which was built long before Antony, at least as early as the Asmonean family (*Ant.* XV, xi, 4). This castle commanded a view of the Temple courts and sacrifices, which was a great grievance to the zealots (*Ant.* XX, viii, 11). So here the castle on the north of the temple not only commanded the approaches and the outer walls, but looked along the temple courts up to the temple itself. These close resemblances cannot be only accidental; the place was intended to be a model of Jerusalem, and a substitute so far as possible for that ideal city of the race.

CHAPTER V

TELL ER RETABEH (RAAMSES)

36. IN the middle of the length of the Wady Tumilat, about twenty miles from Ismailiyeh on the east, and rather farther from Zagazig on the west, stands a wide dusty mound of ruins knows as Tell er Retabeh. As in other ancient sites, so here, the natives remove large quantities of earth to lay upon the fields. But instead of this destructive custom exposing the earlier remains, as is the case on other sites, it makes the lower levels here even more inaccessible. Any pit in this region is quickly filled up with sand from the desert, and the holes made in one year are levelled up again in the next. At first sight the mound looks untouched; but a large part of it is now a honeycomb of old pits filled with sand. This makes work here unprofitable, as it is needful to dig through so much depth of running sand in which nothing can be found. The soil itself also is poor in objects in the untouched parts. The mound is not an accumulation of house ruins, as such mounds usually are; but large parts of it only contain a few enclosing walls, and the area seems to have been largely left open, and then gradually filled up with ashes and blown dust. This filling indicates that the place was rather a fortified camping ground, for the shelter of troops, than an ordinary town.

Twenty years ago Dr. Naville had made some excavations here, and found scarabs of the XVIIIth and XIXth dynasties, and a bronze falchion of that age. But his conclusion was as follows: "The whole place indicates a camp, probably of late Roman times. It must have been one of the military stations posted along the canal leading to the Red Sea, and it may have been another of the garrisons mentioned in the *Notitia Dignitatum*" (*Goshen*, 25); and here the subject had rested, without any further endeavour to settle the history of the site.

The work of the past winter has shown that, so far from being a Roman camp, this is the oldest site known east of Bubastis, and that it has not had any Roman occupation. The stone vases of the Old Kingdom, and the weight and scarabs of the IXth to the XIIth dynasties prove the early date of occupation. The human sacrifice under the oldest wall points to its being held by Syrians rather than Egyptians. The depth of about twelve to fifteen feet of ruins beneath the buildings of the XVIIIth and XIXth dynasties is solid evidence of the early importance of the town. Of

later age we found here a temple of Ramessu II with sculptures in red granite and limestone; part of a tomb of an official who was over the store-houses of Syrian produce; and the great works of Ramessu III. All of these discoveries exactly accord with the requirements of the city of Raamses, where both the second and third kings of that name are stated to have worked, and where a store-city was built by the Israelites along with that of Pithom, which is only eight miles distant. The absence of any other Egyptian site suitable to these conditions, which are all fulfilled here, makes it practically certain that this was the city of Raamses named in Exodus. Of later times the cemetery of the XXIIIrd dynasty has yielded us many interesting small objects.

37. The site should be first described, and after that the objects will be noticed in historical order. On the plan, Pl. XXXV, it will be seen that there are walls of three ages. I could not succeed in completing this plan on the north-west, as deep sand drifts covered the low ruins of the walls. Along the north I could only find one wall, and that so much consolidated by rains that the sizes of the bricks could not be seen. On the east the course of the second wall was clear, and traces of the third upon it. The south side was far better preserved than the others, but here we were working the whole time that I was at the place, in order to trace out what is shown. At the south-west corner the outside and its deposits are entirely lost; and the only deposit which I could recover was at the south-east, and for that a man worked for a week before he could find it. All of the lower walls are of such earthy marl, and so much soaked with wet, that it is difficult to tell them from the earth around. The previous plan of the town (*Goshen*, Pl. XI) is largely drawn by guess work; and the very thick wall at the west of it is really the thickness of the gateway bastions, one of which was cut through instead of tracing the face of it.

The first fortifying of the place was by an irregular wall, marked here wall 1, which lies inside the later town and askew to it. Its thickness in two places was 123 and 124 inches. No further continuation of this to the east could be found, although we made large clearances. The long straight line has a bastion near the west end projecting 48 to 53 inches; of this 33 inches width is of the grey bricks of the wall, and 68 inches more has been added on the east in black bricks. The wall bends just beyond this, runs west for 160 feet, and then bends again, at another bastion which has been patched like the first. This bastion projects 46 to 50 inches ; the older part is 70 wide, and the patch of yellow bricks is 36 wide. Beyond this corner the wall takes a slight bend, and continues till it reaches past the later gateway. Then it ends at what was doubtless the earlier gateway, almost exactly in line with the entrance to the temenos of the temple.

38. Beneath the last-named bastion corner we mined inward in search of a foundation deposit. No deposit was· found such as is usual in Egyptian buildings. But constructions appeared which were entirely new to us in their character. First a stack of bricks, of which the plan and section are given in Pl. XXXV A ; five below, then four, then three, and two on the top. Nothing was found beneath these, and they seem to form the mark which was used in setting out the walls. But just east of these, and parallel to the wall, was a small arched brick tomb of a child, buried at full length, head to the east. As the grave is only 30 inches long, and the body did not fill the length, it must have been quite an infant. The bones were very slight, and so friable in the earth that I could not preserve them. There were no objects with the body. This grave is clearly ceremonial, and not only a stray interment. It is placed by the side of the corner mark so closely that it must have been built at the same time. A pit had been sunk in the bed of clean gravel which underlies the wall, and after the two structures were built the pit was filled with rather dirty gravel. Over the whole lay the final five inches of sand on which the bricks rest. This burial, or child sacrifice, was a custom in Syria, known both by record and by recent discoveries of Mr. Macalister ; the custom was succeeded by that of the burial of a burning lamp, the flame of which was extinguished instead of extinguishing the life. But such a custom has never been found among the Egyptians, and hence we must rather look to a Syrian occupation as the cause of this earliest fortification. To judge by the early age of remains here we might look to Syrian invaders after the VIth dynasty as likely builders ; and as this is a brick fort, and not an earthwork, it is more likely to belong to such people than to the barbaric Hyksos.

39. The town ruins and ashes accumulated to a depth of as much as about fifteen feet by the time of the XVIIIth dynasty. Of that age must be a large house which we entirely cleared out on the highest point of the mound. It contained scarabs of the XVIIIth dynasty (see Pl. XXXIII, no. 11), and

pottery down to about the XXIInd dynasty, and the occupation probably lasted from about 1400–800 B.C. The plan of this house is given on Pl. XXXV A. The entrance was in the middle of the north side ; the passage rose up steps now destroyed, then turned to the west up the broad brick wall, and so reached the upper floor of dwelling rooms. The lower rooms here remaining had probably been the cellars, to judge by their differences of level. At the south side is a curved retaining wall which banked up the earth on which the house was built. The views of this south wall from each end are given on Pl. XXXII A. The most important things found here were the small and large jars containing silver, see Pl. XXXVI mid right side, and a jar at base of Pl. XXXV C. Unhappily for us the silver had been entirely smelted, and not a single fragment had any work upon it ; so no one was the better except the workman, who received the metal value. The silver had been in two cloth parcels sealed with the seals shown in Pl. XXXIII, 9, 10. The various small objects from here are marked 10 in the plates, and one group found together is marked 23.

40. The next period is that of the building of the temple by Ramessu II. From the beginning of our work we endeavoured to find the temple site ; and as it was to be presumed that Ramessu had built on an older sacred site, I naturally began on the lowest ground, along the east end, as temple sites are generally lower than town ruins. Extensive clearances here led to no temenos ; but we were rewarded by finding half of the front of the temple, which had been dragged away to use for building-stone, but never broken up. This is shown in Pls. XXIX, XXX, representing Ramessu II smiting a Syrian before the god Atmu. We also found many blocks which had formed the whole top course of the front, and from these we can see that the opposite side had a similar scene with the god Set instead of Atmu, see top of Pl. XXXI. Some other blocks were also found in the stone lining of a later well a little north of this. All of these sculptures are described in detail in Section 43.

After abandoning this end of the place I worked more at the north-west region, where the natives repeatedly said that there were large stones. We tried for weeks in every place that was pointed out to us, and I offered ten shillings for every block of granite that a native could show us, but in vain. I was much attracted by a massive brick wall with a great gateway in it, and a large jamb of brick down the north side of the entrance. On trying to trace a continuous temenos wall from this, we were disappointed to find that whenever a wall was tracked downwards it came to an end very soon; no walls here would go down to bottom levels. At last the finding of granite blocks near the surface proved that Ramessu had built his temple on fifteen feet of town rubbish, and so no temple need be expected lower. The nature of the site could then be grasped and understood. The front wall north of the entrance is in fine condition. It is 40 ft. 7 in. long to the inner corner; on the outer side it has been anciently broken. The counter wall south of the entrance is 62 ft. 9 in. along the inside; it has no jamb at the entrance, and is built of black bricks, all in one piece with the side wall to the south, and with the wall parallel behind the front. Both sides of the front have a parallel wall 14 ft. 2 in. behind them. Inside this wall on the northern side is a large building, filling that side of the temenos. Further in the temenos lay fragments of a limestone doorway, and beyond these the lower part of a great stele of red granite, see Pls. XXVIII, XXXII; and parts of a red granite dyad of Ramessu II and Atmu standing, the upper half roughened, see Pl. XXXII, the lower part almost destroyed. This group is apparently that seen by the pilgrim in 380 A.D., which was of stone like the Theban statues; she was told that it represented Moses and Aaron. Two other defaced blocks of red granite lay to the south of these nearer to the wall. The base of a limestone column found at the well was 30 across on the top, 34 below. We shall refer again to the details when noticing the plates. Behind the granite monuments is a wall of yellow brick, like that along most of the south side of this temenos, and this appears to have been the back of the temenos, which was thus about 100 feet long and 115 feet wide inside. It will be seen that it stood almost axially on the line from the town gate of the first wall. A later wall has been built straight through the gateway of the temenos.

41. The next step in the history is the outer fortification built by Ramessu III. It may seem strange that this was not built by his greater predecessor. But probably Egypt was safe from the risk of invasion then; while later the Syrian league against Egypt, rendered it prudent to fortify the frontier towns. This second wall ran far outside of the first wall at the south-east; it just touched the outside of the first wall at the south, and then ran further out at the south-west, and turned up to a

gateway between massive brick bastions. Probably the north wall is also part of this fortifying. Under the south-east corner lay the foundation deposit, in a group about 14 inches across; the centre of it was 28 inches to the east outside, and 42 inches to the south. The pans and cups were irregularly laid in the sand (Pl. XXXV C), bones of a sacrifice lay between them, and the glazed offerings of oxen, heads and haunches, ducks, cartouche plaques, scarabs, and beads, had been roughly cast in over all. For these see Pls. XXXII A, XXXIV.

The last stage that we can trace is that this wall of the XXth dynasty was greatly denuded, down to within a few feet of its base, and the west gate had almost vanished, when a third wall was built nearly on the same lines; this was slightly inside the older wall at the south, upon the line and the gateway at the west, and there overlapped the old first wall. The gateway axis was blocked across, and it led only to a narrow passage along the face of the first wall. This passage was 50 inches wide, and then was narrowed by a block to 22 inches wide. Thus there was a narrow entrance for persons in single file. But on the south side a stone gateway had been built, of which the foundation hollows are visible as here marked, and the chips lie thickly around the place.

42. The thicknesses of the walls, where best preserved, are:

1st wall	.	.	123, 124 inches.
2nd wall	.	.	374 inches.
3rd wall	.	.	347, 351, 352 inches.

The third wall is rather open in the building, with spaces between the bricks in some parts; but they are regular and even, not tilted as has been represented.

The sizes of the bricks average:

1st wall	.	.	14·8 × 7·2 × 3·3.
XVIIIth dynasty house	.	15·4 × 7·5 × 3·4.
2nd wall	.	.	18·4 × 8·1 × 4·0.
Low in W. gate	.	.	18·1 × 8·7.
Jamb, wall of temenos		17·4 × 8·1 × 3·7.
3rd wall	.	.	17·1 × 8·5 × 5·3.
High in W. gate	.	17·1 × 8·3 × 5·5.
S.W. wall, temenos	.	14·0 × 6·5.

43. PL. XXVIII. Having now described the site in historical order, the plates will here be followed in noticing the objects, so as to be more convenient for reference. At the top is the inscription from a granite column base of the portico of Ramessu III at Tell el Yehudiyeh.

Below is the lower end of a large granite stele, which will be described under Pl. XXXII.

PLS. XXIX, XXX. The large scene is of Ramessu II smiting a Syrian before Atmu, the god of this eastern side of the Delta. The god holds a falchion, which he is presenting to the king. This scene was on the spectator's left hand of the doorway of the temple; and on the right hand was a similar scene of the king, before the god Set, of which some of the top row of blocks were also found, shown at the top of Pl. XXXI. Along with these are carved the upper parts of two pairs of large feathers. These feathers certainly surmounted cartouches, and these were over the doorway. From these remains we can tolerably restore the front of the temple. It was not free-standing, for the brick wall of the fore-court joined the ends of the front. Between these fore-walls the front measured 166 inches (nearly 14 feet), and stood about 112 inches high to the foot of the cornice, or probably about 12 feet over all. The scenes at the side had a plain wall dado about 56 inches high below them, as is usually the case on temple fronts. The doorway was only 22 inches wide, or possibly a little less.

This façade of the temple was brilliantly painted in red, blue, yellow, and perhaps other colours; much of this colouring is still well preserved in parts. Atmu was in a blue dress, and blue kilt with yellow border, and yellow shoulder-straps and belt. His armlet and tail were also yellow, his collar white and yellow, and the *ankh* was blue. The king's dress was less distinguishable, but his collar and beard were of yellow. The captive wore a striped tunic of red and blue, with red belt and ends, and a blue kilt. All the bodies were painted in red as usual; many of the hieroglyphics were in red also, the *Maat* figures and square of throne, the *mer*, *du*, and *nekht*. The ground of the scene was in yellow.

On the scene we read "Lord of both banks, User·maat·ra, approved of Ra, the strong bull loved by Maat, all protection and life behind him," and "Atmu lord of Succoth gives him all valour and all strength." The work is better than on most of the sculptures of this king, and is equal to the usual style of his father Sety.

Pl. XXXI. The top of this is from the temple front already described. Below this is a fine head of Ramessu III, showing that he also wrought sculptures here as well as building the city wall. To the left are two pieces, which must be from the pylon gateway, being on so much larger a scale than the temple front.

They bear part of the titles of Atmu "lord of Succoth" and of the king "Ramessu, living eternally." Next is a column of inscription, "Adorations to thy *ka* the . . ." Then comes a piece of a doorjamb from a tomb, which was re-used for stone in the town. It reads, "Chief archer, keeper of the granaries, keeper of the palace, USER·MAAT·RA·NEKHTU·NE·THUKU; Chief archer, keeper of the granaries of Ta·nuter, USER·MAAT·RA·NEKHTU·NE·THUKU." Ta·nuter here probably refers to Syria, as in some other cases, and not to its principal meaning of Arabia. That there were granaries here for storing the Syrian produce, is important, as showing that this was a store-city of Ramessu II. The name of the official is in honour of the king "mighty in Succoth." The Semitic word *succoth*, booths, was rendered by the Egyptians as *thuku*; and as it was not a native word, it was blundered as *thu* on the scene, Pl. XXIX, and here as *thk*. Lastly, on the right is the *ka* name from the temple front, as on Pl. XXIX.

Plate XXXII. The dyad of red granite certainly represents Ramessu II and Atmu, to be worshipped as the joint gods of the city Raamses. Below it is the red granite stele, on which we read, . . . *ur shefitu, aa nerau, em tau . . . her kheset uayu suten baty User·maat·ra·sotep·ne·ra Si Ra Mery·Amen·Ramessu du ankh kheryt aat em ta ne Shasu, haq f nay sen thesut, sma her sen, qed em demau her ran f er zet ta*— "mighty in powers, great in terrors in lands . . . on distant deserts, the king User·maat·Ra, approved of Ra, son of Ra, loved by Amen, Ramessu, giving life; (of the) great enemies in the land of the Bedawyn he plundered their hill fortresses, slaughtering their faces, and building in cities upon which his name is to eternity." This allusion to building in the various cities called after Ramessu suggests that this city was one of such—that is, Raamses.

44. At the right are selected amulets from various tombs, the drawings of the same objects being given in their groups in the following plates. The Ptah-sokar with feathers on the head is unusual in amulets (20 in XXXIV A); Bast with feathers is also rare (18 in XXXIV A). The earrings are of silver, as also is the aegis in the centre. The four scarabs and two rings are from one tomb, the whole group of which is on Pl. XXXIII, 22.

Below is a good set of later amulets, grave 318; and a necklace of *uza* eyes, grave 117. At the base is an unique blue glazed bowl, also shown in drawings, Pl. XXXIV B. Round the brim are nineteen frogs, others are jumping up the sides, and a crowd going toward the mouth, while a large frog sits on a pedestal in the middle. The spout is in the form of a lion's head, and a passage leads from the bottom of the bowl through the thickness of it. The frog is the sign for multitudes, it is said by Horapollo to be the emblem of the human embryo, and it is the animal of the goddess Heqt who gives life to the infant (*Deir el Bahri*, ii, XLVIII); hence this bowl may well have been for giving magic drink to ensure fertility. The plan of the tomb where it was found is on Pl. XXXV A.

PL. XXXII A. This shows objects described elsewhere, the weight of Khety in noticing Pl. XXXIII and the foundation deposit in Pl. XXXIV, and the large house in Section 39.

PL. XXXIII. The greater part of the scarabs were found loose in the town rubbish, there being but few in the late cemetery which we excavated. 1 is probably of Mentu·hotep II. 2 is of Amen-emhat I, and is another example of the writing of the name in its true order, Sehotep ab ra, as is known on two other scarabs of this age. 2 A is a rare instance of two circuits of scroll pattern; the central sign is not known as a hieroglyph. 3 reads *Ptah·uas·nefer ankh·du*—"May Ptah give strength and good life." 3, 5, 5A are all of the Hyksos age. 4 is the splendid weight of King Khety of the IXth dynasty, made of polished red jasper: it gives the name as Khety·neb·kau. The weight has probably lost about a twentieth by chipping; allowing for this it was about 1850 grains, and dividing by the numeral 9 on the end, the unit was 205 grains, the well-known gold standard usual in these early square weights. 6, 7, 8 are probably contemporary with Tahut-mes III. 9, 10 are clay seals, from the parcels of melted silver found in the great house (Section 39). 11 is of Amenhotep III. 12 with Anhur, 13 with Ra, 14 with the sphinx, 15 with the crio-sphinx, 16 with Set, and 17 with Mentu, are probably all of Ramessu II. Of the others we may note the degradation of the lotus-flower in 26, 27, copied from 25. 28 to 37 are all of the XXth to the XXIIIrd dynasties.

The large group of tomb 22 contained five scarabs, 38-42; 40 is of a rich Prussian-blue glass, like the large beads 62, of which there is a long graded necklace. From the style of the pierced rings, 60, 61, this group belongs to the XXIInd or XXIIIrd dynasty. At the base of the plate are scarabs bought at Zagazig; 66 is a diorite plaque of Ramessu VI.

PL. XXXIV. The groups of amulets found in the tombs are placed here in approximately their historical order. All of the tombs in the cemetery, a quarter of a mile north of the town, had been plundered anciently, and the remaining objects were found scattered. The tombs were in groups of brick chambers, much like those at Nebesheh (*Tanis*, ii, XVI); the more complete and interesting of these are given on Pl. XXXV A. In the more perfect part of the cemetery the walls are still three to four feet high, further west there is but a foot or a few inches depth left, and west of these there is only bare marl earth, and probably the tombs in it had been entirely denuded away. We worked so far as the sand drift allowed, but there are doubtless other burials now covered by the sand heaps.

The tombs 19 and 8 may probably be of the XIXth or XXth dynasty, see the pottery on Pl. XXXV C; in 19 the beads are of garnet and carnelian, in 8 they are of green glaze and carnelian; but the iron bracelet is remarkable at so early a date. The foundation deposit of Ramessu III was found beneath the corner of his wall, as described in Section 41. The group of tomb 5 has a scarab of the late Ramesside type, but touches the XXIInd dynasty by the plaque of Bast. The beads of ala-baster and notched glaze in tomb 1 are characteristic of the XXIInd and XXIIIrd dynasties.

PL. XXXIV A. Tomb 20 contained some of the best objects, the figures of Ptah-sokar and Bast, the silver aegis and earrings, and the glass spot beads. Tomb 14 had a serpentine palette, probably taken from a XIIth dynasty tomb; the double-cone beads of glass belong to the XXIInd dynasty, as seen in tomb 22, Pl. XXXIII. In tomb 27 the silver earring and *uza* eye are of this age. In tomb 24 is a piece of bronze rasp, and a peculiar red pot (last); the globular bottle is of the same Cypriote class as the pilgrim bottles. The little plaques of the *uza* eye in tomb 18, with the names of Tahuti, Nebhat?, and Uazet, are like those from Zuweleyn near Tanis (*Tanis*, i, XII, 18-22). The open-work basket, tomb 15, was a special attribute of Bast. She carries it on her arm, and there is sometimes a figure of a cat in it. This may be the form of basket in which the sacred cats were carried about in the temple of Bubastis. In the last group, B, it is curious to find the name Hotep·hers on a scarab, as it is not otherwise known beyond the IVth and Vth dynasties.

PL. XXXIV B. We here reach the age of the quadruple eyes, as on Pls. XIX B, C, of Yehudiyeh.

Among the separate objects at the lower part, there is the inscription of an ushabti with an unusual formula, " Says the Osirian the third prophet of Bast, keeper of the estates of Sekhet, Hor, *maa kheru.*" This was the only ushabti found at Retabeh, and it was in the great house, and not in the cemetery. It is remarkable that no ushabtis were found in the cemeteries of Yehudiyeh or Retabeh, nor in even one in a hundred of the Saft graves. The frog bowl has been described under Pl. XXXII, Section 44.

PL. XXXIV C. The figures of gods and amulets that were found separately are drawn here; most of these are from the town. At the right of the top are two groups of Shu and Tefnut, with "good life" on the back. In the second line is a figure of the goddess Hatmehyt of Mendes, with the fish on her head. The large piece in the middle is a figure of Bes, showing the lion's-skin wrapped round him.

PLS. XXXV, XXXV A have already been dealt with in Sections 36 to 41.

45. PL. XXXV B. The bronze here is of various ages. The knives are probably of the XVIIIth dynasty; the rasps are probably about the XXIInd dynasty; and the bracelets at the bottom are later. The glass spot beads are about the XXIIIrd dynasty. The ivory pin may be later; it is not a hair-pin (such as is common in Roman times), but was used for some textile work, in which it became deeply cut diagonally by the thread. The bent pieces of lead are net-sinkers.

PL. XXXV C. This pottery was found with groups in tombs, and is therefore approximately dated. Tomb 6 contained the scarab 25 (Pl. XXXIII). The forms in tomb 8 show that the types of the XVIIIth dynasty still survived, along with an iron bracelet, Pl. XXXIV. Tomb 13 is of the same age. The foundation deposits of Ramessu III were found with the glazed figures on Pl. XXXIV, see Section 41. The pan in tomb 4 was with the group in Pl. XXXIV and the foreign flask XXXVI, 17. The group of tomb 1 included the beads and scarabs on Pl. XXXIV. At the base is the pottery of the XVIIIth dynasty onward, found in the great house, 10. The last flask is of Cypriote form.

PL. XXXVI. Many examples of foreign pottery were found at Retabeh, mostly in the town. 1 is the lower part of a leather-bottle form of black ware with white lines, of the early XVIIIth dynasty. 2 is part of the edge of a dish of light red with dark red pattern, recalling the style of the XVIIIth dynasty cist at Yehudiyeh, Pls. XIV A, XV. 3 is a triple

bottle with two necks, with the same decoration; the fragments were found in a tomb. The piece of buff Cypriote bowl, 6, was found in the N.N.E. of the town on the washed-down earth of the walls, before the town rubbish had accumulated. This shows that before this pottery came in there was a long period of desertion of the site; this was probably during the Hyksos age, when no frontier was needed. The triple handle in 7 belongs to the XIXth dynasty age, see *Illahun*, XVIII, 51; XIX, 11. The globular pilgrim-bottles, as 4, 12, 13, 15, are a later type, probably of the XXIInd dynasty, the beginnings of which may be seen in the XXth dynasty (*Mound of the Jew*, XIII, 3; XV, 13). The thick lumpy pottery flasks, as 16, 17, are akin to the last on the previous plate, which type is found at Sharanba and in Cyprus. It is there attributed to as late a date as about 550 B.C. (*Jour. Hellen. S.* XVII, 159; fig. 12, 1); there is no positive evidence against this, but such forms were not found with the Cypriote pottery of 600–500 B.C. at Nebesheh (*Tanis*, ii, *Nebesheh*, Pl. III), and from a general impression I should have put these one or two centuries earlier. The piece of bowl, 18, is certainly VIIth century Greek. At the bottom are some rude figures of pottery, of probably foreign make about 1000–800 B.C.

PL. XXXVI A. This large pottery is of various ages. Probably we may assign it to the following dates: XIXth dynasty, 4, 5, 6; XXIInd dynasty, 7, 8, 13, 14, 15, 16; XXVIth dynasty, 2, 3; Ptolemaic, 1, 9, 10, 11, 17; Arab (?), 12. It was all found in the town. The small jar 13 was placed inside the large jar 14, and so is contemporary.

PL. XXXVI B. This smaller pottery was likewise all found in the town. As there is no evidence about the ages it is here classed according to form. The stands, 53-6, are probably fire pots, for carrying lighted charcoal from house to house. Some of these forms, as 54, 55, will stand independently, and may have been used also to support cooking pots over the fire; but others, 53, 56, will not stand, and having a handle they seem intended to carry embers.

46. PL. XXXVI C. The stone vases here show the early occupation; the cylinder, 1, of white and grey granite, is probably of the Old Kingdom; the alabaster, 2, is of the VIth or VIIth dynasty (*Diospolis Parva*, XXVIII); the diorite kohl pot, 3, is probably of the same age; the alabasters, 5, 7, are of the XIIth—4 is later, perhaps of the XVIIIth dynasty (*Dios.* XXX). 9 is perhaps of the XIIth dynasty;

5

8 is of the XXVIth. 12 is a model capital of limestone. 13 is part of a curious limestone box on four legs, with patterns which are more Syrian than Egyptian. The alabaster toilet dishes, 14, 15, are of the XVIIIth dynasty.

The weights, 16–22, are of interest, as this is the only place worked during this year, where such were found. The materials, weights, and units are as follows :

		Grains		Units
16, grey limestone, almond	669 ÷ 3 =	223
18, white „ cone	1134	5	227
20, „ „ conoid	911	4	228
21, basalt square	1387	6	231
22, white limestone, conoid	1348	6	225
23, serpentine	688	3	229

These yield a unit averaging 227, the regular shekel known as the Phoenician standard ; and the varieties fall on the most usual range of this standard (*Tanis*, ii, *Defenneh*, XLVIII).

19, white limestone, square	2414 ÷ 12 =	201
Khety, jasper, in XXXIII, 4,	1850 (?) 9	205

These belong to the gold standard ; but the Khety weight is of the unusual multiple 9, as marked upon the end of it. This suggests that it was probably of another standard originally, and was subsequently marked for the gold standard. It may be that it was 8 of the standard of 231 grains, the old Syrian standard which was later adopted for the Phoenician coinage. Multiples of this by 8 were found at Naukratis. Possibly of this same standard is a cast bronze plaque with a. walking lion upon it, which I bought at Zagazig ; it weighs 870 grains, or 4 × 217·5.

One example of the Assyrian standard occurs, from Saft.

Sandstone, square, 1569 ÷ 12 = 130·7.

But among all these ten weights there is not a single one of the official Egyptian standard, the *deben* and *qedet.* This shows how much the eastern road was under Syrian influence, and that the traders and merchants were Syrians rather than Egyptians.

The spindle whorls, 23-32, drill caps 33, 34, pounding stones 35-41, and loom weights 42-8, do not need description.

47. The skulls were collected, whenever their condition permitted, at Tell el Yehudiyeh ; but the damp ground had left few in movable state, and none of the Hyksos period were found unbroken. The measured examples date from the XVIIIth dynasty to Ptolemaic times, and there are not enough to distinguish changes, so that we can only regard them as an average of this locality. At Saft Mr. Duncan collected many skulls, but unfortunately all the numbers were weathered off before I arrived to measure them. I could only roughly divide them into early and late, according to the grouping as they were discovered ; the earlier excavations being generally of the XVIIIth dynasty, and the later excavations being mostly Roman. The number from Yehudiyeh is 7 male and 8 female ; from Saft the earlier are 7 male and 22 female, the later are 14 male and 16 female. The division of sex I estimated on each skull, as well as I could, when measuring. These numbers of examples are so small that the distribution of varieties cannot be examined, and I here only publish the median of each group.

	MALES.			FEMALES.		
	Yehud.	Saft early.	Saft late.	Yehud.	Saft early.	Saft late.
Length, Broca . .	185	176	178	178	173	170
„ Flower .	182	176	176	180	173	170
Breadth, maximum .	136	137	133	135	132	133
„ biauricular .	120	115	116	115	114	113
„ bizygomatic .	—	126	129	—	118	122
Height, bregma .	133	136	131	132	124	127
Basi-nasal . . .	103	101	102	99	95	95
Basi-alveolar . .	97	96	94	92	91	87
Nasi-alveolar . .	71	70	67	62	66	62
Nasal height . .	53	53	52	47	50	49
Nasal width . .	25	24	24	23	23	22

The larger size in every dimension of the Yehudiyeh skulls, over those of Saft, is very marked ; yet the places are only 25 miles apart, and are under similar conditions. Comparing the early and late skulls from Saft the most distinct difference is that the face becomes wider at the cheek-bones, and the whole facial bones diminish in the height and projection of the jaw. This is probably due to a better preparation of food diminishing the grinding required.

The importance of Saft as the nome capital of Goshen rendered it certain that a cemetery of some size must be in its neighbourhood. I therefore visited the place, and found the sandy rise of the cemetery. So soon as Mr. Duncan and Mr. Gilbart-Smith were at liberty they accordingly went there, and the excavations were done by them as described in the following pages. I finally visited the work myself for the dating of the objects.

CHAPTER VI

THE CEMETERY OF GOSHEN (SAFT)

By J. Garrow Duncan, B.D.

48. To the east of Zagazig in the Delta, about half-way between the small stations of Abu el Akhdar and Abu Hammád, and close to the eastern bank of the Ismailiyeh Canal, lie the ruins of an ancient city, on whose site now stands the modern town Saft el Henneh. Twenty years ago, Dr. Naville, in his excavations on this site, conclusively proved that this was the city whose name in hieroglyphic inscriptions was Pa-Sopt. He also showed that it was known about the XXXth dynasty as Kes, (Greek Pha-cusa), in the Septuagint as Kesem, and in the Old Testament as Goshen. The town contained a temple built by Ramessu II, and the most important discovery Dr. Naville made was that of the fragments of the beautiful shrine dedicated to the god of the place by Nectanebo II of the XXXth dynasty. The Sanctuary was known as "the Abode of the Sycomore," this tree being regarded as sacred in the district.

Though in the XVIIIth and XIXth dynasties there were probably wide stretches in this region consisting of sand or rough uncultivated and marshy ground, now at the present day it is one of the most fertile and beautiful portions of the Delta; in all probability the whole of the sandy rises and ruins will soon be absorbed in the rapidly advancing cultivation, which artificial irrigation has recently done so much to promote. Already a considerable portion of the ruins lies under the level of surrounding fields, which when irrigated are partially under water, so that there is not much hope of the possibility of further work being carried out. The whole district is scattered over with trees, the most prominent of which are the sycomore, the acacia, and the date-palm. About three-quarters of a mile to the south of Saft el Henneh, between it and the village of Suwa, there exists still a considerable stretch of sandy *gezireh*, the western and eastern sides of which are employed as modern burial-grounds. This gezireh became the scene of our operations from the middle of February to the first week of April; and the results attained showed that it had been used as a cemetery more or less intermittently from the early XVIIIth dynasty down to the period of the Roman occupation of Egypt.

Much of the oldest part of the cemetery has already been laid under cultivation for the growth of henneh, a considerable produce of these villages; and in some parts the sand had been so completely carried away by *sebakhin* that in a large number of the sand-pit tombs which we examined, the skeleton, pottery, and other objects were barely covered. In some cases, the tomb-filling had been so denuded that no trace of bones was left; and the fact that there had been a burial there, was attested simply by the presence of scattered beads or other small objects, found a few inches under the surface; while in other cases we actually found that the bottoms of upturned vases had for some time formed part of the surface of the pathway, over which the traffic between the surrounding villages passed from day to day. It would appear therefore, that by the merest accident, or through the entire lack of enterprise and observation on the part of the natives living around, this gezireh had been left to us to be a source of information and historical data, as well as of many objects of value.

49. On the 18th of February we pitched our tents on the top of the broad brick wall on the eastern side of the ancient town of Goshen, intending to spend some time in examining the ruins of the place; but the tale that the ruins had recently become the property of a relative of the *omdeh* compelled us to leave this part, and we therefore began operations at once on the gezireh.

On examining the cemetery we adopted the most thorough method of spreading the workmen over it, allotting to each pair a space of four or six metres wide, and beginning at the extreme eastern edge. By frequent measurement and recording of the work of each group throughout the day, the workmen were enabled to deposit the sand immediately behind them, so that at the close of operations the aspect of the gezireh remained comparatively unaltered, though almost every foot of it had been turned over and carefully examined.

At a later period we transferred our operations to the western edge, and followed the same method, working towards the centre, until we found burials of so late a date and so uninteresting a character, that we decided to abandon this place for the gezireh of Suwa about a mile distant.

In the work during part of the time I had the valuable assistance of Mr. Gilbart-Smith, who undertook the measuring and helped me with the recording; and later of Mr. T. Butler Stoney, who rendered great service in drawing a portion of the objects found; the greater part were drawn by Mrs. Petrie. We shall now describe the character of the interments, and then proceed to the details of the more distinctive graves.

50. THE DISPOSITION OF THE BODY. The body was almost invariably placed on its back, with the hands by the sides, or folded over the breast, as the large quantities of beads and bracelets found above the pelvis show. In a few graves, the body was found on its left or right side, but these were not the rule. In the majority of the graves, the head was to the west or north-west, with the face up; though in a few cases, the face was turned to one side or the other. No trace of mutilation of the corpse was found. From the abundant remains of decayed cloth, we infer that every body was wrapped in cloth before burial, and where we did find cloth in any state of preservation, it was manifest that the body had not been simply dressed in a single garment, but swathed in' many folds of linen. In graves of men, usually nothing but a few pots were found. With the women, on the other hand, there seem to have been buried a selection of domestic utensils and personal ornaments, such as they would have used and worn during their lives. Large quantities of beads, which must have belonged to some sort of beadwork, were often found on the chest, rings on the fingers, earrings at the ears, valuable stone beads at the neck, hair-pins, and hair-rings under the head. A curious feature, frequently observed, was that the bronze bracelets and anklets, often mixed with coins and rings, were placed together on the breast, or by the ear. Pots, vases, and other things of domestic use, were variously arranged around the corpse, but, as a rule, a space was left for such things at the head of the grave; and, where the corpse was covered with bricks, before the sand filling, the pottery was usually placed above the bricks, just over the face of the corpse. In the pot-burials of children, the pots averaged 3 feet in length. The same practice was observed in nearly every case; the body had been wrapped in cloth, and wore the beads, bracelets, scarabs, and other ornaments which had been worn by the child in its lifetime. It was usually inserted at the bottom end, head first, and, where the pot was too small, the body was doubled up to fit it; generally the pot was placed so that the child's head was towards the west or north-west. When the neck of the pot was broken off at the shoulder, the body was inserted feet foremost, and the bottom of the pot left intact. In the earlier burials, this held good almost universally; in the later pot-burials of the Roman period, the same

attention was not paid to the direction in which the body lay; and sometimes as many as five pots, each containing the skeleton of a child, were found in one pit, lying in all directions.

Very few cases of contemporary double burials were found. Occasionally, the bones of an infant were found mixed with those of an adult, a mother and child having probably been buried simultaneously; and in one case (grave 242), four skeletons (two complete and two in part) were found doubled up and placed crossways in an ordinary brick-lined grave. In pot-burials, if other pottery was in the grave it was invariably outside the coffin.

51. [Before referring to the ages of the various graves, it should be stated in what manner the dating was settled. Mr. Duncan had placed the grave number on almost every amulet, group of beads, and pot. I subsequently dated each of these by what I knew from other sites. Differences in the age attributed to any grave were very few; and after the pottery was classed and arranged on these plates a final complete list was made of all the datings for each grave, and all the graves in which each type occurred. There were only two cases in which the estimated age of a pot required alteration. A large pan is classed now as an extra size of no. 225 instead of in the XVIIIth dynasty; the base of it should have settled this before. And the new form 198 A belongs to the XXVIth dynasty, instead of the XVIIIth; there was no precedent to guide the determination. It is satisfactory to find that out of hundreds of examples of new collocations of forms and objects there is so little remaining to be learned.

In only six graves did there seem to be a mixture of earlier pottery re-used. But it should be noted that in making the broad division between XXVIth dynasty and Ptolemaic pottery, there are instances where a grave may have its contents classed differently owing to its belonging to the XXVIIth—XXXth dynasties. We have not yet sufficient accurately dated examples to make a whole class of the Persian period; hence the pottery of this age appears under either the XXVIth or Ptolemaic according to its affinities. The following graves seem to belong to this age. At Saft 514; at Suwa 39, 58, 61, 106, 121, 134, 135, 180, 205, 238, 256, 262, 267, and these are called XXXth dynasty in the descriptions.

The selection of the following material has been made from a larger list drawn up by Mr. Duncan, and revised in accordance with the conclusions from a comparison of the final lists, with reference numbers to the plates as I have arranged them.—W. M. F. P.]

52. TYPES OF GRAVES. The graves of the Cemetery of Goshen fall into the following classes:

I. *The ordinary sand-pit burials.* The body was laid in the sand, and covered with sand, without any brick building or coffin in any shape or form.

II. *Side-scoop sand-pits.* A hole was excavated in the sand to a certain depth, and a place was scooped out on one side of it, of sufficient size to admit the corpse. The entrance to the grave proper was usually built up with bricks after the burial, and the hole then filled.

III. *Brick-built and covered burials.* The bottom of the sand-pit was usually lined with single bricks, so as to form a narrow trough, just wide and deep enough for the reception of the body. This was afterwards covered over with bricks and plastered close with mud. Occasionally, a brick bottom was first laid, and the body placed on it, and in such cases, we found the skeleton firmly sunk into this hard brick mass, owing to the weight of sand above it. Usually, however, the body was laid simply on the sand, without any brick floor. This type of grave is still the usual form of burial in the modern cemetery near by, employed by those who do not possess brick-built mastabas. In these graves, the pottery offerings were all placed above the brick covering of the corpse.

IV. *Slipper-shaped pottery coffins.* These belong to the XVIIIth and XIXth dynasties. Most of them bore a modelling of the face and hands of the deceased, and several were well painted. Pottery offerings were placed outside of these, at the head or at the sides.

V. *Double Ziyeh burials.* Two large pots, each from 3 to 3½ feet high, and about 2 feet in diameter at the top, were placed mouth to mouth with the body enclosed within them.

VI. *Half-pot burials.* In three graves, bodies of adults were found buried with the upper portion of the body laid inside a large pot about 3 feet long, 14 inches in diameter at bottom, and 26 inches in diameter at the mouth. The rest of the body was unprotected.

VII. *Pot burials of children.* These formed a very numerous class in this cemetery. In almost every case, a large water or oil jar, or later, a wine jar was employed. The bottom was knocked out, the child placed inside, with its head invariably at the mouth end, and both ends were then closed by clay saucers or broken pieces of jars.

VIII. *Stone coffins.* Very few of these were found, and in no case were they inscribed.

IX. *Clay oblong coffins.* In one case, an oblong box of clay, dried in the sun, was employed for the burial of a child.

X. *Wooden coffins.* In several graves, a flooring of wood under the skeleton, and fragments of decayed wood were found, from which it would appear that wooden coffins were also used.

We now proceed to the description of selected graves, taking the classes in the above order, and following the date in each class. For references to the plates, the pottery is all numbered consecutively 1 to 355, referring to Pls. XXXIX B, C, D, E, F, G, H, J and K; the scarabs are marked S. 1 to 57, referring to Pl. XXXVII; the amulets are marked A. 1 to 57, referring to Pl. XXXVIII.

53. I. SAND-PIT GRAVES

XVIIIth dynasty.

Grave 1. An ordinary sand-pit burial, close on the edge of the henneh fields, and with the sand so denuded by *sebakhin* that the skeleton was only a few inches down. It was that of a woman laid on the back at full length, with the head to the west. At the head, one roughly decorated pot, and a red baked saucer were found (see 41, 79 in Pls. XXXIX C, D); the latter containing the vertebrae of an infant. Under each ear was a large silver-gilt hair-ring (Pl. XXXVIII, and Pl. XXXVII A as no. 26).

Grave 5 resembled grave 1 closely in every detail. The pottery is of the leather-bottle Cypriote type (Pl. XXXIX B, 10). The pans nos. 27, 46, 47 were with it.

Grave 6. The arrangement of the body was the same. The grave contained one red baked pot, no. 50, a saucer of the same kind with a flat bottom, no. 42, and one porphyry vase. A gold-encased scarab, S. 5, and an oblong glazed bead, S. 16, inscribed on both sides, were found at the neck. Another scarab with scroll pattern surrounding a scorpion, A. 1, and set in a silver ring, was found by the side. Some tiny carnelian beads complete the contents found.

Grave 95. The skeleton lay on right side, head to west, hands on sides, face to south, body fully stretched. One flat glazed bead, S. 41, ¼ inch thick, with a scarabaeus on each side, a scarab, S. 12, tiny carnelian beads, and one long cylindrical glazed bead were found near the head.

Grave 123. The skeleton lay on left side, with

head to west, arms and legs stretched to full length, and face to north. Glazed beads, green and yellow mixed, very tiny beads, a bronze bracelet, and two scarabs, S. 13, 35, were found about the neck and chest. A small bronze ring was also found at a higher level in the sand filling.

Grave 151. The skeleton lay on back with head to north-west, and face up. A considerable quantity of blue glazed flat beads were found at the pelvis. One blue glazed figure of Bast, A. 26, two smaller glazed pendants, and a black scarab, S. 28, and another, S. 36, complete the contents.

Grave 168. The skeleton lay on back, head to west, and face to south. A large quantity of flat glazed beads, coloured blue and black, were taken from the pelvis. These particular beads of about ⅛ inch in diameter were found in a large majority of the graves in the same position. At the right wrist were found glazed bars with four holes pierced in them, which had been used to form a bracelet of four strings of these beads, the two bars being employed to keep the strings in position. At the left wrist, six glazed scaraboids were found, being part of another bracelet, and, under the chin, glass beads of three colours, blue, white, and black.

Grave 172 was a burial of the usual sand-pit type. The skeleton lay on back, head to west, and resting on left cheek. Under the right ear were found a pair of silver-gilt hair-rings, as A. 11. Five small, round, and slightly larger cylindrical carnelian beads were found in the neck. A bronze mirror, the wooden handle of which lay in pieces beside it, had evidently been placed in the right hand, and was found inside the right arm. On a level slightly higher than the brow, at the head of the grave, was a false-neck pot, no. 15, and Pl. XXXVIII A, about five inches high, with red painted bands round it, and double ears and spout.

Grave 246 was a very shallow burial, the surface having been removed by *sebakhin*. It measured 50 inches × 20 × 20. The skeleton lay on back, with head to west. Five kinds of beads were found:

(1) The blue glazed type of flat round beads found at the pelvis;
(2) Tiny glazed beads, coloured yellow, brown, and black, found at the neck;
(3) Carnelian lotus-seed pendants found at neck, see A. 7;
(4) Glazed pendants; and
(5) Small round carnelian beads.

All except the first and fifth classes were found at the neck, and composed one necklace, the pattern of which was as follows,—two carnelian pendants alternately with two glazed pendants; each pendant separated from the next by four of the tiny glazed beads of varied colours. The small carnelian beads were found at the right wrist, and had been mixed with beads of class 1, probably to form a bracelet of several threads.

Grave 376 measured 60 inches × 30 × 30. The skeleton lay on back, with head to west. In this tomb a large quantity of the blue glazed beads commonly found at the pelvis, were found on the left shoulder and under the back. Under the chin, tiny glazed beads, black and yellow, and near the arm small carnelian and other beads were found. From the large numbers of the blue glazed beads found strung together these would seem to have belonged to a bead-embroidered veil or shroud. The tiny glaze and carnelian beads probably alternated to form a three-string necklace, as ivory bars triple-bored were found at the neck.

Grave 393, 60 inches × 40 w. × 50 d. The skeleton lay on its right side, with head toward the west. The red pot no. 62 was at the head. A beautiful blue glazed bracelet was made up of six figures of gods, a Horus eye, and an uraeus, separated from each other by seven crocodiles of the same material. There was also a small red pot, and tiny brown and yellow beads.

Grave 394 contained some beads apparently of the same type, and also traces of iron, which is unusual if so early.

Grave 438 was a double burial. The pit measured 60 inches × 30 × 30. The skeleton of the adult lay on its left side, with head to the west. The bones of an infant were found on a piece of potsherd lying above the pelvis of the adult. With this were blue glazed and carnelian beads.

Grave 448 measured 60 inches × 40 × 30. The skeleton lay on back, with head to the west. A quantity of beads, white and black, were found on the chest. The bronze rings found by the right ear beside a ring of white material (probably coloured glass) were perhaps hair-rings, resembling them exactly in shape.

Grave 489 measured 60 × 30 × 30; the skeleton lay on back, and with the head to the south-west. In this tomb the fine terra-cotta figure of a woman seated, playing the mandoline, was found (see Pl. XXXVII B). This unique figure is decorated with a diamond check pattern in black lines on the chest, and the musical instrument with a double wavy line, crossing and re-crossing to form a series of small circles. It is a piece of very clever modelling. The profile and the pose of the head and neck give to the figure an absorbed expression, which is striking when we consider the very simple treatment. The piece shows evidence of Cypriote art, and probably dates from about the XIXth—XXth dynasty.

Grave 561, 50 × 40 × 30 w. Head to west, normal. The skeleton found belonged to a later burial probably, since at a considerable depth below it a quantity of XVIIIth dynasty tiny blue glazed beads were found. With these beads were two white glazed bars, eight-fluted, showing that the beads had formed a bracelet of eight strings. The bars had originally been blue.

Grave 846 measured 60 × 40 d. × 30 w. Skeleton on back, head to west, a normal sand-pit burial. The body lay against the west side of the pit. In the left corner at the head was a rough red pot of the commonest type, no. 74. At the knee a red saucer, no. 38, bottom up, and an alabaster pot (XXXIX L, 1) beside it; on the left hand a jasper ring, A. 21, and jasper beads, small and flat with bevelled edges, alternating with tiny amber beads complete the contents.

54. XIXth dynasty.

Grave 45. At the head a red pot, no. 60. A three-tubed kohl-pot (Pl. XXXVIII A) of blue glaze, two bronze bracelets, some beads, and fragments of blue glaze were also found.

Grave 499 measured 50 inches l. × 30 w. × 10 d. The skeleton lay on its back, but the direction of the head was to the south-east, which was unusual. With it was a blue glazed kohl-pot of two tubes joined together (upper one on Pl. XXXVIII A).

Grave 673 : 70 × 30 × 30. Skeleton on back, head to west. A fair specimen of a male burial. One pot, no. 84, of a XIXth dynasty type, lay at the head. In most burials of males nothing was found.

XXIInd dynasty.

Grave 93. Skeleton lay on left side, head to west, face to north, hands by sides, body fully stretched. Tiny carnelian beads, a Horus eye of carnelian, and small porphyry beads were found.

Grave 602. A child's sand-pit burial, normal, except that four large bricks had been laid around and above the head to keep off the sand, while the rest of the body was not specially protected. A glaze Bes, 2 univalve shells, and 2 beads were found in it.

Grave 649 measured 70 × 40 × 30 w. Skeleton on back, head to the south. At the neck were a small Bes figure and five white beads, which are of a type unusual in this cemetery.

XXIIIrd to XXVIth dynasty.

Grave 126. Here the surface had been so wasted away, that the bottom of the grave was only some five inches down. Three bronze bells, A. 41, a black and yellow glass double-faced amulet, A. 44, some iron, and several glazed beads were found.

Grave 311. Sand-pit burial of a child, 60 inches × 30 × 40 d. Skeleton on back, head to the north-east. Beads mixed at neck. A small red elongated pot, no. 201, bronze bell (Pl. XXXVII A), glaze figure of Bes, a double-face pendant of black and yellow glass, A. 43, and two iron bracelets were found on a ledge at the head of the tomb.

Grave 381 measured 40 inches × 50 d. × 30 w. Large carnelian, black and white (probably glass) beads, a large Bes figure, a large double-face pendant black and yellow as A. 44, and a piece of ivory, were found at the head.

Grave 231, probably of the Persian period. The skeleton of a young girl lay on back, with head to north-west. At the feet bronze anklets, and at the wrists iron bracelets were found. A quantity of beads were picked up from under the head, and among them two interesting scarabs, S. 50, 51, the one representing the Living Ram, the other the Living Thoth.

Grave 323, 60 inches × 50 × 40 d., was probably Ptolemaic. The skeleton lay on back, with head north-west. In the centre of the tomb a heap of pottery was found, comprising rough red pots (no. 292), and saucers (no. 226), all broken, 5 blue glaze saucers (XXXIX L, 9, 10, 13, 14), an alabastron broken at the top, and a ring pot-stand. Apparently no sort of arrangement had been intended. All were deposited in a heap above the lower part of the body.

55. Roman.

Grave 277 measured 50 inches l. × 30 × 30. The skeleton of a child lay on back, with head to south-east. Beads were found in the following order, 8 carnelian (of 6 different types), 1 quartz, 1 glass, and 8 glaze (of 5 different types). A few small beads were found scattered.

Grave 291 : 40 l. × 30 × 20 d. Child with head to west. Beads of several kinds and sizes were found under the chin, of which the only pattern discernible was that of gilt beads and resinous alternating. Cloth wrapping, and pieces of wood were found at the head, and a string of skin knotted as it had been used for stringing the beads.

Grave 341 measured 60 inches × 30 × 40 d. Skeleton on back, with head to the west. Small green glass beads, small silver paste beads, and amber beads were found mixed together on the chest. A quantity of small bronze hair-pins, and a bronze hair ornament lay at each side of the head.

Grave 439 measured 60 inches × 40 × 30 w. The skeleton of a young girl lay on its back, with the head to the west. Bronze earrings with bead pendants lay at the ears. In the pendant the arrangement of beads was at bottom a small amethyst, lozenge-shaped drop, above it four beads, paste, blue, green and black, strung on thin bronze wire. In the necklace the order seemed to have been green, carnelian, and yellow in rotation. A small bronze spoon of the Roman period was also found, and a pin of bronze, A. 50.

Grave 490 is a normal sand-pit burial, but it was remarkable for the deep layer of what looked like fine bluish ashes, under and over the whole skeleton to a depth of three inches. It was most likely the dust of the decayed folds of wrapping which had originally enclosed the corpse. A similar layer was in graves 566 and 588. Five large coloured beads were found, two under each ear and one on the chest.

Grave 492 : 50 inches × 30 × 15 d. The skeleton lay on its back, hands by the sides as usual, and the head to the west.

The grave is remarkable for the many and varied ornaments taken from the neck and under the head. There were found :

(1) A large bronze *toq* round the neck, badly corroded.

(2) An ivory toq about ½ inch broad and ⅜ inch thick, in pieces.

(3) Twelve ivory pendants, one a head and face, two barrel-shaped 'and pierced through in parallel rows of three holes each, two crosses (Coptic), and the others more or less rudely shaped and ornamented.

(4) Large amber beads, mixed with small paste beads. These two alternated types of beads seemed to have formed a necklace along with the ivory pendants (3).

(5) Several bronze and silver rings mixed.

(6) One large blue glass (?) bead, probably used as a hair-ring.

(7) A collection of iron rings under the head (as noticed before), which had been anklets or bracelets.

(8) A coil of the bronze wire used to thread the beads, with several beads on it.

The custom of piling all the ornaments and jewellery in a heap by the head is not observed in earlier burials.

In grave 494 the following types of beads were found under the chin. Small round yellow glass beads, small blue beads evidently strung separately, larger glass beads imitating amber, amber beads (large), blue glaze flat beads of the kind found at the pelvis in earlier burials, glaze beads of the same make but coloured yellow, brown, black and light blue, long thin cylindrical beads of blue glaze, all so inextricably mixed up that no clue could be got as to the original pattern. Bronze earrings, and bracelets (plain ring and wire twisted) and iron anklets were found also near the head.

Grave 630 measured 60 × 50 × 30 w. Skeleton on back, head to the west. On the right breast lay a fine bronze writing-case, Pl. XXXVII B. Like the brass writing-case in use at the present day, it was made evidently to be carried at the waist. The bronze cylinder held the long, thin reeds for writing, the end below the ink pot retaining it in the belt. Thus the ink pot was upright ready for use. The conical top of it had a small hole to slip the reed through, and the black powder of ink is still inside. At the head lay a glass bottle about 14 inches long, its body being uniformly about 2 inches in diameter, and the neck short and narrow in proportion (see Pl. XXXVII B, middle of group).

Grave 660 contained carnelian and other stone beads in a heap at the neck, a broad bronze bracelet at right hand, 2 bronze rings on left hand, a bronze bell at the right hand, and 2 large rings on the mouth, which may have been bracelets, but more likely nose-rings.

Grave 662 had amber beads at neck, iron rings, probably nose-rings, on the mouth, bronze bracelets at wrists, and iron anklets.

Grave 666 : 60 × 30 w. × 20 d. Skeleton on back, head to the west. Above the face a small glass bottle with vertical fluting at the neck, a bronze toq flattened and pierced at one end, and a pair of bronze horns (A. 55 and Pl. XXXVII A).

Grave 678, head to west. On right arm two bronze armlets, on left breast a bronze bell, at left ear a large thin bronze ring and finger-ring, at right ear one earring, under the chin a coin and beads were found. The bones in this burial were of a peculiar pink colour due to the action of some chemical, or perhaps to the dye of wrappings now decayed. This same feature was observed in only one other tomb.

Grave 725 contained several glass vessels. A large glass jar is decorated round the bowl in a diamond pattern of raised glass threads (see Pl. XXXVIII A, base); the neck was lost. This jar was about 8 inches in diameter. Near it lay a smaller glass bottle 3½ to 4 inches long, flat, decorated down the middle of both sides with a glass band, which at the shoulders formed an ear at each side (see above the jar). The large black glass bracelet is about ¾ inch in breadth, decorated with raised parallel ridges all round (see over previous figure). Another small round glass bottle, plain, and many fragments of broken glass were also found in this tomb. Ivory hair-pins (as A. 51) and ear-plugs of wood (as A. 24) lay at the head. The glass was all found behind the head.

56. II. SIDE-SCOOP GRAVES

These were enlarged sand-pit tombs, but instead of the body being placed in the bottom of a square grave, it lay in a hole scooped out on one side of the pit and usually built up with bricks afterwards. There were very few of this class in this cemetery, and no two of the same period. They will be more fully discussed in connection with the Cemetery of Gheyta.

Grave 545, 50 l. × 40 × 40 inches, was of a child, with head to east. Iron anklets, bronze bells, univalve shells, and glazed figures lay in a heap at the feet. The figures included a Bes and a crocodile, A. 37. There was also one glazed bell pendant, and another of bronze, A. 41. Three flat saucers of a rough make were taken from the filling. They were of the type commonly used as lids for larger pots. The contents indicate a burial of the XXVIth dynasty.

Graves 417 and 485 were both child-burials of this class. The hole was scooped out on the west side of the pit. They measured each about 50 inches l. × 40 w. × 40 d. In 485 bronze and iron bracelets and anklets, and beads were found, all of types that would indicate a Roman date. The head was to the north.

Grave 662 is best classed with these. The shaft (40 inches l. × 20 w. × 60 d.) led down to two underground rooms, one on the west and one on the north side, cut into hard *gebel*. The rooms had been walled and roofed with sun-dried bricks, and the entrances from the shaft had been built up. The skeletons lay with head to west. A silver earring, A. 18, and bronze pin, A. 49, were with them.

57. III. BRICK-LINED AND COVERED GRAVES

XVIIIth dynasty.

Grave 139. The brick lining and covering were complete. Two rough red pots, no. 73, about 14 inches long, flat-bottomed, were laid across the face alternately with the bricks. The cakes of black mud in the bottom showed that they originally contained liquid of some sort. On the left shoulder was a small alabaster pot about 4 inches high (XXXIX L, 4), and a fine blue glaze oblong bead inscribed on both sides.

Grave 330 measured 80 inches × 30 × 30. The skeleton lay on left side, with head to the west. At the head stood a small one-eared pot, no. 101, of whitish ground with red bands. At the right wrist was a bracelet of small glaze pendants, A. 6, and four scarabs, see S. 10, 17, 19, 26, 34; a small bronze mirror lay at the waist; alabaster hair-rings, A. 12, and ear-plugs, A. 23, 24, beads, and two rings from the head, show that this was the grave of a woman.

Grave 355 was 80 × 50 d. × 40 w., brick-lined and arched. Skeleton on back, with head to west. At the head the bricks of lining, instead of lying across the tomb formed a triangle in which space lay the head. From this triangle the arch sprang, but so as to leave a clear space outside of it, in which were deposited two red pilgrim-bottles, nos. 110, 111, and a small one-eared white pot.

Grave 378 was 80 × 40 d. × 30 w. Skeleton lay on left side, head to west, face to the east. The body had been swathed in cloth. On the chest and under the back were blue glaze beads, such as were usually found at the pelvis, tiny glaze beads, black, brown and yellow; small round carnelian and garnet beads which alternated to form a necklace, and a small scarab, S. 24, were found. The brick lining was complete, but the covering had gone.

Grave 437: 60 × 40 × 30. The skeleton lay on back, with head to west. The grave was brick-lined all round. At the wrist of right hand, tiny glaze beads—yellow, brown, blue, and white—and at the pelvis, a quantity of the usual blue glaze type were found.

XIXth dynasty.

Grave 150. Skeleton on back, head to the southwest. Two blue glaze figures of Bast, A. 35, a small red saucer, and a jar, no. 62, lay at the right side.

6

At the north corner of the grave, a considerable distance away, lay a pot, no. 104.

XXIIIrd dynasty.

Grave 304 measured 60 inches × 40 d. × 30 w. Skeleton on back, head to west. Under the head were two figures of Bes, two bronze bell pendants, A. 41, one double-face pendant black and yellow, A. 44, and one large bead with projecting knobs, A. 42.

XXVIth dynasty.

Grave 308 of this class was normal, but is notable for the fact that the skull was found deposited outside of the tomb proper, and on the top of the brick covering, as if the head had been cut off at time of burial and purposely buried separately. Beside the skull were found bronze bracelets, and a small scarab, S. 45, with the uraeus and "Son of Ra." Under the skull were iron anklets.

Ptolemaic.

Grave 242 contained parts of four skeletons laid across a normal sized grave, with the heads towards the west. The grave measured 60 inches l. × 40 w. × 50 d. The bodies lay on their left sides. Two complete ones in the south end, with the legs doubled up to fit the space of 40 inches. The third seemed to have lain on right side facing these two, but the skull lay on its face. The vertebrae showed the original position of the body. The legs had completely disappeared if they were ever there. Of the fourth skeleton only the skull and a few vertebrae remained. The skull lay face up, and the body probably lay on its right side.

At the left ear of the first complete skeleton a bronze earring, between the two a small red pot, no. 202, and where the knees of the second and third would have met a large red pot with short neck and abruptly bulging shoulder, as nos. 104, 109, were found.

Grave 101. The body lay on the back, with head to the north. Under the ear a large jasper pendant, A. 27, and two carnelian hair-rings, as A. 13, and in another part a pot, no. 283, and a usual Ptolemaic flask, no. 327. This burial if not of mixed dates has certainly re-used earlier objects of the XVIIIth dynasty. The brick sides were complete, but the brick covering, as in most cases, had mingled with the sand.

Grave 663 was on the western edge of the gezireh. The body lay on its back, with head to the north-west. To keep the head in position, a brick was placed at each side of it, between it and the brick lining. The brick lining and covering were complete.

At each ear was found a gold earring of considerable weight, A. 57, with a spherical gold pendant covered with globules; see also XXXVII A. Another flattened gold earring was picked up in the filling. On a finger of right hand was a bronze ring of double-snake pattern, A. 54.

Roman.

Grave 672 was at the north-west corner of the gezireh, where the sand filling was almost completely removed. At the head of what had been a brick-lined grave were found a ribbed drinking pot, no. 346 A, a red ribbed bowl about 4 inches deep, no. 346, and inside the latter, a small glass bottle.

58. IV. POTTERY COFFINS—PLAIN AND ORNAMENTED—SLIPPER-SHAPED

XVIIIth dynasty.

Grave 8 contained a red pottery coffin about 6 feet in length, placed with head to the north-west. The skeleton lay face down. A scarab, S. 14, was the only thing found inside. Outside the coffin, at the head, were two pots, nos. 57 and 80.

Grave 211. The coffin lay with head to west, measured 6 feet in length, and had a woman's face moulded on the top of the lid. The lid measured about 2 feet in length. The skeleton lay on its back. At the ears were found silver-gilt hair-rings, as A. 11, at the neck, carnelian beads and pendants, as A. 7, and, at the waist, three small scarabs, S. 29, 30, 31.

Grave 331. The coffin lay with head to the west in a grave 80 inches × 40 w. × 50 d. Body on back. At the wrist a blue glazed bracelet of *uza* eyes was found, A. 8. Outside the coffin at the right shoulder stood a rough red pot, no. 43, of a common XIXth dynasty type.

Grave 507. The pit measured 80 inches × 60 d. × 40 w. The head was toward the west. At the right hand corner outside of the coffin a rough red pot, and inside two carnelian hair-rings, as A. 13, were found. The coffin lid bore a woman's face.

Grave 821 contained the finest pottery coffin found in this cemetery. It measured 7 feet in length, and was very fairly painted and inscribed, the lid bearing a woman's face. The pit was 100 inches × 50 d. × 40 w. At the head on the right side and outside the coffin stood a large red double-eared amphora, which appears to be a later Roman burial, no. 342. But in the filling was found a small red pot of the XVIIIth dynasty, no. 58.

Grave 269 contained a pottery coffin with the face of a woman on the lid and lying with head to north-west. The grave measured 80 inches × 30 d. × 40 w., and the coffin was about 6 feet long. Outside of the coffin at the right shoulder were placed a red saucer, and a tall red pot, no. 63.

Roman.

Grave 446 contained a plain coffin evidently of the Roman period. Near the head inside were found a silver(?) bracelet, amber beads, 20 bronze hair-pins, and a large quantity of small round glass beads, coloured yellow, green, blue and white. The head was to the west.

In all these coffins the lid was a separate slab about 2 feet long, fitting neatly into a hole at the thick end of the coffin, just over the head of the body. Where there was a face it was on the lid, and had been evidently moulded in clay separately, and then affixed to the lid before it was baked. The face often came away as a separate piece.

Probably every one of these coffins had been more or less rifled at an earlier period. Some of them were found only a few inches down, and the *sebakhin* might discover them when an ordinary pit tomb would escape their notice.

59. V. DOUBLE ZIYEH BURIALS

Only two of these were found in this cemetery. They were frequent in the Cemetery of Gheyta.

In grave 650 two large pots, each 36 in. long, placed mouth to mouth, enclosed the body. The pots were of a very rough type and evidently belonged to a late date. The head was to the west. Nothing but the skeleton was found in them. The tomb was on the far west side of the gezireh.

Grave 679 was in the same part of the cemetery. The head was to the north-west. The skull was quite separate and stood with face to the north-west end of the pot. The skeleton seemed to have lain on its face. The pots were very rough. Both burials probably belong to the Roman period.

VI. HALF-POT BURIALS

In grave 292 the upper half of the skeleton (from skull to pelvis) lay inside a large pot, about 3½ feet long, and about 26 inches in diameter at the mouth. The lower limbs were unprotected. A complete iron knife in a leather sheath was found at the feet. The burial is of Roman date. The head was to the west. The pot was of a late date and very rough type.

Grave 477. The pot was of slightly different shape and of an earlier type. It measured 5 feet long, and 30 inches in diameter at the mouth. Nothing else was found to indicate the date.

Grave 482 is another of this class, and settles the date of them. The pit measured 70 inches long × 30 × 30. The head was to the west. The bronze earrings, beads, and bronze bracelets found belong distinctly to the Roman period. Only these three instances of this type were found. They appear to be unusual, and to belong to the poorer classes.

60. VII. POT BURIALS OF CHILDREN

In grave 154 there was a red pot of XVIIIth dynasty type, containing a few tiny glaze beads of the same age, with an infant's bones.

Grave 334. The pot measured about 3 feet long, with neck broken off at shoulder, and bottom complete. The body of a child was inserted feet first; and being too large for the pot, the legs were doubled up, to make it fit in. The head was to the west.

Grave 823 contained a three-handled jar, no. 124. The head of the child was at the mouth, and to the north-west. In the pot were found a few fine jasper beads of XVIIIth dynasty.

Of about the XXIInd dynasty there are the following :

Grave 118. Here a pot with a face of Bes had been used. It was found broken; and near it a small red pot, no. 98.

Grave 119. The pot measured 30 inches long, and 15 inches wide at the widest part. The neck was too narrow to admit a body. The bottom had been broken off, the body inserted head first from bottom end, and both ends closed afterwards with sherds. One large bead like four round beads joined side to side, three glazed beads, and a figure of Bast were found.

In grave 147 the pot was rather rounder below than no. 123; it was actually worn through by the continual traffic of people passing over it. There was found in what remained of it, the complete skeleton of an infant, along with three bronze brace-lets, four carnelian beads, a rough white bead, and a rough scarab bead.

In grave 416 the pot was a plain wide-mouth flat-bottomed pot, no. 121, 28 inches high, and 20 inches greatest width. The skeleton lay with head in the bottom of the pot, and toward the west. A large basin, no. 26, covered the mouth. Beside it stood a globular jar, no. 103. This pot closely resembles the type of which we found so many at Sharanba. Iron bracelets were found beside the skeleton.

Roman.

Graves 553, 554. The pots were of the dark brown and ribbed type, no. 354. They were usually broken across at the shoulder; sometimes the neck and shoulder were complete, and the bottom end broken for the admission of the body. Both ends were closed in the usual way, with sherds. In grave 553 the narrow mouth of the jar was sealed with clay—the skull lay in the bottom, and towards the east. A small vase, no. 314, was taken from the filling. In 554 the skull was at the mouth end.

Grave 657. The pot had a rounded bottom, as no. 82, and the body was of uniform width up to the shoulder, where it was broken as usual. A red band of decoration ran round the lower part. The mouth was closed with the bottom end of a similar pot. Beside the pot were placed a small glass bottle, and a two-handled, ribbed drinking pot, with the usual spout. The head of skeleton was to the south-west, otherwise normal.

Grave 830 contained the burial in a jar, no. 350, which is inscribed with what seems to be a mixture of Greek and Roman letters, doubtless a record of the wine which it had contained. A scarab, S. 54, in this grave had the *ankh* in the middle surrounded by a row of concentric circles.

In part of the gezireh, close to the east fence of the market-place, very few burials of adults were found, while pot burials of children abounded. Sometimes as many as five or six of them were buried in one pit, and dozens are passed over here because they simply repeat the above details. With very few exceptions, the head was at the mouth end of the pot and usually toward the west, though they do not seem to have paid so much attention to the direction of the body in the case of children. Where the pot was large enough, the body was never doubled up, but lay quite straight.

No case of mutilation in any form was found, and the bodies had apparently in every case been wrapped in cloth before burial.

61. VIII. STONE COFFINS

Only two stone coffins were found in this cemetery. The one in grave 363, was a fine limestone coffin cut in one block, 80 inches long × 20 × 20, and about 3 inches in thickness all over. It lay north and south, but had evidently shared the fate of most of the pottery coffins. The natives had grubbed down to it, and rifled it. No trace of the lid was found, and there was no inscription on it, nor bones inside. It was surrounded on every side by graves of the XVIIIth and XIXth dynasties.

Grave 684. Our attention was drawn to the other by the natives of the village at the far west side of the gezireh. They had unearthed and reburied it. It was not, like the former, cut out of a solid block of stone, but was evidently made up of slabs appropriated from some building, and cut down to suit. The front side of it, and the lid, were entirely gone. The corners had been plastered. There was no inscription, or other indication of its date.

IX. OBLONG CLAY BOX COFFIN

Grave 384 was unique. It contained the burial of a child in a hard clay oblong coffin measuring 45 inches l. × 20 w. × 8 d. The sides were about $1\frac{1}{2}$ inches thick. The head was to the north.

Inside a small bronze mirror was found. The burial belonged probably to the XVIIIth or XIXth dynasty.

X. WOODEN COFFINS

Traces of wood were quite common throughout the cemetery, but in a few cases there was so much as to suggest that originally wooden coffins had been used.

In grave 379 a complete wooden floor was found under the corpse, and traces of decayed wood in the filling. This was an XVIIIth dynasty burial; the pit measured 60 inches l. × 30 × 30. The head was to the west. At the neck two blue and white beads alternated with two yellow to form a double string necklace. A quantity of the usual blue glazed beads was found at the pelvis.

62. THE CONTENTS OF THE GRAVES fall into three main classes, (1) Domestic, (2) Personal, (3) General.

(1) To the first class belong most of the larger pottery found in the graves. What the exact uses of these pots were, it is not easy to say. Many were doubtless water-jars, especially the class of peg-bottom Roman pots. Many of the later pots, including those described, would have been wine-jars. Others served as cooking pots, and seem to have been buried just as they were taken off the fire, with their bottoms burned black. Some even of the very small pots, with rounded bottom and short wide neck, were burned black. Others were probably used to hold meal and flour, and oil.

The contents of every pot were carefully examined and noted when emptied. It was very common to find a cake of mud in the bottom of some, especially the common rough red pots of the XVIIIth and XIXth dynasties, showing that the pot had originally contained some liquid, now completely evaporated. These cakes may yet be analyzed. Many were found sealed with a lump of mud on the mouth. They (graves 313, 382) were usually large pots, and had contained something of flour, or meal, or grain. Traces of grain were found in several. The largest pots were, of course, those used to contain the burials of children. Basins and saucers of many forms, dates and sizes, were found ; and one particular class of small rough saucer, with abrupt out-sloping sides, about 1½ inches deep, were undoubtedly used as lids for various large pots. They had been used for cooking pots, as well as for pots that required to be sealed.

(2) The class of personal ornament is much more varied.

(a) The beads of many varieties and materials were of the utmost value in dating the graves. The most common materials of the earlier period were glazed pottery, blue and other colours, carnelian, and jasper ; and, of the later period, glass, paste, carnelian (rough) and amber.

(b) Finger-rings, earrings, hair-rings, hair-pins. Finger-rings were found of silver, bronze, blue glaze, and carnelian. Earrings of gold, silver, and bronze. Hair-rings had a slit on one side for the admission of the hairs of the tress on which it was placed. The finest found were also of the oldest period. They were of silver, and gilded (see Pl. XXXVII A, fig. 26). Hair-rings of carnelian, jasper, and lime-stone, were common ; and occasionally large ring beads seem to have been worn in the same way. Hair-pins of bronze were found, sometimes as many as 20 or more in one grave. Ivory hair-pins were not so common as bronze.

(c) Mirrors, bracelets, toqs, and anklets. These were extremely common in bronze. The fine bracelet of glass has been referred to in sand-pit graves, Roman, 725. Many iron rings were found, which were apparently heavy bracelets and anklets. Bracelets of ivory were also very common, and in children's tombs, sometimes anklets of ivory were found, and small finger-rings.

Toqs of bronze, for wearing round the neck, were found in some of the Roman burials, and in one case a toq of ivory.

(d) Pendants and scarabs. A great variety of pendants in blue glaze, carnelian, and jasper were found. The commonest were the glaze figures of Bes and Bast, found mostly in children's graves.

The finest is a necklace of carnelian face-pendants (see Pl. XXXVII A, no. 82) ; another of carnelian pendants, of the lotus-seed form, A. 7, and others of jasper of the same type.

The double-face pendants, black and yellow in colour, A. 43-7, bronze pendants, cats, Isis and Horus, were not uncommon. The bronze bells so usual in children's graves ought, perhaps, to be included in this class.

The scarabs are all reproduced in Pl. XXXVII. The following are notable : one of Unas of dynasty V, one of Queen Thyi, and one where Ramessu II is represented as being carried on the shoulders of the priests (grave 50) in the sed festival (Cairo Museum).

Throughout the whole examination of these various burials, strict watch was kept as to the class of graves containing scarabs, and all were found in burials of women or children. In no case can we say a single scarab was found in a man's grave ; but this is probably only a result of the general rarity of any objects or ornaments in men's graves.

(e) Ear-plugs were quite common in the earlier period. They were of limestone, wood, and ivory (see Pl. XXXVIII).

(3) General. Under this head we must class the stone vases, and small ornamented pottery vases (see Pl. XXXIX L), the various terra-cotta figures, Roman lamps, Roman glass bottles, bronze writing-cases, iron knives, ushabtis, and tables of offerings. The large pot no. 355 was not found in the cemetery, but was purchased in a house near by, where it had been used by three generations for the storage of henneh leaves. The ears are both inscribed with apparently early Arabic writing.

63. On a comparison of the dates of these graves, it will be at once remarked, that the burials of the XVIIIth and XIXth dynasties, and those belonging to the period of Roman occupation, greatly outnumber all the others. There are few belonging to the XXIInd or XXVIth dynasty, and the contents of these are not very decisive ; while the XXXth dynasty does not appear to be represented at all. We are free to infer from this, that the town of Goshen was a flourishing place in the XVIIIth and XIXth dynasties, and I feel sure, that what we have found is a mere remnant of what might have been found here, before the henneh fields made such inroads upon

the gezireh. It is a safe inference also, that the town was a place of some importance in Roman times. But, because the period intervening between these two is so poorly represented here, it would not be justifiable to infer that the place was almost abandoned then.

From Dr. Naville's work, we know that Goshen was of considerable importance in the XXXth dynasty, and the second king of that dynasty was the donor of its famous shrine. It may be that the portion of the gezireh used in that period for burial, was absorbed by the surrounding cultivation. But it is more likely that the intervening burials were in the Cemetery of Suwa, which we are next to describe, where the vast majority of the graves belong to the XXVIth dynasty and Ptolemaic times, while those of the XVIIIth or XIXth dynasty and the Roman period are very scarce. The two cemeteries are but a mile apart, and they seem to be complementary. What would tend to confirm this is that there are no ruins of a Ptolemaic or XXVIth dynasty town anywhere near to the Cemetery of Suwa, except the ruins of the ancient Goshen. Two miles to the east of Suwa, beside another little modern town, which would stand full two miles south of Saft el Henneh (Goshen), we found a patch on the edge of the gezireh (now used as a modern cemetery), which was simply packed full of XVIIIth dynasty interments; and away further south, on another portion (see tombs 217-47, Suwa Cem.), where all the surface sand had been just piled in a large heap, preparatory to cultivation, we found burials of the same period (220, 223, 231). When we consider that the only town of importance in this district, at this period, was Goshen, and that no remains of any other ancient village are visible— the district being then practically uninhabited (according to the inscription of Merenptah), we are almost driven to the conclusion that all these burials belong to the same town.

In the Cemetery of Saft, the part nearest to the ancient site and the modern Saft contained the graves of the oldest date. As our men trenched inwards to the south-west, the burials became later and later, till close on the market-place they were all Roman, and most were pot burials of children. Nothing earlier than Ptolemaic was found on the far western edge. Traces of mummy pits like those of Suwa were found, these containing piles of bones all inextricably mixed up, and traces of mud plaster, coloured white and pink, on the sides of the pits.

One of the striking features of the cemetery is the vast preponderance of the plain sand-pit grave over all the other types. It is hardly likely that cheapness is the explanation of this, in a country where bricks cost next to nothing. In any case it shows that there was no religious idea of keeping the body apart from the earth. The slipper-shaped coffins date mostly from the XVIIIth or XIXth dynasties, and were contemporaneous with the sand-pits. Whether it was that they had all been opened, and the sand got in then, or not, every one of them, even the few which appeared to be intact, were packed full of sand. Similarly, in the pot burials of children, again and again they seemed so carefully closed that no sand could get in, and yet every one was full of sand. Often we felt convinced that the pot had been filled with sand at the time of the burial. On the other hand, in the case of the brick-lined, and all the pot-burials, it is difficult not to see an attempt to separate the body from the soil. The same motive, which made them swathe the dead in linen or cotton, and which in several cases made them place four or six large bricks as a protection to the face in a sand-pit grave, led to the protecting of the upper part of the body with a large pot (half-pot graves), and to the double ziyeh burials, and probably to coffin burials of every type.

Judging by the contents, it would appear that all the slipper-shaped coffins were burials of women, and most of the brick-lined and covered graves contained skeletons of men. The men appear to have been buried without any accompaniment, except here and there a pot or two at the head. With the women, on the other hand, there seemed to have been buried everything in the way of dress and ornament and household utensils, on which they set any particular value. The same holds true of the children's burials. What a mother might be expected to keep as a memento, was buried with the child—the beads, bracelets, anklets, rings, and scarabs, which the child wore, were all deposited in the grave. Child-burials probably belonging to the XXIIIrd dynasty have frequently a curious black and yellow double-face pendant bead or charm; and in nearly all of them were found glaze figures of Bes, the protector of infants.

It will be seen most of the pottery was found in the brick-built graves, and the pots were generally placed at the head on the same level as the brick covering of the grave. Often, however, small pots were found inside the brick lining, and sometimes it appeared as if there had never been any brick covering.

More that a dozen graves showed very clearly the cloth wrapping of bodies, and two were specially notable for the thick pink-coloured layers of decayed cloth found in them.

CHAPTER VII

THE CEMETERY OF SUWA

By J. Garrow Duncan, B.D.

64. About one mile south of the gezireh of Saft el Henneh, is another large stretch of unreclaimed gebel, with several villages built on the edge of it. The village of Soweh or Suwa is one of the largest and most beautiful of these. It stands on a part of the gezireh which was a cemetery much used in the later dynasties, and in Ptolemaic times. During our work here, our road led us through lovely groves of palm-trees, and the district around is probably one of the best wooded and watered parts of the Delta. Here and there one comes upon a village pond, with trees and shrubs down to its very edge, and looking more like a small lake, than a mere pond for the convenience of the villagers and their cattle. The Romans have left very distinct traces of their work, in the shape of deep brick-built draw-wells, and brick-built side outlets for irrigation from a canal, which must have been in use in their time, the course of which can still be easily traced. In a walk through this beautifully wooded region, I came upon several such indications of the presence of the Romans, but I found also, several basalt and limestone blocks, one of which bore part of the cartouche of Ramessu II.

On the western side of Suwa, the gezireh has been so much denuded by *sebakh* diggers, that most of the graves here were utterly destroyed, fragments of bones being visible all over the surface. One small part, however, remained, close on the edge of the henneh fields; and this, as will be seen later, was sufficient to show that the burials in this denuded part had all been of Ptolemaic and Roman dates. A much greater part, and probably the more important and valuable, has been put under cultivation for the growth of henneh. When taking in a piece of gebel for cultivation, the natives begin by removing two or three feet of the surface sand, with a kind of flat-bottomed drag, drawn by oxen, and they pile the

sand in heaps, using it up gradually for various purposes. In this way, they sometimes begin cultivating at a level only a few inches above graves, that probably contain valuable information, which is thus lost to the world, at least for the present, if not for ever. It was very annoying, in passing through the henneh fields, actually to see the rings of pot-mouths or pot-bottoms on the surface of the path, and yet be unable to unearth them. This lower portion of the gezireh west of Suwa, and close to it, was of comparatively soft sand, and easily worked, which explains why so much of it had been denuded. The higher portion was of very hard gebel, and the tombs there are accordingly of totally different classes. We began work on the higher gebel, between Suwa and the modern cemetery to the west, and adopted very much the same methods as at Saft, where practicable.

65. The graves of this cemetery fall into the following classes:

I. Sand-pits.

II. Square pit graves, which had originally been covered probably with a dome roof of bricks, to a few feet above the ground; these were plain, or lined with coloured plaster, or mummy pits.

III. Four-chambered square pits, which had been roofed like Class II, and which had a built shaft for entrance. The chambers all communicated with each other.

IV. Deep shaft-pit and chamber tombs; these all contained mummies of the Ptolemaic period.

Modes of burial:

I. Cloth wrapping.

II. Mummifying.

III. Clay face coffins. Most of these were found in square pit graves of Classes III and IV.

IV. Wooden coffins.

V. Stone coffins.

The following is a description of the selected tombs:

66. I. Sand-pits. This class of burial was found only in one portion of the cemetery. On the north-eastern edge of the lower part, skirting the henneh fields, a narrow ridge of sand had been left, much less denuded by the *sebakhin*. Here about 70 graves were opened and recorded. They belonged to what had been an extensive cemetery, covering all the lower and the softer part of the gezireh on the west of the village; but, as already mentioned, by far the greater part of this lower cemetery had been destroyed through the removal of vast quantities of sand by the *sebakhin*. Here and there the remains of a grave

were found containing enough to indicate that they belonged to the Ptolemaic and Roman periods, like the rest of the graves found on this ridge. The depth measurements frequently show that there had been considerable denudation on the ridge too. The arrangement of the body was the same as at Saft el Henneh.

Grave 47 was 60 inches l. × 40 w. × 25 d. The body had lain on its back, with the head to the west. Two red pots, about 14 inches high, nos. 130, 210, another form, nos. 338, 339, which may be conveniently referred to as the two-eared cooking pot, and a very small red pot, about 5 inches high with short out-sloping neck, were found in the tomb. The first type was similar to the pottery found at Sharanba, but rougher. It had been used apparently for holding some dry material, such as meal or flour, and the neck, narrow in proportion to the body, was just wide enough to admit a woman's hand. XXVIth dynasty.

Tomb 59 : 70 × 50 w. × 40 d. The skeleton lay on the south side of the pit, head to the west. Along the north side, from the top corner downwards, were arranged a wide-mouthed rough red pot, no. 263, followed by two other, no. 210. Both were burned black as if they had been used for cooking, and on one lay a saucer of the "lid" type, no. 229. The tomb contained also a black saucer of Ptolemaic make, as no. 218.

Tomb 61 measured 70 × 50 × 40 w. The skeleton lay on back, with the head to the west. Under the feet was a deep rough red basin with flat bottom, no. 225 ; and between the left leg and the side of the tomb a red pot with pointed bottom, no. 132, a jar, no. 154, and a smaller pot with two black bands, no. 293. XXXth dynasty.

Tomb 63 was normal, and contained two long pots, no. 205, which had held grain, and were sealed with mud. They stood by the left foot and right shoulder. At the left shoulder stood a long white double-eared water-pot, with pointed bottom, no. 212.

Tomb 79 : 60 × 40 d. × 30 w. Head to north-west. No bones. Ptolemaic coin from centre. Five glazed figures from where the skull had been, including one Bes, two double-face pendants, and one pot, no. 205.

Tomb 83 contained the potsherd with the three lines of demotic inscription, XXXIX L, 16 ; the same words being written three times with slight modification.

Most of these sand-pits had been rifled before, as is plain from the complete absence of bones from many, and the way the pots were found in them.

The pottery was frequently lying in a heap in the centre, and as often bottom up as otherwise.

67. II. Pits, Plain and Colour-plastered. On the higher gebel there was a large number of square-pit graves cut in the hard soil. Sometimes the sides of these were plastered with plain mud plaster. A few were covered with a finer plaster, and coloured blue, white, or pink, or contained coloured clay coffins. Both types are varieties of one class. Often the pits were so denuded that it was impossible to say with certainty what class they belonged to, and several of them were simply masses of bones from broken mummies. In one part of the cemetery, where grave robbers had left a hollow of considerable size, the sides of the hollow showed bones protruding in confusion, and in such numbers, that the place had the appearance of having been used as one large grave, into which bodies had been packed till it could hold no more. Among some of these, where bodies had been piled above each other with evidently nothing between, our men found such quantities of blue glaze beads of various forms, as took sometimes two days' steady work to separate from the soil.

A. *Coloured plaster tombs.* Grave 1 was a pit 60 inches × 50 w. × 30 d., and contained at least 4 skeletons, three side by side—two with head to south, one head to north. A fourth lay under one of these. They had not been mummied, but all appeared to have been enclosed in plaster and mud coffins. The sides of the pit were covered with pink-coloured plaster.

Grave 39 had its sides similarly plastered, measuring 80 × 60 × 25 inches deep. Traces were found of two skeletons, lying on right side with heads to west. Scattered over the tomb were eleven pots, nos. 163, 165, 200, 249, 259, 319. Most of them were full of hard mud, as if they had contained liquid. XXXth dynasty.

B. *Plain pits.* Some of these had contained mummies ; others were plain burials with the corpse placed inside a brick-built coffin ; and in others we found complete clay faces, which had been affixed to the lids of rough clay coffins.

Grave 99 was an ordinary pit of this class, and had been rifled. In it were found two small blue glazed figures and a clay moulded face, covered with white plaster, and painted green.

The glazed figures are unquestionably XVIIIth dynasty work, and give us thus a date for these clay faces. They must at least have been used at that period.

Grave 23 was a square pit, which probably had an arched roof above ground ; but it is quite possible that it had been originally a deep shaft-pit grave. Inside were several mummies laid one above another, all more or less destroyed. Between two of them lay three inscribed altars, Pl. XXXIX. Three small rough red pots, no. 147, were found in the filling. XXVIth dynasty.

Grave 89 was close on the edge of the modern cemetery. It was almost entirely wasted by *sebakhin*. In it was found a bronze situla (XXXVIII A) with a thick mud cake in the bottom.

Grave 95 was a large square brick-lined pit, now about 40 inches deep, and 80 inches each side. It must have been roofed with bricks originally, which had fallen in. The skeleton lay on a brick-built ledge in the centre, and was bricked round and overhead. Above the brick covering over the right shoulder and arm, were laid three bronze situlae (XXXVIII A). Half-way down the filling was a rough red bowl, no. 251. The clay face of a woman, plastered white, with eyes and eye-brows done in black, and a blue glaze *uza* eye, complete the contents. The grave had been opened before, though the skeleton remained evidently untouched in its brick-built coffin. It lay on the back, with head on right side, and to the west. Probably XXVIth dynasty.

Grave 101 measured 80 × 80 × 40 inches. In it were found a limestone figure of Bast (?) and a limestone bead, a blue glaze *uza* eye, fifteen small pots and a small altar of offerings all scattered in the filling. The pots represent altogether twelve different types, nos. 149, 157, 158, 159, 167, 177, 179, 189, 194, 195, 198 A, 265, the most notable of which is the small pot with the dwarf ears, which serve also as the ears of a Bes face incised on the side of it. A clay face, plastered white, was also found in it. XXVIth dynasty.

In grave 131 were found a green glaze elephant pendant or charm, a blue glaze *uza* eye, dark blue cat and Bast pendants, and several small flat glaze beads. XXVIth dynasty.

Grave 171 was perhaps the best specimen which we found of a square pit brick-built and arched over. It was roofed with red burnt bricks about three feet down, and the men cut through the roof. No trace of any other entrance could be found. There were at least twenty-nine skulls in the tomb. Nothing else was found but a few *uza* eye beads of the XXVIth dynasty colour.

Grave 205. In this tomb several pieces of blue glaze Naukratite ware were found, of which one piece was decorated with the Assyrian winged lion. The rest of the saucer showed other traces of Syrian influence, no. 16. The bowl 242 was here also.

Graves 25 and 26 contained masses of mummy bones, in an inextricable jumble. In 25 were found three glaze figures of a necklace, and at the pelvis, beads of the usual type. In 26 were six skulls, and two small pots, nos. 280, 322, and a blue glaze figure of Bast. The small round pot contained caked mud. Both are of Ptolemaic date.

Grave 90 measured 70 inches × 60 w. × 30 d. One side of it contained a skeleton on back with head to the south. A mud face, finely moulded, lay on the face of the skull. A blue glazed necklace was found at the neck. Ptolemaic.

Grave 128 was Ptolemaic. It was brick-walled, and the shaft entrance remained also brick-built, showing how these graves were entered. A red saucer, with ring bottom, several flat blue glazed beads, a crystal bead, several glaze figures, and a remarkable bearded double-face pendant were found scattered in the tomb. It had been rifled.

68. III. FOUR-CHAMBERED SQUARE PITS. The surface of these had in some cases been so worn away, that the chambers were often not more than 40 inches deep. Originally the body of the tomb had been excavated in the hard gebel. Walls of sun-dried brick were then built in, dividing it into four rooms of about equal dimensions, and in each wall a door was left so that one could walk round the whole enclosure from any one of them. The whole had afterwards been roofed with brick, the roof taking the form of a dome or arch. This type of tomb is well known at Nebesheh and Retabeh, of the XXIIIrd—XXVIth dynasties.

On one side a square pit with or without steps led down to the only entrance. Tombs of a very similar class are built at the present day on the south-eastern edge of the gezireh of Saft el Henneh; they are usually altogether underground, and covered over with sand except the entrance pit. It is easy to see that tombs of this class would be an easy prey to the spoiler.

Tombs 106 and 108 were adjacent chambers of a pit of this class. The other two chambers were empty. The whole was 18 feet square, and about 42 inches deep. The dividing brick walls were 3 feet thick, and the chambers were all closely equal in size. Bones were found in both, and the skeletons were apparently arranged in the usual way, with the head to the south-west, and lying on the back. In tomb 106 three pots were found (nos. 151, 177, 309), all of them XXVIth dynasty types, and fine blue glaze pendant figures.

In tomb 108 there were masses of bones belonging to at least six skeletons. Six clay faces, painted black and white, and two of them with red were found, though not all complete. Three blue glaze figures, a lead earring, and one *uza* eye bead were also picked up in the filling.

Tomb 135 adjacent contained seven pots of similar types and a bronze bracelet. Of these pots one had distinct traces of burnt ashes inside. In another traces of grain, in another of mud, and in another a lump of bitumen were found. For types of pots, which were all scattered, see nos. 139, 154, 195, 196, 287, 296. The stand no. 113 may be an earlier piece re-used. XXXth dynasty.

Tombs 109, 114, 115, 116 formed another such tomb. The whole measured 19 feet square and 36 inches deep. The dividing walls were 34 inches wide, and the rooms practically equal in size. The bodies lay as usual on back and with head to the south. In 109 one skeleton had been on a raised brick ledge running down the centre. Two others, or more, had been buried, one on each side of it. On the east side a large quantity of glaze beads, of 5 different colours, were taken from the pelvis of one skeleton. They were of the type usually found in the same position. A well-made red pot tapering to a blunt point at the bottom, and with mouth broken, lay at the head. One clay face, a blue glaze bird pendant, and a blue glaze figure of Bast were also found in the filling. At the head of the burial on the western side were found a small flat limestone slab, well-finished, measuring about 8 inches square and 1 inch thick, and what had been the base or capital of a small limestone pillar. This latter measured about 5 inches square at bottom, and the circular part above it was about 4 inches in diameter (see A. 76). Neither was inscribed. Behind these two stones at the very head of this burial on the western side three pots stood— one a curious red baked drinking pot of the XVIIIth dynasty (see Pl. XXXVII A), with a gazelle's head at the bottom. The other two were of much coarser types and distinctly of a late make, no. 318. No beads were found.

In the centre the skeleton lay in a brick-lined space, and had been covered over with bricks, another burial having been placed on the top of it at a later date. At the pelvis of the lower skeleton a large quantity of beads of the usual type were found. In tomb 114, jar no. 213 was found.

Tomb 115 was the south-west chamber of the group. On the east side of it, with the head just at the door leading into tomb 116, the body evidently of a woman had been buried. At the chest and pelvis large quantities of glaze beads were found, of five different kinds. Those found at the pelvis were of the usual type, and coloured red, blue, and black. At the chest beads of this type were mixed with small round glaze, single and double, beads. In this same chamber at the door leading into tomb 109 three small vases of the Greek black and red type were found, nos. 17, 18, 19. They had evidently been buried at the feet of a skeleton, which had entirely disappeared, and they lay quite close to the three pots found in tomb 109.

In all these four chambers the skeletons lay on the back, and the head invariably pointed to the south-west side of the tomb. They were not mummies, the bones were all white, and they had probably all been originally enclosed in rough mud coffins with clay modelled and painted faces on the lids, as in neighbouring tombs of the same type.

Tomb 190 (S.W. corner) contained bronze rings, blue glaze pendants, and a black and yellow double-face pendant.

69. IV. SHAFT-PIT AND CHAMBER TOMBS. These were all mummy tombs of the Ptolemaic period, and naturally they were found in the part of the gezireh where the ground was hard gebel. There had at one time been a great many more than now exist, and we left many unopened. At several places the natives, not caring to seek the shaft, or in the process of carrying away the black earth for *sebakh*, had worked straight in from the face of the upper part of the gezireh, often thus clearing away the shaft and all the earth above the roof of the chamber, so that we found chambers of shaft-pit tombs on the present ground-level. Several of these had elaborate stairways down to them to a depth of 12 or 15 feet, but usually there was simply a shaft of about 30 inches square leading straight down. At the bottom of the shaft the doors of the chamber were invariably built up with brick. As a rule no jewellery or pottery was found in any of these, nor any indication of the date beyond what the mummies themselves afforded. In one or two altar slabs were found. They will be noted afterwards.

Tomb 143. About 10 inches down the shaft an inscribed flat altar was found in the filling, which had evidently been thrown back at the last moment when the tomb was rifled. At the bottom of the shaft, close to the brick-built wall which shut the door of the chamber, was another complete limestone altar, and under the bricks a portion of a third was found.

Tomb 146. At the bottom of the shaft the door of the chamber had been built up with burnt bricks, afterwards covered with a thick coating of mud plaster and painted red. Several mummies were found in the chamber, all badly broken. Near the side wall of the chamber two more of these flat altars, one inscribed, were found (no. 42). A small black pot, neck broken, was also found in the filling.

Tomb 21. Here the shaft was about 12 feet deep and the chamber measured 8 feet × 4. Two bodies lay side by side on back with heads to the west. They were finely gilded mummies of the Ptolemaic type, but so brittle that even the heads could not be removed entire.

Tomb 41. The shaft was quite cut away here by *sebakhin*. A terra-cotta figure of a woman with a large aureole behind the head, was found in the filling only 30 inches under the present surface : this type is common in early Roman times.

70. THE DISPOSITION OF THE BODY. From the various burials described, it will be seen that, in the disposition of the body, five methods were followed in this cemetery.

(1) Wrapping. In the sand-pits, the body had simply been swathed in linen, and placed on its back, with the hands by the sides, and the head as near as possible to the west.

(2) Mummifying. After the body was preserved, it was wrapped in many folds of coarse linen, plastered on the surface, and painted and gilded. The body was laid in the usual direction, head to west.

(3) Clay face coffins. In all the square pit tombs, whether four-chambered or not, the bodies seem first to have been wrapped in cloth, then placed in a rough clay coffin, one of which we found complete. On the lid of the coffin, above the face of the dead, a clay face, modelled and painted, was affixed evidently by wooden pins. The holes where these had pierced the faces could be seen. From the variety of types found, it appears that the clay faces were intended to reproduce the features of the dead. The arrangement otherwise was as usual. Great quantities of beads and pendant figures (glazed) were found in this class of burial.

For clay faces see graves 15, 30, 90, 99, 101, 102, 108, 118, 119, 155, 173.

(4) Wooden coffins. In some cases wooden coffins were used, and one complete wooden coffin was found in grave 28, enclosing a mummy of a type belonging to the Ptolemaic period.

In tombs 1 and 12 particularly distinct traces of wooden coffins were found. The arrangement otherwise was normal, and the burial in a square pit.

(5) Stone coffin. Only one such was found. It seemed to have been buried at the bottom of the shaft of tomb 23, where the first limestone altars were found. It measured 9 feet long × 3 w. × 3 d., and contained a mummy. The coffin had been hollowed out of a single block of limestone, and the lid was so massive that it needed five or six men to remove it. There was no inscription inside or out.

71. THE GRAVES AT ALI MARAH. Two or three miles to the south-east of Suwa along the gezireh there is a village named Ali Marah, close to which is an ancient cemetery now almost entirely within the bounds of the modern cemetery. Twenty-two graves were examined here on the confines of the modern cemetery, and every one proved to belong to the XVIIIth or XIXth dynasty. They were all plain sand-pits or brick-lined graves, and in all details of arrangement closely resembled the burials of the same date in the gezireh of Saft el Henneh.

Grave 217 was a pottery face coffin burial (slipper-shaped), and contained ten small pots of various types belonging to the XVIIIth and XIXth dynasties, two scarabs, blue pendants and other beads, a small white glaze pot with mud in the bottom, and some bronze. The pots included two of the Cypriote type, no. 6, one double-eared, see no. 111, and other foreign vases, nos. 4, 5, 7, and 8, three alabaster pots (XXXIX L, 2), and five larger, nos. 55, 56, 61, 93, and 106. A coffin face and two small red saucers completed the contents. The burial was normal in arrangement.

In graves 226 and 232 gold earrings were found.

Graves 228 to 247 were all in this place, and the pottery and beads found in them are all of the same period. In 237 three gold earrings, and two XVIIIth dynasty pots, three scarabs, and blue glaze pendants of same date were found.

A little further to the south in a patch of sand just being prepared for cultivation, several graves were found belonging to the same date.

Graves 220 to 223 were situated here. 220 was brick-lined to the height of the body, and brick-covered, and contained one pilgrim-bottle, no. 111.

Grave 221 was a shallow and narrow mud brick grave, and contained one red pot of XVIIIth dynasty, full of caked mud, and a large white basin of the same period.

Grave 222 was a pottery coffin burial with the head to the west. Inside of it were found two jasper hair-rings.

Grave 223 was a brick-built and covered grave. Outside of the covering at the head stood a large red pot of the same type and date as in grave 221.

The graves of Ali Marah and this patch of gezireh have already been commented on in my notes on the Cemetery of Goshen.

INDEX

Printed by Hazell, Watson & Vine , Ld., London and Aylesbury.

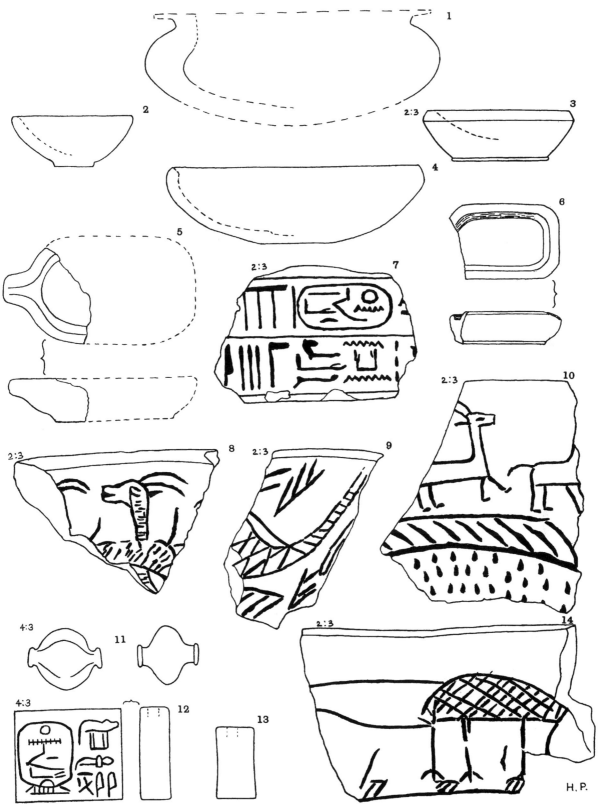

H.P.

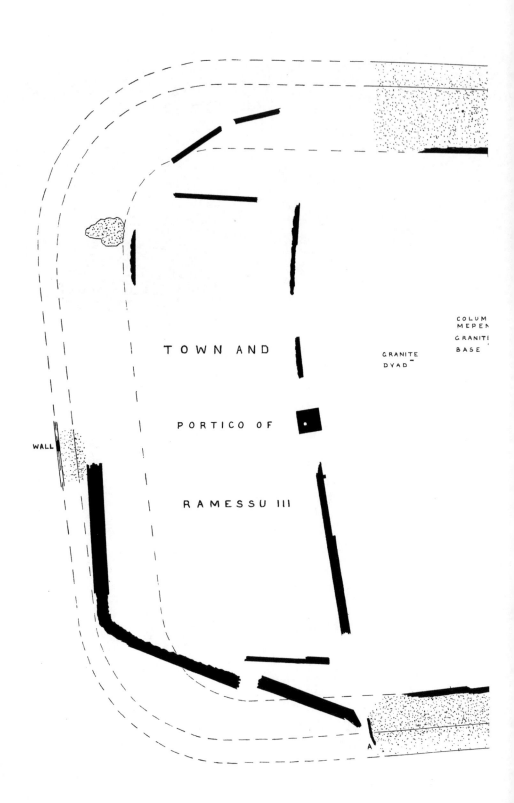

TOWN AND

PORTICO OF

RAMESSU III

WALL

GRANITE
DYAD

COLUM
MEPEN

GRANITE
BASE

A

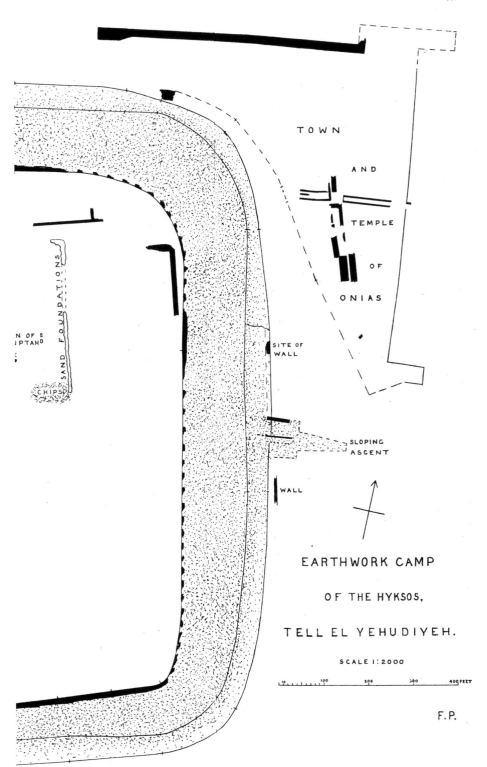

II.

TOWN

AND

TEMPLE

OF

ONIAS

SITE OF
WALL

SLOPING
ASCENT

WALL

SAND FOUNDATIONS

N OF
IPTAH

CHIPS

EARTHWORK CAMP

OF THE HYKSOS,

TELL EL YEHUDIYEH.

SCALE 1:2000

10   100   200   300   400 FEET

F.P.

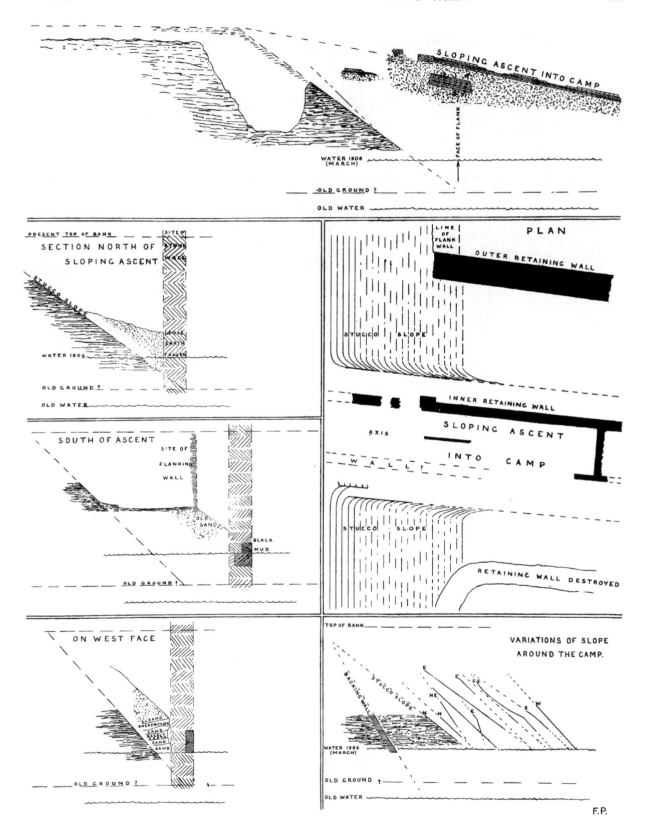

F.P.

MODEL OF HYKSOS CAMP, SHEWING EASTERN ENTRANCE.

THE STUCCO SLOPE.

THE SAND EMBANKMENT AT PRESENT.

RETAINING WALL INSIDE STUCCO SLOPE.

INNER SIDE OF SAND EMBANKMENT.

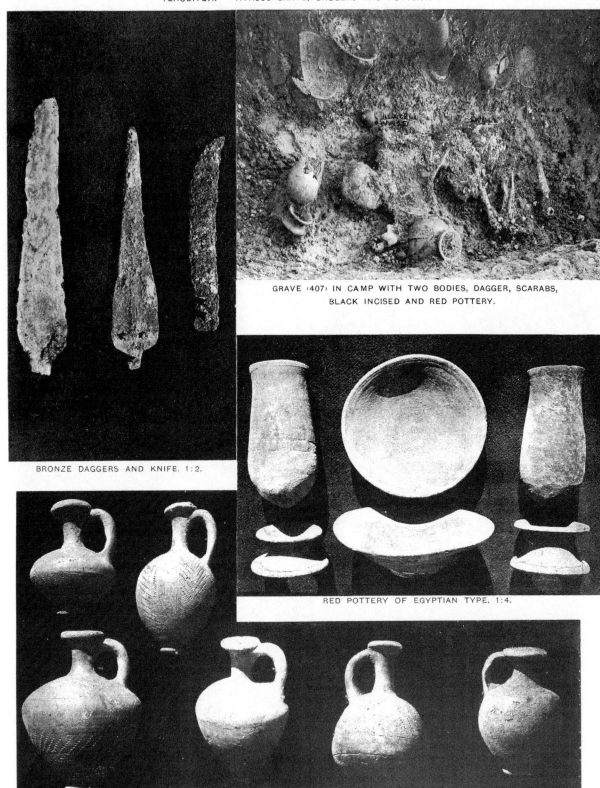

GRAVE (407) IN CAMP WITH TWO BODIES, DAGGER, SCARABS,
BLACK INCISED AND RED POTTERY.

BRONZE DAGGERS AND KNIFE. 1:2.

RED POTTERY OF EGYPTIAN TYPE. 1:4.

BLACK INCISED POTTERY OF FOREIGN TYPE. 1:3.

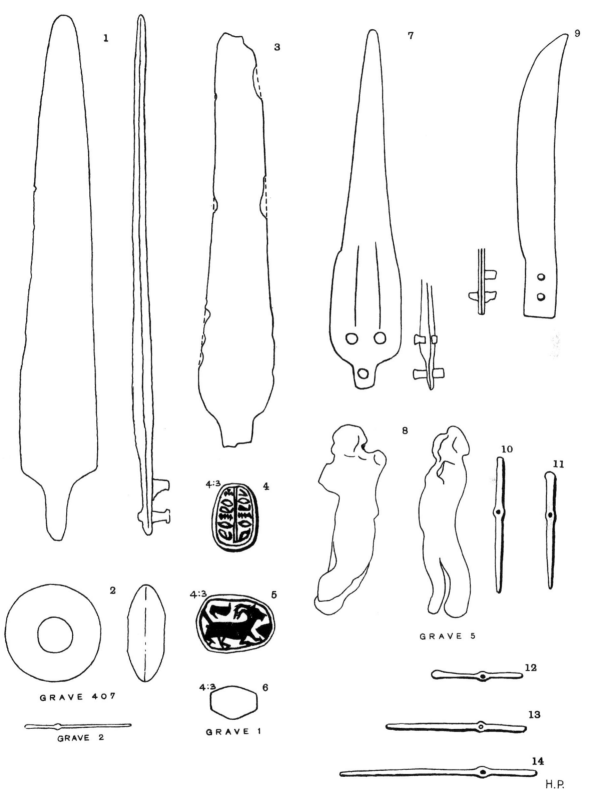

GRAVE 407

GRAVE 2

GRAVE 1

GRAVE 5

H.P.

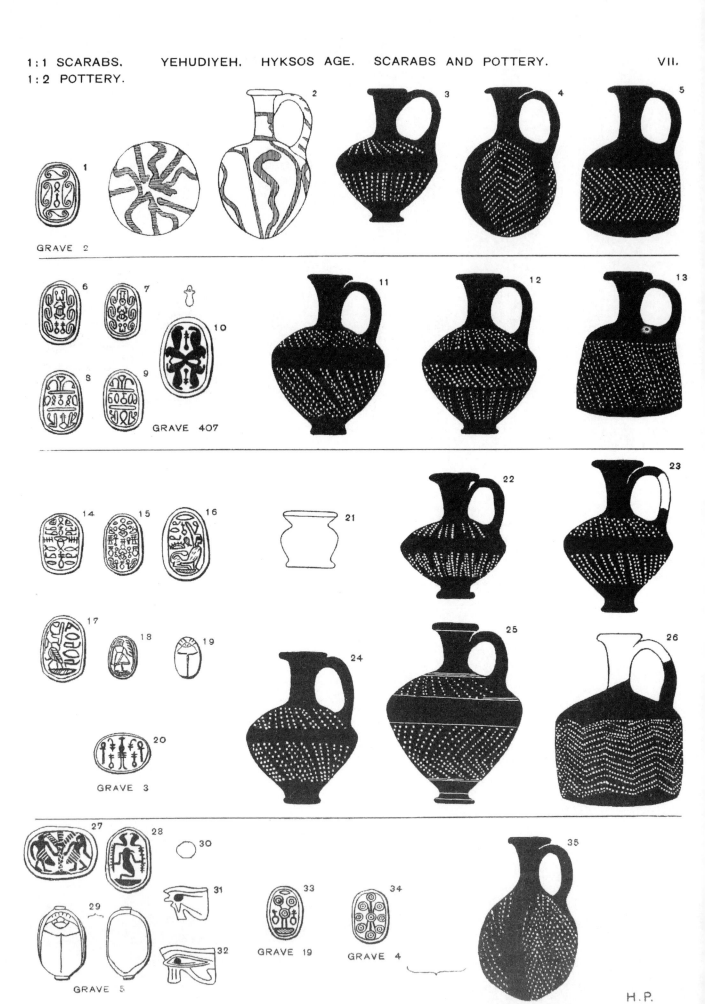

GRAVE 2

GRAVE 407

GRAVE 3

GRAVE 19   GRAVE 4

GRAVE 5

H.P.

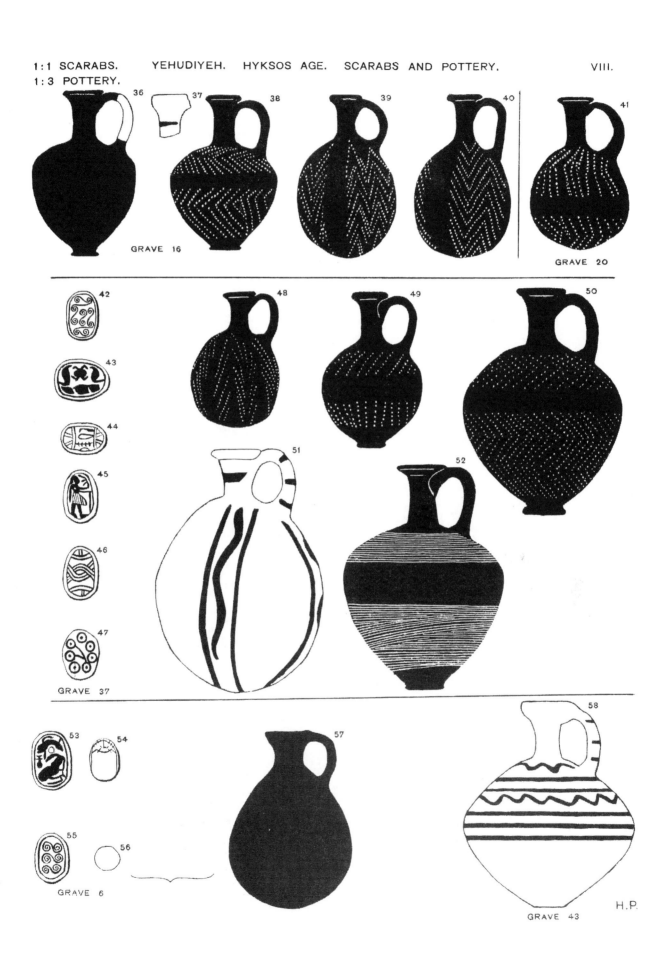

GRAVE 16

GRAVE 20

GRAVE 37

GRAVE 6

GRAVE 43

H.P.

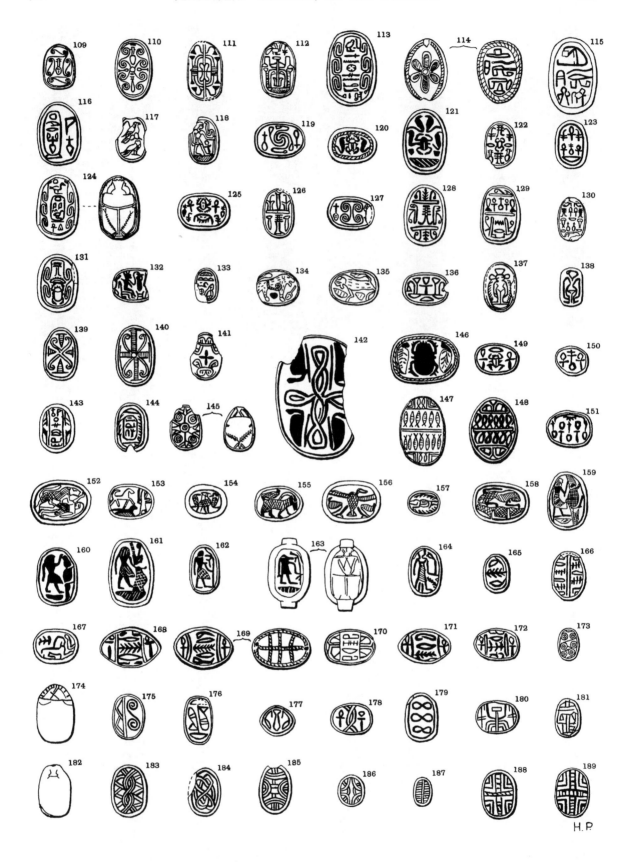

H.P.

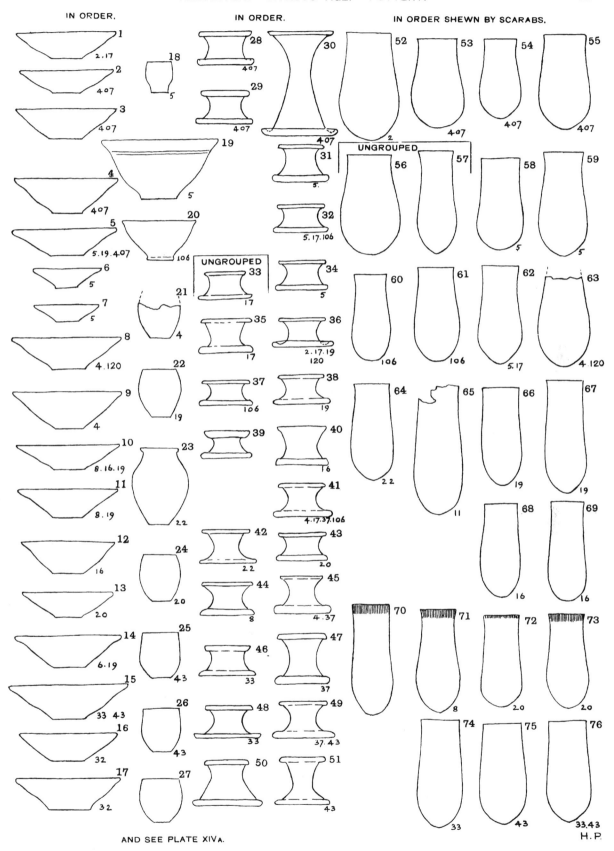

IN ORDER.　　　　　　IN ORDER.　　　　IN ORDER SHEWN BY SCARABS.

UNGROUPED

AND SEE PLATE XIVA.

H.P.

jar handle

plaster cap of jar

with iron spear

H.P.

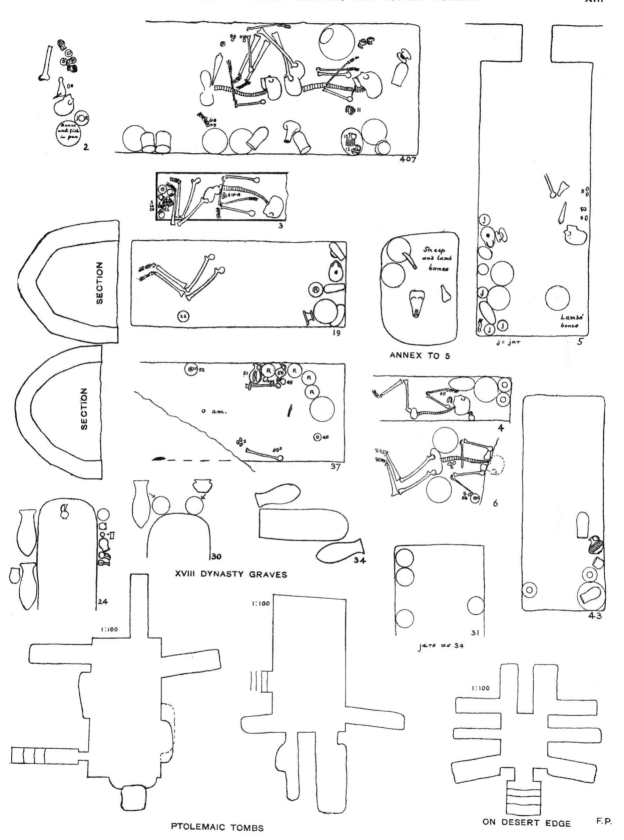

SECTION

SECTION

ANNEX TO 5

j = jar

Sheep and lamb bones

Lamb bones

Bones and fish in pan

2

407

3

19

5

37

4

6

43

30

XVIII DYNASTY GRAVES

24

1:100

1:100

31

jars as 34

34

PTOLEMAIC TOMBS

1:100

ON DESERT EDGE   F.P.

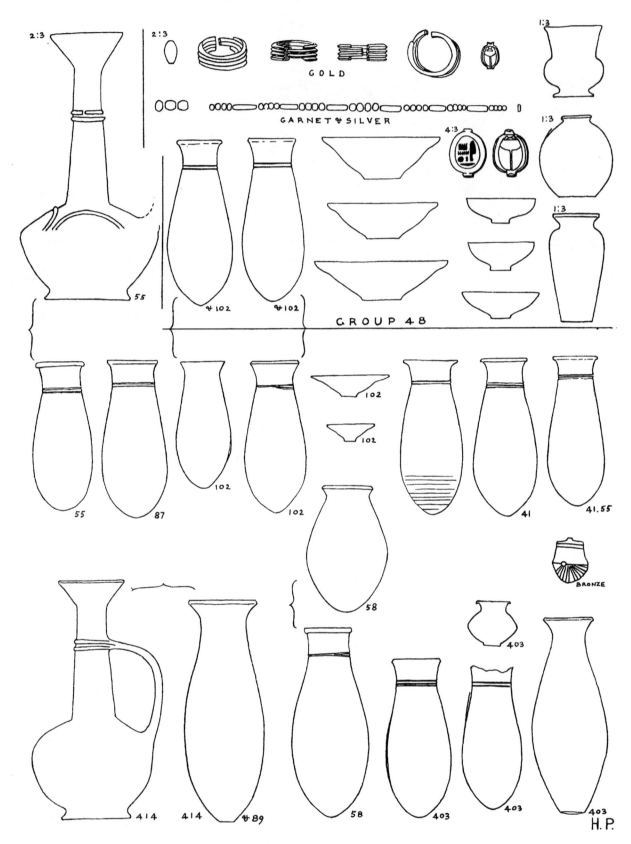

GOLD

GARNET & SILVER

GROUP 48

BRONZE

H.P.

H.P.

KNEELING FIGURE OF HOR, ADMIRAL OF THE MEDITERRANEAN UNDER PSAMTEK II.

SIDE OF COFFIN OF MEN.

LID OF COFFIN OF MEN.

POTTERY COFFER, TAHUTMES III.

QUARTZITE CORN GRINDERS.

H.P.

H.P.

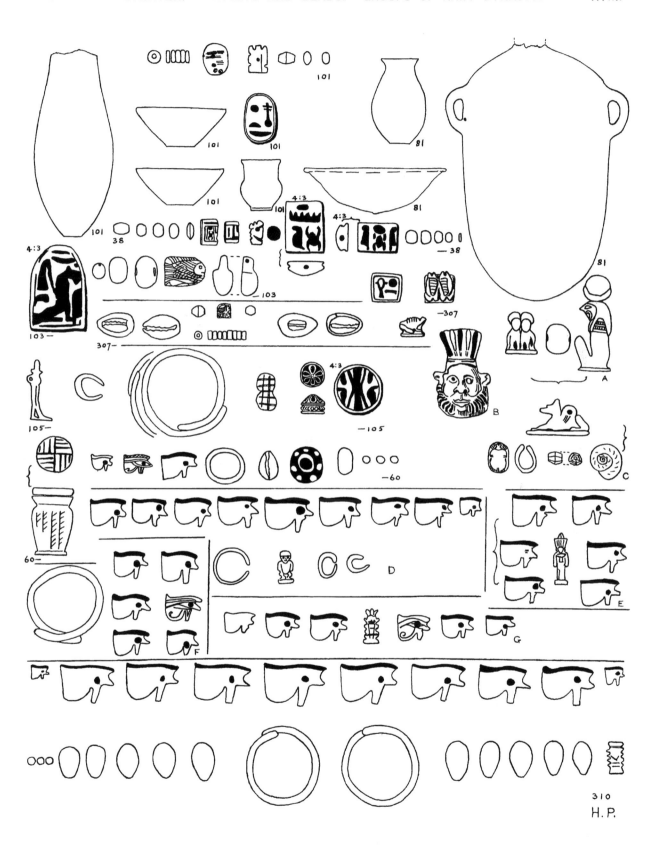

310
H.P.

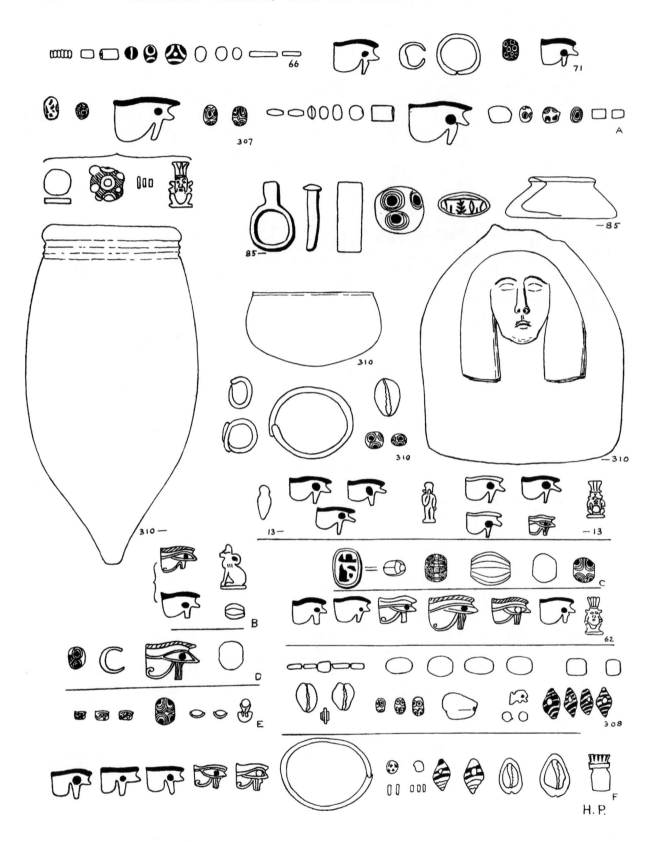

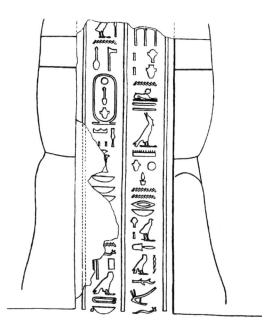

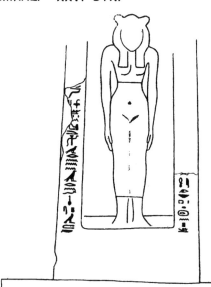

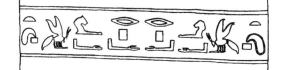

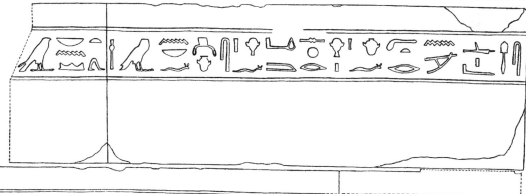

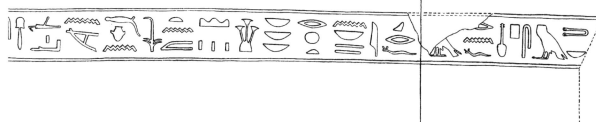

H.P.

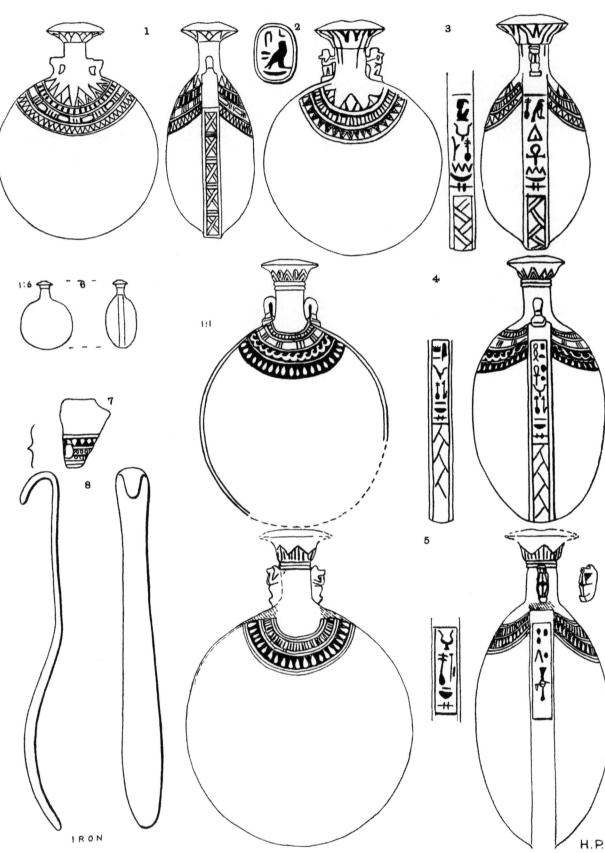

IRON

H.P.

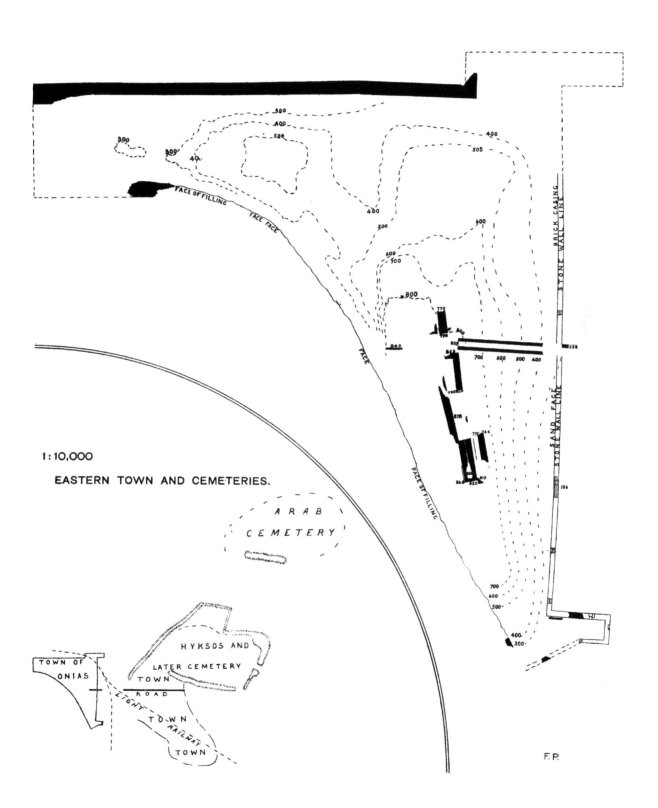

1:10,000

EASTERN TOWN AND CEMETERIES.

FACE OF FILLING

FACE   FACE

FACE

FACE OF FILLING

BRICK CASING
STONE WALL LINE

STONE WALL FACE
SAND FACE

ARAB
CEMETERY

HYKSOS AND
LATER CEMETERY
TOWN OF
ONIAS
TOWN
ROAD
LIGHT
TOWN
TOWN
RAILWAY
TOWN

F. P.

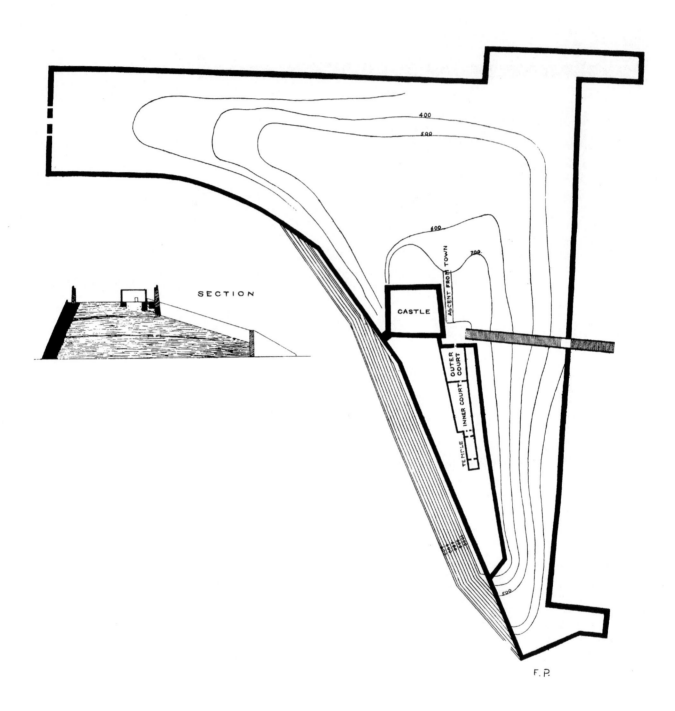

SECTION

CASTLE

ASCENT FROM TOWN

TEMPLE INNER COURT OUTER COURT

400
500
600
700
500

F. P.

MODEL OF RESTORATION, FROM THE EAST SIDE.

BRICKING ROUND OFFERING CYLINDER.

OFFERING CYLINDER BARED.

WEST FACED, SHEWING STRATIFICATION.

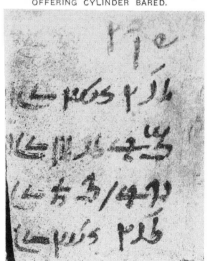

BRICK ACCOUNT OF BUILDERS.

EAST FACE SHEWING GREAT STAIR ↑ FROM EASTERN ROAD.

MODEL FROM SOUTH END.   STAIRWAY SIDE SOUTH WITH PLASTER.   STAIRWAY WITH ROAD LINE BELOW.

CORNICE OF EASTERN WALL.

FRAGMENTS OF ARCHITECTURAL DECORATION.

GREAT WALL ON EASTERN SIDE.

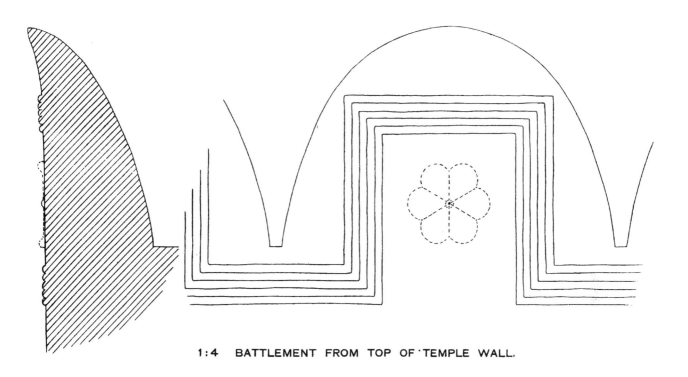

1:4   BATTLEMENT FROM TOP OF TEMPLE WALL.

F. P.

1:40   ELEVATION OF EASTERN FRONT WALL.

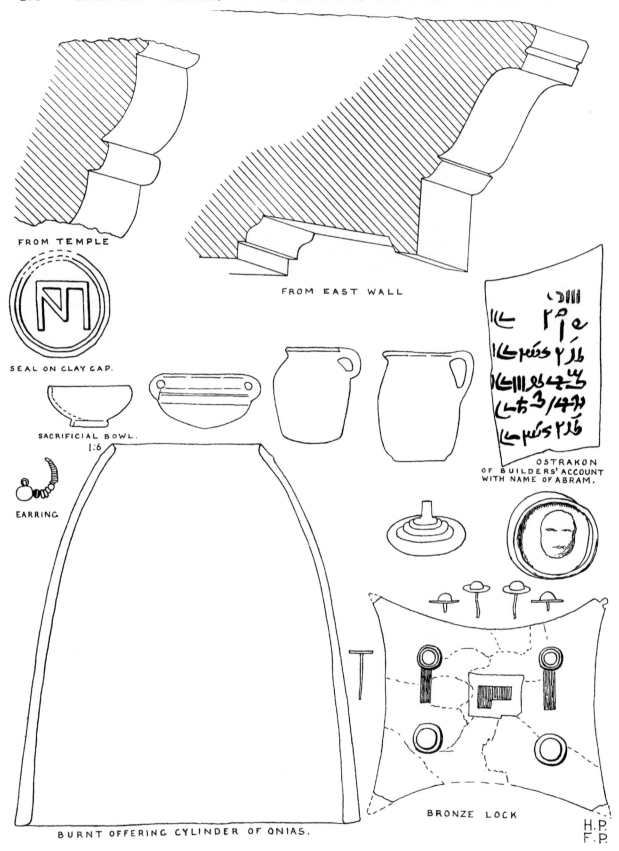

FROM TEMPLE

FROM EAST WALL

SEAL ON CLAY CAP.

SACRIFICIAL BOWL.
1:6

EARRING

OSTRAKON
OF BUILDERS' ACCOUNT
WITH NAME OF ABRAM.

BURNT OFFERING CYLINDER OF ONIAS.

BRONZE LOCK

H.P.
F.P.

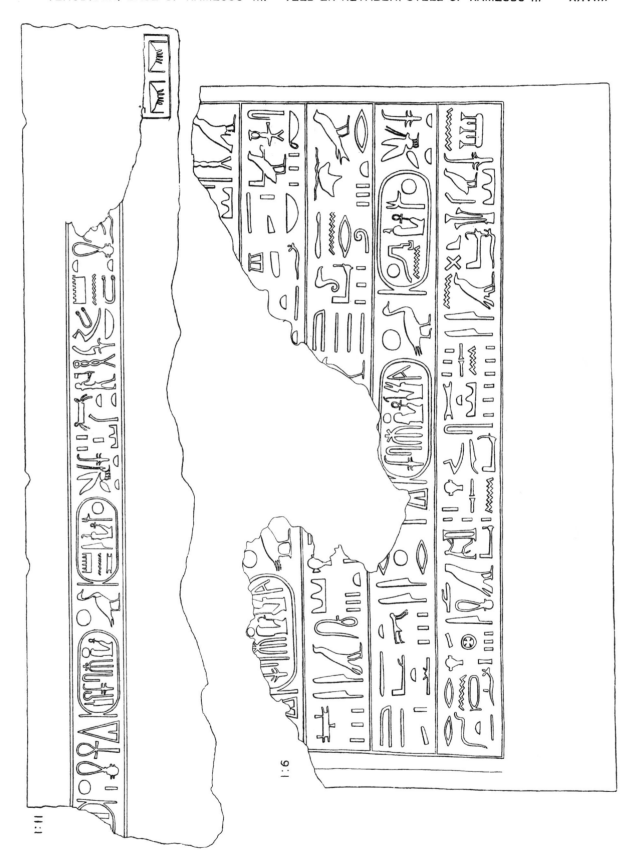

H.P.

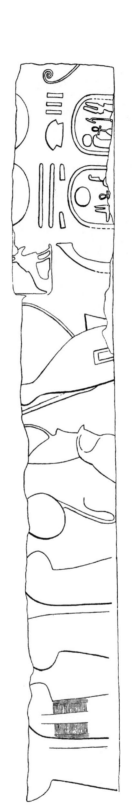

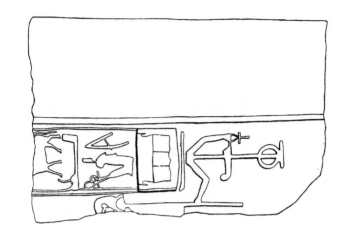

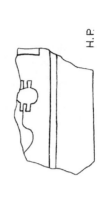

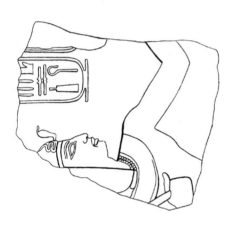

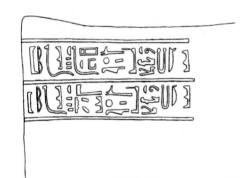

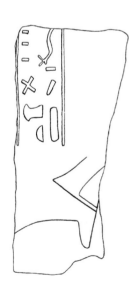

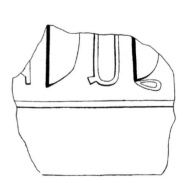

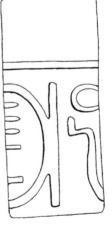

AMULETS, XXII DYNASTY.

GRANITE DYAD RAMESSU II AND ATMU.

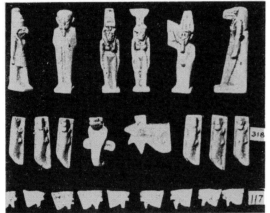

AMULETS, XXVI DYNASTY.

GRANITE STELE RAMESSU II.

BLUE GLAZED FROG BOWL, XXII DYNASTY.

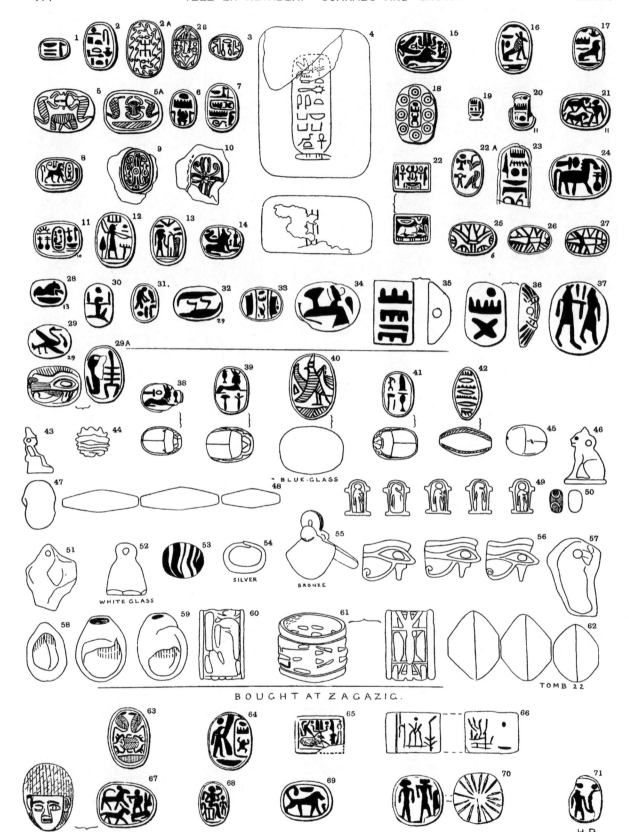

BLUE·GLASS

SILVER

BRONZE

WHITE GLASS

TOMB 22

BOUGHT AT ZAGAZIG.

H.P.

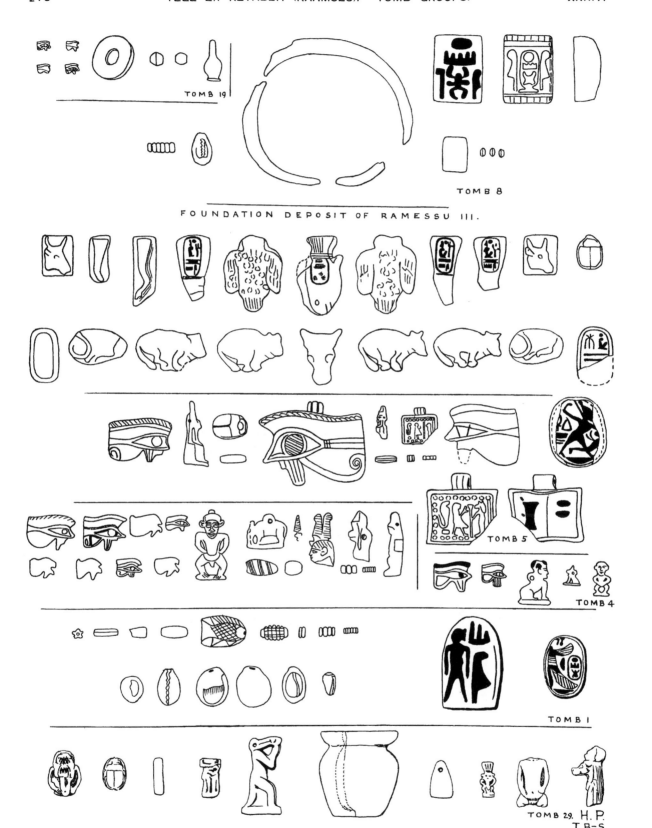

TOMB 19

TOMB 8

FOUNDATION DEPOSIT OF RAMESSU III.

TOMB 5

TOMB 4

TOMB 1

TOMB 29.   H. P.
T. B-S.

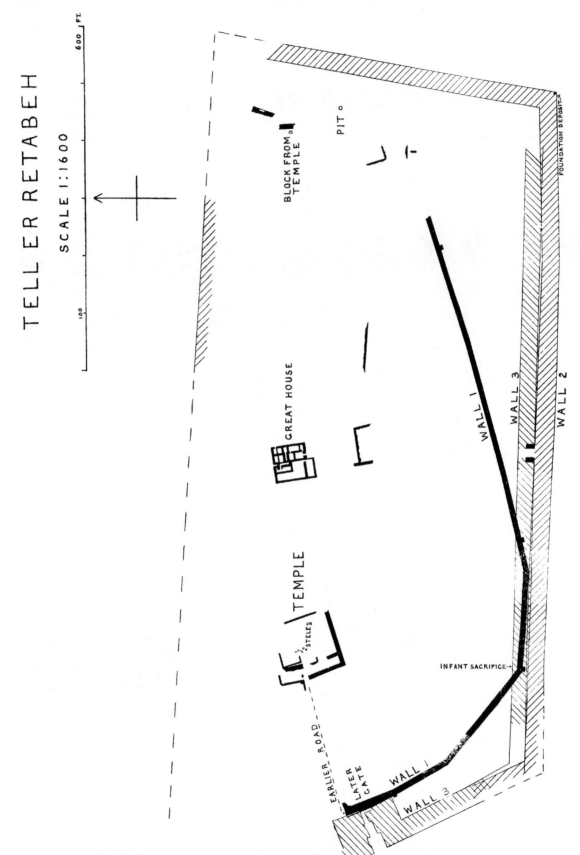

TELL ER RETABEH

SCALE 1:1600

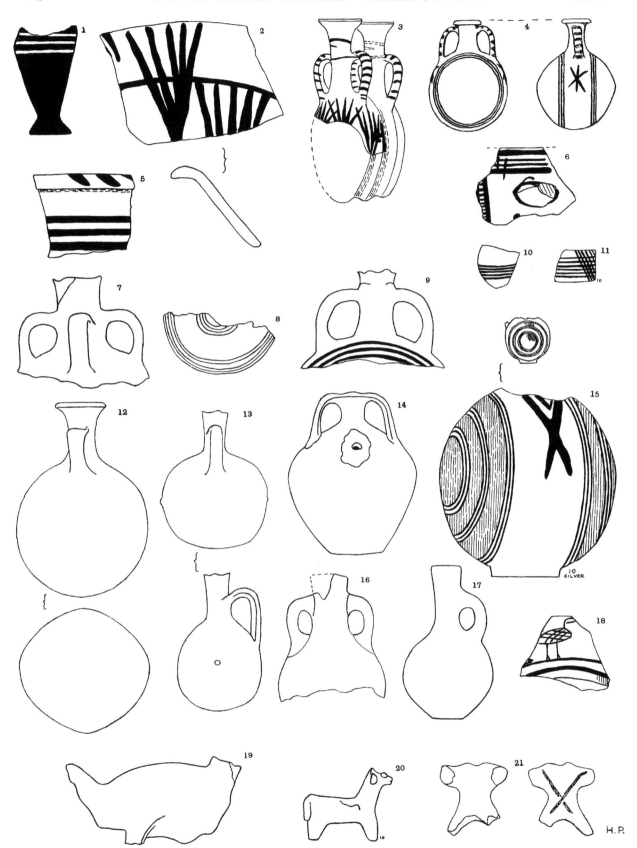

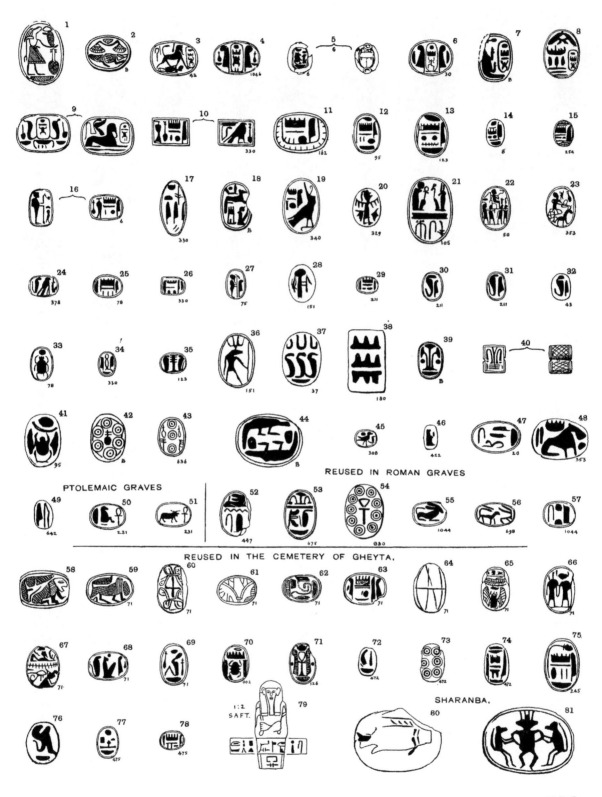

PTOLEMAIC GRAVES

REUSED IN ROMAN GRAVES

REUSED IN THE CEMETERY OF GHEYTA.

1:2
SAFT.

SHARANBA.

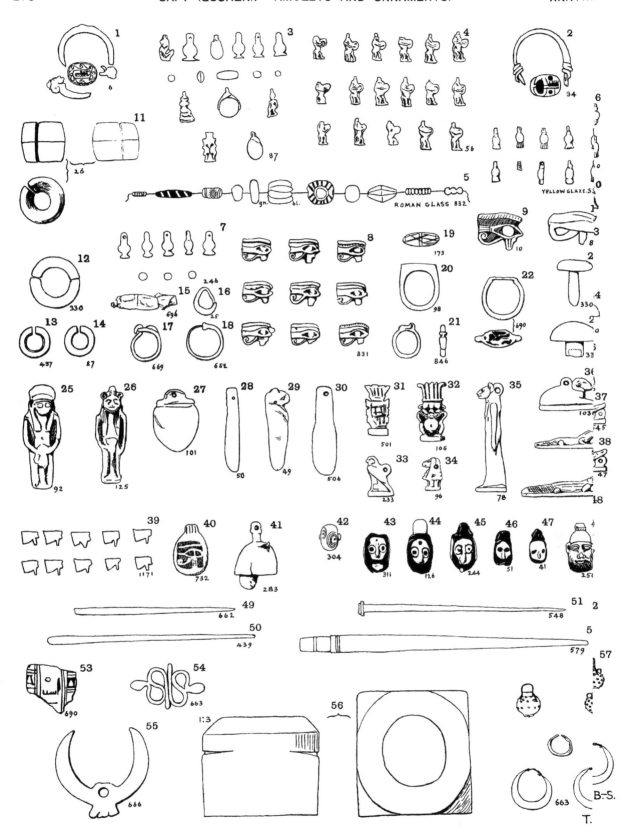

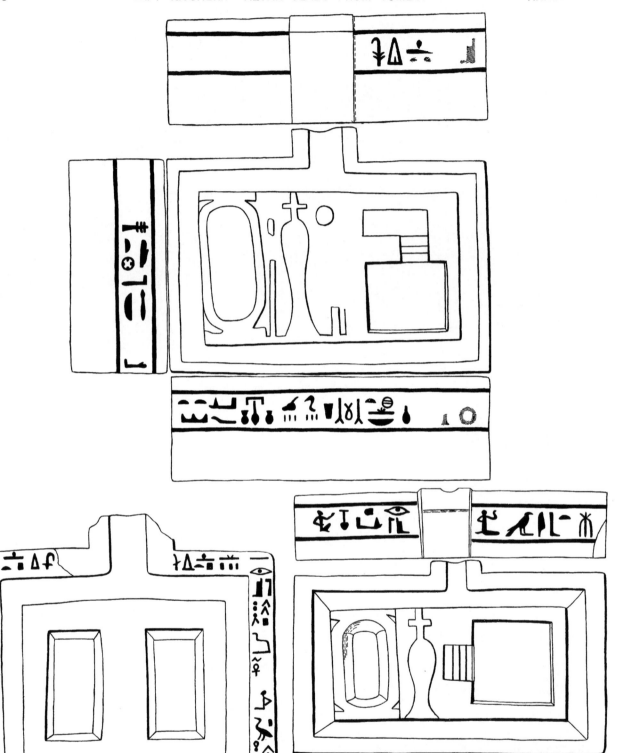

H.P.

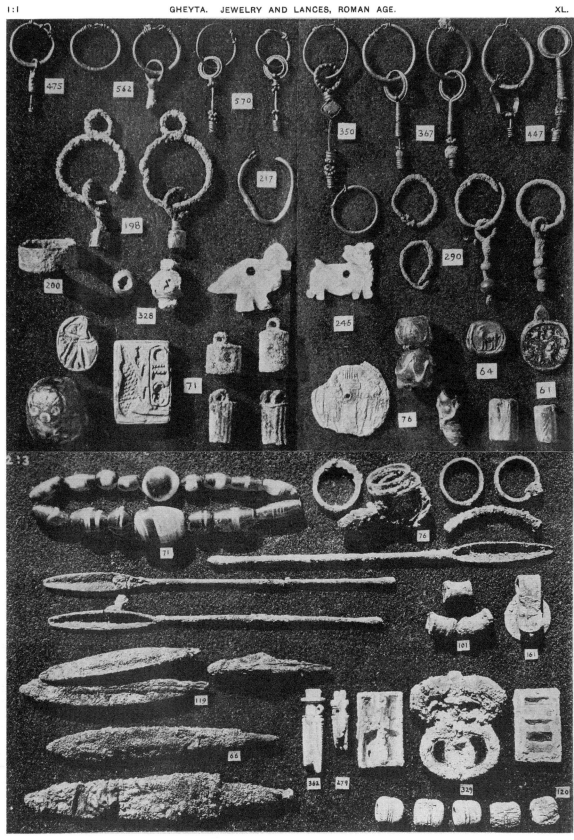

Printed in Great Britain
by Amazon

38600767R00106